SPEY FLIES

Atlantic Salmon Fishing *by Chet Reneson*

SPEY FLIES

And How To Tie Them

Bob Veverka
Color Photographs by Michael Radencich

STACKPOLE
BOOKS

To Diane, with love,
Take life as it comes,
Specialize in having fun!

Copyright © 2004 by Stackpole Books

First published in paperback in 2015 by
STACKPOLE BOOKS
5067 Ritter Road
Mechanicsburg, PA 17055
www.stackpolebooks.com

Printed in China

First paperback edition

10 9 8 7 6 5 4 3 2 1

Cover photos by Michael Radencich
Cover design by Caroline Stover
Front cover (top to bottom): Red King, Lady Caroline, Rough Grouse,
Gold Riach from George Kelson's The Salmon Fly, *tied by Bob Veverka*
Back cover (top to bottom): Glentana (zebra turkey wing), Balmoral, Double
Akroyd, Gardener from George Kelson's The Salmon Fly, *tied by Bob Veverka*

ISBN: 978-0-8117-1500-3 (paperback)

Library of Congress Cataloging-in-Publication Data

Veverka, Bob.
    Spey flies and how to tie them / Bob Veverka.—1st ed.
      p. cm.
    Includes bibliographical references (p.   ).
    ISBN 0-8117-0032-1
      1. Flies, Artificial. 2. Fly tying—History. 3. Salmon fishing. 4.
    Steelhead fishing. I. Title.
    SH451 .V49 2004
    688.7'9124—dc21
                                    2003011429

CONTENTS

FOREWORD

ALMON FLIES HAVE ALWAYS BEEN HIGH ON MY LIST in fly tying, and I suppose one could even say that I have been having a love affair with them for years. And I'm not the only one. Since the sixteenth century, even before Izaak Walton's book *The Complete Angler* was published in 1653, the old masters have written about their experiences dressing salmon flies as they were needed then, and they continued through the centuries and generations to teach the wonderful art of fly tying.

So when I look at my bookcases and scan the many titles dealing with all aspects of fly tying, I wonder if there really is a need for yet another book. Then I remember what my old tutor, the late William F. Blades, said to me: "Fly tying is a school from which we never graduate." So perhaps our needs are never ending, and as the contemporary fly tiers develop their skills and start sharing their knowledge in books of their own, we will surely have to make room on our shelves for their contributions.

Now that we are in the beginning of a new century, we find ourselves in the midst of a new breed of fly tiers. They are sophisticated and well educated in the art of dressing almost any fly you will ever need. The foremost of this new breed of tiers is Bob Veverka. His work with Spey flies is the result of many years of study. He began by learning the basics of tying the trout flies for his own use. But like most fly tiers, Bob wanted to expand his skills at the vise, and as he began to study the art of dressing the salmon fly, he discovered that in working with these gaudy full-dressed classic flies from the Victorian era, he had entered into a whole new school of fly tying.

First of all, he found it difficult to obtain the materials he needed to tie the flies as described in the pat-terns of old masters. And then if he could locate the materials, they were expensive. As Bob developed as a salmon fly tier, he learned that to participate in the deep-seated traditions of salmon fly dressing, one must learn the correct placement of each material on the hook. It's not like dressing a trout fly, in which case the tier is at liberty to change the anatomical structure to suit his fishing needs.

Salmon fly tying has become an art. The full-dressed flies of the Victorian era are framed and hung on walls to be admired rather than fished. I am not an angling historian, but when I read the old books on salmon flies, it appears that in 1910, when Mr. A. H. Chator and Mr. Ernest Crosfield invaded the field with sparsely dressed flies and introduced us to more primitive flies based on simplicity and economy of materials, salmon anglers started to use these simpler flies with great success. Thus, they concluded that the fancy feathers were no longer needed.

This new trend of simplicity has also reached the anglers on American and Canadian steelhead rivers, and new patterns are being developed and fished with good results. As evidence, Trey Combs's book *Steelhead Fishing and Flies* was published in 1976, followed in 1991 with his book *Steelhead.*

Bob Veverka became fascinated with the West Coast flies, particularly the Spey fly dressed by Syd Glasso. By studying Glasso's flies after long hours of practicing and experimenting with different hooks and materials, Bob has arrived at a style of tying the beautiful Spey flies found in this book, which surely places him among the world's most accomplished salmon fly tiers.

—Poul Jorgensen
Roscoe, New York

ACKNOWLEDGMENTS

IRST I WOULD LIKE TO THANK JUDITH SCHNELL and Stackpole Books for the chance to publish this book with them. Thanks, Judith, for believing I had the passion to do this book.

As important are the fly tiers I have met and tied with over the years. And a special thanks to the ones that took the time to tie flies for this book—they include Bob Aid, Megan Boyd, Fred Brand, Brad Burden, Mark Canfield, Bill Chinn, Pat Crane, Syd Glasso, Steve Gobin, Jon Harrang, Joe Howell, Alec Jackson, Walt Johnson, Randall Kaufmann, Jerome Malloy, Dave McCullogh, Scott Noble, Marvin Nolte, Paul Rossman, Mark Sageser, Stack Scoville, Gary Selig, Marty Sherman, Merlin Stidham, Derl Stovall, Bob Warren, Mark Waslick, Dick Wentworth, and Rick Whorwood.

A special thanks to Mike Radencich for taking the great photos of the flies and materials that appear in this book, Walt Koda for his friendship and his fine pencil sketches that are included throughout the book, Chet Reneson for the paintings in the front and back of this book, and Poul Jorgensen for writing the foreword to this book about spey flies and for writing his revolutionary *Salmon Flies* back in 1978. It started the careers of many of the fine salmon fly tiers practicing today.

Thanks to the hook makers who supplied me with hooks over the years, especially to the grandfather of American-salmon fly hook makers, Eugene Sunday, the man with a flair for hook making, and Ron Reinhold, who strives to make the finest salmon fly hooks available anywhere in the world today. Thanks also go to Paul Rossman for providing some of the materials that appear in the plates.

Others who have helped me over the years include Bill Hunter, Dave Woolrich, Dave Zincavage, Phil Castleman, Dave Mcneese, Gary Selig, the leader specialist, and Colin Simpson for his help with information about River Dee fly tiers.

Some that are no longer with us but are not forgotten and had some type of influence are Bill Cushner, whose interest in the history of flies and the people who tie them brought us together, Joe Bates, who let me study his extensive collection of salmon flies, and Syd Glasso. Though I never met him, his style of flies led me down a road that has filled my life for over twenty years.

INTRODUCTION

My introduction to Spey flies happened a long time ago and probably couldn't have come in a better place. While trout fishing in the Catskills, I heard of the famous fly tiers Harry and Elsie Darbee. They lived on the Willowemoc River and ran a small fly shop, one of the most famous in North America. This was back when a fly shop usually consisted of part of a fly tier's home.

Whenever I was in the area, I would stop and buy some flies and just kind of rubberneck, taking in all the neat stuff the Darbees had lying around—bins of flies, all sorts of tying materials, rods, reels, and lines. What really caught my eye was the angling art that had shadow-boxed flies. I'd never seen flies displayed that way and with appropriate artwork.

A large watercolor of a salmon river with a string of shadow-boxed salmon flies hung in a back room. One fly in particular stood out from the rest. It wasn't a very colorful fly, but the way the materials flowed out past the hook caught my eye.

"What kind of fly is that?" I asked Harry.

He gave me an inquisitive look and said, "You like the way it looks? That's called a Spey fly."

I can still faintly picture the shape and proportions of that fly. Of all the flies in their shop, that one caught my eye.

Visiting the Darbees's shop opened my eyes to all the different varieties of flies. Something happened to me there, and I started to look into some of the other styles of flies and types of fishing.

I was always fascinated by artificial flies. All the tying I had done up to that time consisted of trout flies for my own fishing. I was self-taught and didn't even own a book on fly tying. I wanted to improve my flies, and books seemed the best teachers. My first fly-tying book was Art Flick's *Streamside Guide to Naturals and Their Imitations*. I worked on perfecting my dry flies,

and after some practice I got pretty good at tying them. Then I wanted to try some other styles.

I bought *Steelhead Fishing and Flies*, by Trey Combs, when it was first published in 1976. The flies were very colorful and looked easy to tie. The last plate showed ten patterns by a man named Syd Glasso. They were the most beautiful flies I'd ever seen, and they would turn out to be those that would have the most influence on my own tying. I read about them and found out that they were Spey flies. This made me think back to the fly that I saw at the Darbees's shop.

Glasso's flies looked different from the others in *Steelhead Fishing and Flies*, and I wanted to tie flies like them. I tried to, but the materials I had wouldn't let me tie a fly in this style. I was getting a lesson about materials and how important they are, and how frustrating it is when you don't have the right ones. I tied many of the flies in that book, but I still wanted to do some Spey flies and wasn't about to give up.

Then Poul Jorgensen's book *Salmon Flies* was published in 1978. Poul's flies were beautiful, and they came on the scene at the right time for me. They really got me into tying salmon flies and learning about their materials. I learned that most of the original materials were no longer available, and again I experienced the frustration of not being able to tie certain flies that I wanted to make. Since many of the hairwing Atlantic-salmon patterns seemed similar to the steelhead patterns I'd already tied, I started with that style.

All this salmon and steelhead tying and fishing fascinated me, and I began to think it was time to move to the Pacific Northwest to tie flies and fish for steelhead. That didn't work out, and I moved to Vermont in 1980. The lakes near my new home held landlocked salmon, and my interest turned to the fly patterns tied for them. I spent time studying and tying all the different styles of bucktails and streamers.

I continued to dabble in steelhead and salmon flies, working on the hairwing patterns until I could turn out a dozen examples that all looked the same. The classic salmon dressings were the biggest challenge to tie, and their history fascinated me. My favorites, though, were still the Spey and Dee flies. I tried all the different styles and found that each had a way it should look, and that I had to tie a number of each style before I achieved the look I wanted. At this time I started to sell flies, tying dozens and dozens of hairwing salmon flies for fishermen going to Canada, Norway, and Iceland. Production tying taught me a lot about flies and materials.

I also started to raise many of the exotic pheasants, grouse, partridges, and quail whose feathers I needed. It was an enormous amount of work but well worth the time spent because my birds provided a steady supply of good materials.

Experience taught me that the most important aspect of fly tying is the quality of the materials you start with. Good materials make all the difference. Tying with inferior materials is frustrating; they don't handle easily and they make for lousy-looking flies.

Equally important, I learned, is the quality of the hooks you tie on. The hook is the foundation of a fly, and it should complement the style of the pattern you're tying. Likewise, the fly should accent the shape and balance of the hook. Start with the right hooks and your flies will look better.

Learning about feathers, hooks, and other materials takes time. It's a process of elimination; with experience, you will learn to judge materials and to figure out what works and what doesn't. This is perhaps the hardest lesson to learn in fly tying, and it's not something that someone else can teach you. It's a hands-on process; you must go through lots of materials and pick out the best, and then know which feathers and their special properties you are looking for. What makes a great salmon-fly material is its length, shape, texture, and brilliant color. The ability to recognize these qualities comes only with time and tying many different styles of flies.

Bill Hunter helped me a lot during the early 1980s. Bill fished for salmon and ran a small fly shop in New Boston, New Hampshire. He was the first person I knew who stocked some of the original materials for the more exotic Atlantic-salmon patterns. Bill is also an excellent tier, and the photos of his salmon flies in his yearly catalog caught the attention of fellow fly tiers.

Bob Veverka Spey Flies

Purple Heart Spey

Royal Blue and Bronze Spey	Thunder and Lightning Spey

Purple Crow

Purple Sol Duc	Steelhead Sunrise

Golden Orange Crow

Copper Heron	Claret Shoveler

Steelhead Dog

Steelhead Sunset	Golden Argus Spey

My flies are influenced by the flies that Syd Glasso tied for Trey Combs's 1976 *Steelhead Fishing and Flies*. Most were tied during the early 1980s when I was tying many classic Atlantic-salmon flies and used some of the rarer salmon materials on my Spey patterns. I like my flies to have lots of movement in the water, strong bold colors, and some type of flash or inner glow. Translucent feathers such as golden pheasant crests, Indian crow, and toucan add a sparkly special effect (hot spot) to the fly when veiled over a tinsel body.

This created a demand for salmon flies and the materials to tie them. Even then, twenty years ago, Bill knew about all types of salmon-fly materials and how to dye them to get exactly the right shades. Bill was also the first teacher I knew who held fly-tying seminars devoted to salmon flies. His materials, knowledge, and classes helped start a renaissance in salmon-fly tying in North America.

Syd Glasso died not long after I met Bill Hunter but not before he had created some of the finest steelhead and salmon patterns ever tied. At the time, about the only fly fishers who knew of Glasso's work were those who had been closest to him, his friends in the Pacific Northwest.

Bill Hunter had corresponded with Glasso and had a few of his flies and some photos of Glasso's classic salmon patterns. Bill showed me a photo of a Jock Scott that Glasso had tied. I was awestruck. I'd seen many beautiful sights in nature, but here was something man-made that struck me the same way. Glasso's flies were the most pleasing and graceful I'd ever seen. Their materials had a style and flow that matched the shapes of their hooks, and the materials seemed to burst out of the finest, neatest, smallest heads I'd ever seen. The head alone was a mystery—how could Glasso tie so

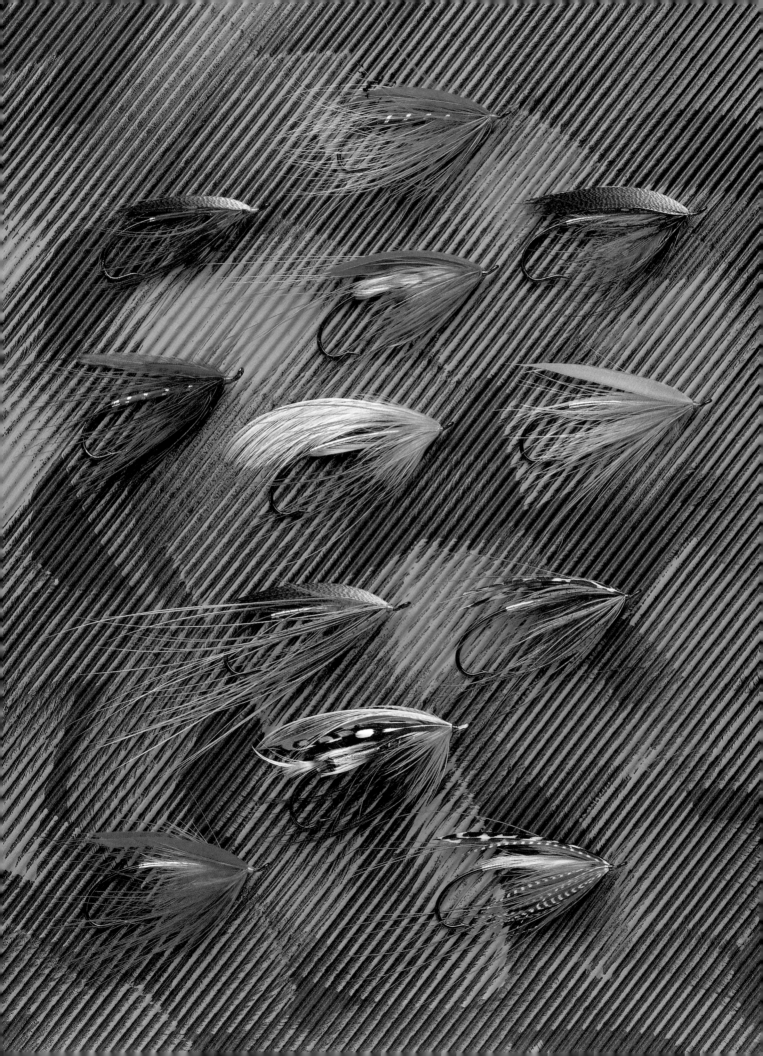

many materials on a hook and still build such a small head? I asked Bill, but he just shrugged. I would find out in time that not many people, even among those closest to him, had actually seen Syd Glasso tie a fly.

All of these experiences led to an obsession that has lasted more than twenty years. I tied flies every day, often spending eight to twelve hours at the vise. In the process, I learned to tie all the styles of steelhead and Atlantic-salmon flies. I traveled out to the West Coast and tied with folks from that area, and I attended many shows on the East Coast at which salmon-fly tiers demonstrated their skills. I tied flies with some of the most talented fly tiers in North America and had one hell of a good time doing it.

I also met a lot of interesting people who shared my obsession. Fly tiers are a bunch of characters, and many are multitalented. I know some who build cane rods or make reels, others who are sporting or wildlife artists, net makers, authors, or hook makers. Quite a few are involved in some type of artsy, sporting-related activity. Many other fly tiers are doctors, lawyers, or common laborers. The fascination with salmon flies and their history brings together many different personalities.

Shortly after Glasso died, I saw an ad for custom-made steelhead and salmon hooks. I dialed the number and talked to Alec Jackson for the first time. He mentioned that he had known Syd Glasso and many of the people who fished and tied with him. That conversation led to several trips out to the West Coast to meet with Alec and some of the other tiers of Washington and Oregon. Through Alec, I got to meet some of the people who had known Glasso. From them, I hoped to learn some of the secrets of Glasso's beautiful Spey flies.

Alec Jackson is a great steelhead fly historian, and we discussed fly patterns, hooks, materials, and Syd Glasso. Alec never saw Syd tie a fly, but he had some flies that Glasso had given him. You can learn a lot by looking at another tier's work, but Glasso's flies were so finely tied and so different from any others I had seen that I could only stare at them in wonder.

I found out that very few of Glasso's friends knew how he had tied his flies. Most felt that their precision was unapproachable. This alone lit my desire to tie flies in the Syd Glasso tradition.

Alec loved the look of the steelhead Speys, but he never tied them. Instead, he developed a series of flies called Pseudo Speys, wet flies tied with a tail, a body of spun herl, and a collar, but without wings. He devel-

oped a unique way to make fly bodies with herl dyed various colors. He'd twist several strands of herl onto a piece of oval tinsel and then wind the tinsel to produce a beautifully shaped body. His Pseudo Speys were clean, soft-hackled wet flies for steelhead.

Alec introduced me to Dick Wentworth and Dave Woolrich, with whom I studied original examples of Glasso's flies. Dick Wentworth had learned to tie flies from Glasso, who had been one of his school teachers. Dick knew most of Glasso's techniques and answered many of my questions. Anyone could see right away that Dick was intense about his tying and fishing. You could also see that Dick really missed his great friend Syd Glasso.

We talked away the best part of a day and swapped some flies. Dick told me stories about Glasso, and we looked at many of Glasso's original fly patterns for Atlantic salmon, steelhead, and sea-run cutthroats. We also looked at many photos that Syd had taken of his flies.

Before I left, Dick took out a small Wheatley fly box that contained three of his flies. They were electric

Syd Glasso Atlantic-salmon patterns (top to bottom: Thunder and Lightning, Gordon, Black Dog)

orange in color, the brightest flies I'd ever seen, with a fuzzy, fireball-orange look like that of the sun going down at the end of a hot, hazy summer day. This was the pattern that Dick had tied in honor of his friend and mentor; he'd named it the Mr. Glasso Steelhead Spey. On March 14, 1981, Dick caught a 21-pound, 8-ounce Sol Duc steelhead on the pattern—a beautiful tribute to his friend.

Around the time that I first spoke with Alec Jackson, I met another man who also would have an impact on my life and tying. He was not a fly tier himself, but he shadowed-boxed sets of flies and ran a little fly-fishing museum on the Cape Breton Trail in Nova Scotia. His name was Bill Cushner.

I visited the American Museum of Fly Fishing in Manchester, Vermont, on a skiing trip in the late 1970s. The exhibits included a number of flies in beautiful gilded frames. The framing, I learned, had been done by a man named Bill Cushner, who had recently moved to Canada. I filed the name in the back of my mind.

Several years later, my wife and I decided to take a trip to Nova Scotia. A brochure about the area we planned to visit mentioned a fly-fishing museum owned and operated by someone named Bill Cushner. A light went on in my head as I realized that this was the same man who had done the frames for the museum in Vermont. When I called Bill, he invited me to stop by and see him if we were in the neighborhood. Our trip to Nova Scotia took on a new meaning.

As we toured the Cape Breton Trail, a winding road that runs along the coast through small fishing villages, I turned into a driveway next to a sign that read, "Bill Cushner's Fly Fishing Museum." Bill greeted us and showed us around. His museum contained many frames with historic fly patterns from around the world. Bill had trout flies by Rube Cross, Edward Hewitt, and the Darbees; stonefly nymphs by Poul Jorgensen and Ted Niemeyer; soft-hackles by James Leisenring; and salmon flies by Charles Defeo and Preston Jennings. Hundreds of frames with historic flies and angling artwork hung on the walls.

We talked for hours about flies and fly tiers. Bill asked to see some of my work. I went out to the car and brought in some flies I had tied. He couldn't believe that someone my age could tie such flies, but he couldn't have known how hard I'd been working at it. Bill asked if I would tie up two sets of my flies for a trade: he would frame one set for himself and the other

Bill Cushner's Fly Fishing Museum, Cape Breton, Nova Scotia

for me. This was a common practice for Bill. Happy for the chance to own a Bill Cushner frame, I agreed.

Our meeting turned into a lifelong friendship. Bill appreciated my tying ability and I admired the artistry of his frames. And, of course, we had a common interest in the history of fly patterns. I knew many fly tiers on both coasts and gave Bill leads to procure flies for framing. I learned that Bill's interest was fueled by his friend Ted Niemeyer, another fly historian and an ocean of information about patterns, tiers, and materials. They had met when Bill lived in New York City and ran a frame shop there.

Bill and I came from two different eras, but fly tying brought us together. We kept in touch through letters, phone calls, and visits.

Not long after I met him, Bill moved to the coast of Oregon, where his daughter and her family lived, and opened a small museum there. Once on the West Coast, he met many of the tiers in that area and traded them frames for flies. Whenever I was out that way, I made sure to stop by and visit with Bill and his wife. When Bill died, I lost a good friend. We learned a lot from each other.

It was also around this time that I started to correspond with Joe Bates, and on a few occasions went to visit him and his fly collection. Joe had thousands of Atlantic-salmon patterns, both new and old. At the time, he was working on a book that dealt with the classic patterns and their artistic appeal. His collection had a number of Glasso's original flies tied on blind-eye hooks, very rare dressings that would prove very help-

The author with Bill Cushner and Ted Niemeyer at a Federation of Fly Fishers Conclave

The author and Joe Bates in Longmeadow, Massachusetts

The author with Eugene Sunday and Mike Radencich

ful to me in figuring out the techniques that Glasso used.

The Art of the Atlantic Salmon Fly was published in 1987. Bates's book showcased both antique salmon flies and contemporary dressings by Megan Boyd, Syd Glasso, Larry Borders, Ron Alcott, and others. It was the first book to show some of the Atlantic-salmon patterns tied by Syd Glasso. One color plate showed some of my Spey flies.

I was really getting into the full-dress classics at this time. You have to spend countless hours tying them before they turn out the way you want. I had tied some in the past that had turned out all right, but they were not in the style I wanted. I didn't have the correct materials and hooks for the look I strived for. Hooks were my biggest problem. I could not find the style needed to dress flies with long, low wings.

During this time, a growing number of fly tiers on the East and West Coasts had become interested in salmon flies and the original materials used in the classic patterns—blue chatterer, Indian crow, toucan, bustard, and others. Most tiers started to work with blind-eye hooks to match the antique flies. Obtaining proper hooks was always a problem. Many tiers converted various types of hooks to salmon-fly shapes and tried to finish them with some sort of black paint.

Then I received a hook from Eugene Sunday. It was in the style that I was looking for, and at first I thought it was an antique hook. Gene informed me that it wasn't; it was one that he had made. He could make any style, and the quest for quality hooks was over. Gene was an artist at hook making, and many tiers started using his hooks.

With Gene's hooks, my flies started to take on the look that I wanted. I tied many of the classic full-dress flies and patterns of my own design. From all the tying I was doing, I learned about all the different materials and the flies tied with them. I started to teach other tiers.

On one of my trips to the West Coast, Dave McNeese asked me to run a two-day class in the construction of salmon flies. Dave owned a shop in Salem, Oregon, and stocked many of the exotic feathers used to tie salmon and steelhead flies. He is an expert fly tier with a vast knowledge of materials and how to dye them. He was also very interested in the history of fly patterns and their materials. Dave had a salmon-fly hook made that was the finest of its time. The entire production run was sold in a couple of weeks, and that was the last time they were available. They are very rare now.

Thanks to my travels on both coasts and in Canada, I was able to take in the entire scope of contemporary steelhead and Atlantic-salmon fly tying. I met the tiers, learned their techniques, and talked with them about the histories of fly patterns and their originators. We traded flies and materials. In the process, I tied thousands of steelhead and Atlantic-salmon patterns for display and fishing. The 1980s saw a lot of activity, and many fine tiers emerged on both coasts. On my trips West I met many of the best fly tiers—Steve Gobin, Ted Neimeyer, Bill Chinn, Wayne Luallen, Joe Howell, and many others.

I also met a number of people who had flies tied by Syd Glasso. By the late 1980s, I'd seen and studied hundreds of Glasso's flies, but I still wondered about the whereabouts of the flies shown in Trey Combs's book, *Steelhead Fly Fishing and Flies*. No one knew where they were, though I was confident that I'd eventually run across them on a trip to the West Coast. To my surprise, they were in Vermont all the time. I was talking with John Merwin during a visit to the American Museum of Fly Fishing in Manchester when he mentioned that he had plates of steelhead flies from the West Coast. I asked to see them. We went upstairs and John showed me a box containing glass panes with steelhead flies glued to them. When I opened the box, I recognized the flies as those from Trey's book. I dug through the plates and on the bottom found the ten flies that Syd Glasso had tied. I'd traveled thousands of miles to see them, and the whole time they were in the same state that I lived in.

In 1991, Judith Dunham's *The Atlantic Salmon Fly: The Tyers and Their Art* was published. It included the work of salmon-fly tiers from all over Europe, Canada, and the United States, and it brought to light the talents of many contemporary fly tiers. Salmon-fly tying had become a beehive of activity.

At about the same time, Trey Combs asked me to supply him with some of my steelhead Speys for his new book, *Steelhead*, published in 1991. It chronicled steelhead fly fishers and fly tiers from the past to the present. Like many other authors, Trey had a genuine interest in the tiers and their fly patterns. Books like his preserve the history and traditions.

Perhaps the grandest of all Atlantic-salmon books, *Fishing Atlantic Salmon*, by Joseph D. Bates, Jr., and

Jock Scott tied by the author

Steve Marl, Joe Howell, Steve Brocco, Dave McNeese, Mike McCoy, and the author tying flies at Dave McNeese's shop

Pamela Bates Richards, was published in 1996 by Stackpole Books. The manuscript of this extensive volume about salmon flies was written by Joe Bates, and after his death was turned into a book by his daughter, Pam Richards. Pam selected all the best antique and contemporary flies from her father's collection and contacted many of the newer salmon-fly tiers for examples of their work, putting together the finest book to date on Atlantic-salmon fishing and fly tying. *Fishing Atlantic Salmon* includes flies from the beginning of salmon-fly tying to those of the present. The flies were photographed by Mike Radencich, and the images show the beauty, exotic colors, and complex makeups of the world's best salmon flies. Joe would have been very proud.

Bob Warren, the author, Mark Waslick, Peter Castagnetti, and Pam Bates tying flies at Mark's camp in Middlebury, Vermont

The Sol Duc Twins, Brad Burden and the author, fishing their favorite flies for steelhead

Mike Radencich did his own book in 1997, *Tying the Classic Salmon Fly*. Along with *Fishing Atlantic Salmon*, Mike's book gives a fly tier all the knowledge he needs to get started.

Interest in salmon flies and their history continues to grow. Every year, many people join the ranks of salmon- and steelhead-fly tiers. The availability of materials keeps improving, and most experienced tiers are happy to share their knowledge and skills, both of which trends stand in contrast to the past. We have a number of great books full of information and beautiful photography.

There has never been a book dedicated entirely to the Spey and Dee patterns and the other flies that those styles have spawned. A growing number of fly fishers are interested in tying and using them. Recent years have seen a boom in the use of Spey rods and Spey casting for steelhead and Atlantic-salmon fishing. The time seems right for a book devoted to these elegant, graceful patterns.

This book includes all the history, patterns, materials, and tiers that I have come across in twenty years of studying and tying Spey flies. I hope my obsession proves as rewarding for you as it has been for me.

—Bob Veverka
Underhill, Vermont
February 2002

CHAPTER 1

Spey Fly History

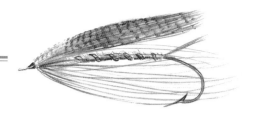

SPEY FLIES WERE ORIGINATED ON THE RIVER SPEY in northeastern Scotland more than 150 years ago. At the time, every salmon river in Scotland had its own set of flies. On many rivers, fly fishers developed patterns characterized by certain colors or unique materials. Along with the style of tying, such features defined a series of flies for a particular river system.

Spey flies were distinguished by their simple dressings and somber colors. They were dressed on hooks that had extra-long shanks. The bodies of Spey flies were made of various colors of Berlin wool blended together, and they were ribbed with tinsel and sometimes with silk. Body colors ranged from all black to shades of olive, green, and purple. The bodies were wound with long-fibered, mobile hackles that had lots of action in the water; Spey-cock and heron hackles were commonly used. These long, flowing body hackles were the most important feature of Spey flies. Various writers have mentioned that Spey flies were tied to look like and have the action of a shrimp when fished. Spey flies were rather simple patterns as salmon flies go, but they had an elegant, flowing appearance, and their action in the water was unsurpassed.

The body hackles of the earliest Spey patterns consisted of feathers taken from the sides of the tails of Spey cocks, specially bred chickens raised along the banks of the River Spey. They were never bred in large numbers and are believed to be extinct today.

Spey-cock hackles ranged in color from cinnamon brown to black. The best hackles were cinnamon brown at the base and a smoky dun color at the tip. They were opaque feathers selected for their mobility in the water. On flies dressed with heron hackles, tiers used either gray or black feathers, according to the pattern.

Early Spey flies had collars made of teal flank, and it was felt that a fly was incomplete without a teal col-lar. The wings were two slips of bronze mallard set low along the top of the hook. Their low, bronze-mallard wings became another distinguishing feature of these flies.

Another series of patterns known as Dee flies also used long, mobile body hackles. These were tied for the River Dee in northeastern Scotland. While Spey and Dee patterns are quite similar in some ways, they also have some important differences.

Dee flies were dressed on very large hooks. Called Dee irons, these hooks were of the largest sizes and had Limerick bends and very long shanks. The earliest Dee flies were dressed with tails made from the red body feathers or the tippets of golden pheasants. Later patterns had golden-pheasant crests, and many sported tail veils made with strands of tippets or other accenting feathers. The original Spey patterns did not have tails.

The bodies of Dee patterns consisted of spun fur in the most brilliant colors of yellow, orange, red, claret, and blue. Most of their bodies were dressed with two or three colors or sections. The earliest examples called for bodies of mohair or pig's wool; later, most tiers switched to seal fur. These body materials were chosen for their beautiful, translucent colors. Dee-fly bodies were ribbed with the broadest of tinsels. When the body material was picked out, it would veil the ribbing; in the water, the combination of picked-out dubbing and wide tinsel made for a translucent or halo effect.

Dee flies were hackled with the longest heron hackles. On large flies, the fiber length of the body hackles could be as much as three to four inches, and the flies were sometimes tied so the hackle fibers would extend past the back of the hook. Both gray and black heron were used. On patterns that had throats, tiers used the longest-fibered widgeon- or teal-flank feathers.

The wings of Dee flies consisted of two strips from some type of wing quill, usually turkey, and were rather thin so as to move in the water with the slightest current. That's why these patterns are often called Dee strip-wing flies. Dee tiers mounted the wings in a special manner, attaching the strips individually rather than together, and tying them flat over the body rather than on edge. The wings were tied on the shoulders of the fly and formed a V when viewed from above. This style of wing has a scissors action in the water.

The original Gled Wing pattern is regarded as the earliest Dee fly. Its wings consisted of two strips from the quills of a gled, a hawklike bird from the River Dee area. Gled was reddish brown in color, with darker brown bars. Its soft texture produced the best action in the water. Like the Spey cock, this bird eventually became extinct, and Dee tiers switched to turkey quills ranging in color from cinnamon to dark brown. Strips of gled were commonly used on flies in the early 1800s, but the bird was extinct before 1895, when George Kelson's book was published.

The best turkey feathers for Dee flies were cinnamon in color with a dun color at the tips of the fibers. A later pattern that used this material and was designed after the Gled Wing was called the Glentana. Many nineteenth-century anglers, however, felt that Dee flies

Antique Spey and Dee Flies

Glentana

White Wing   Akroyd

Dallas

Lady Caroline   Tri-Color

These are examples of (antique) original Spey and Dee patterns. The Glentana is an old Dee fly originated by William Garden of Aberdeen. It is designed from the earlier pattern the Gled Wing. The White Wing is an early Tweed fly originated by James Wright. The Akroyd, another old Dee pattern, was originated by Charles Akroyd, who named it the Poor Man's Jock Scott. The Tri-Color was a standard fly on the Dee, which, when dressed with a red breast hackle from the golden pheasant and white wings, is known as the Killer.

The Lady Caroline and the Dallas are Speys, although the Dallas, originated by John Dallas, included wings of turkey, not the standard bronze mallard used on Speys. The Lady Caroline is first mentioned in George Kelson's *The Salmon Fly*, but who originated it is a mystery. In a much later salmon-fly book, *A Guide to Salmon Flies* by John Buckland and Arthur Oglesby, they mention that the fly is named after Lady Caroline Gordon-Lennox, daughter of the then Duke of Richmond and Gordon at Gordon Castle.

Salmon Fishing on the Dee *by Joseph Farquharson from W. Earl Hodgson's* Salmon Fishing

tied with turkey strips simply didn't fish as well as the earlier patterns made with gled.

Several Dee patterns were tied with jungle-cock sides. They were described as "drooping," because the feathers ran along the sides of the fly slightly below the body. The heads of Dee flies were also tied in a special manner, made as small as possible to cause the water to glide over the head and give the wings their best action or play in the water.

Dee patterns were well-thought-out designs. Everything on each fly had a reason. The tails, body hackles, and wings gave them great mobility in the water. This action or movement suggests life, an important attribute in fishing flies. The bodies were made in the most brilliant colors, which provided attraction, and they were tied with translucent materials, which provided a natural look. Real fish, shrimp, and insects exhibit translucency, and our flies should do the same.

Early books on salmon fishing tell us that each river had its own set of local flies tied by fishermen who lived along the river. Spey and Dee flies can be classified as local patterns because they were developed on the Rivers Spey and Dee and rarely used elsewhere. Patterns regarded as "general flies" were used on any number of rivers.

Like all salmon-fly patterns, Spey and Dee flies evolved over time. Their materials indicate that they date from the early days of salmon-fly evolution. Salmon flies from the very early 1800s employed basic materials—bodies of wool or fur dubbing, body hackles of chicken feathers, and simple strip wings of turkey quill. Their use of such materials places the original Spey and Dee patterns in this time period.

Travel and supplies of materials were limited in those days, and new ideas and materials were rare. Most tiers of the early 1800s used whatever was available locally, often borrowing an idea from one pattern and adding it to another to make a fly fit a particular river or circumstance. With limited materials and ideas, fly patterns took on a similar look. As time went by, of course, some fishermen traveled to different rivers and brought back new (to them) ideas in fly design. For a long time, however, salmon flies evolved slowly.

THE EARLY RECORD

Although fly fishing for salmon dates back to at least the 1600s, patterns we would recognize as salmon flies didn't start to show up until the early nineteenth cen-

---

Early Strip-Wing Flies, Veverka

Summer Fly	Spring Fly

Black Dog, Original

Stoddart's Spey	Toppy

These early patterns, many of them from the Tweed, are tied similar to Spey and Dee patterns and may be the ancestors of the Spey and Dee flies or ones copied from them. The method used to tie on the wings of Tweed patterns and Dee patterns were the same: Two sections of Quill are tied on separately to form a V when viewed from above, which looks like a slightly opened pair of scissor blades that open and close in the water.

George C. Bainbridge's book, *The Fly Fishers Guide*, 1816, was the first to contain color plates of flies, including the Summer and Spring Flies. The original Black Dog appears in Alexander Mackintosh's 1808 book, *The Driffield Angler*. As the salmon fly evolved and entered the Victorian era, the original Black Dog was dressed with a more complex wing with sections of yellow and red goose quill, bustard, and Amherst tail with veils of summer duck and a golden pheasant topping.

The Toppy is one of the most famous of all the Tweed flies, mentioned by John Younger in *River Angling*, 1840. William Scrope made it famous in his 1843 book, *Days and Nights of Salmon Fishing on the Tweed*, Thomas Stoddart included it in *The Anglers Companion*, 1847, and Edward Fitzgibbon, who wrote under the name of Ephemera, included it in *The Book of the Salmon*, 1850.

---

tury. Thomas Barker's *The Art of Angling*, published in 1651, contains the first printed recipe for a salmon-fly dressing. The first salmon fly listed by name is the "Horseleech Fly" mentioned by James Chetham in *The Angler's Vade Mecum* (1681). These two flies are very similar and might be the same pattern. Both authors described a fly that had a large body, a very long tail, and three sets of wings.

In 1746, Richard Bowlker published *The Art of Angling*, in which he listed two salmon flies by name, the King's Fisher or Peacock Fly and the Dragon Fly. Simple in construction and somber in color, both flies probably evolved from trout patterns.

More salmon flies came on the scene in the early 1800s, but they were still relatively rare commodities. One of the earliest nineteenth-century patterns was the original Black Dog mentioned by Alexander Mackintosh in his book, *The Driffield Angler* (1808). This early pattern was a strip-wing fly with a tinsel rib and a hackle wound up the body, very dark and tied in the same style as the Spey and Dee patterns. Mackintosh's infor-

mation dated back to 1765; he mentions catching a salmon that weighed fifty-four and a half pounds in that year.

George Bainbridge's *Fly Fishers Guide*, published in 1816, was the first book to contain colored plates of salmon flies. The flies depicted were the Spring Fly, Summer Fly, Gaudy Fly, Quaker, and the Wasp Fly. They remained standard patterns for a long time. Four of them were tied in the same style, with dubbed bodies, hackles wound up the body, and simple strip wings. The Gaudy Fly was, to say the least, gaudy; it had a tail of peacock herl, a red body with a yellow hackle, and a red wing with a guinea-fowl feather over it.

Some of the oldest patterns tied for a specific river were those used on the River Tweed. I think that the early Tweed flies might have been the forerunners of the Spey and Dee patterns, or were themselves copied from patterns used on the Spey and Dee. The early Tweed patterns were simple in construction: tails made with a tuft of wool, bodies of mohair or pig's wool, a throat hackle, and a pair of turkey-quill wings tied on in a fashion that is very similar to the style used on Spey and Dee patterns. Early Spey and Dee patterns were tied in the same style as the Tweed patterns, but with the addition of a long, mobile body hackle.

The most famous of all the Tweed flies was the Toppy. It was considered a standard fly and one of the best for that river, and it is mentioned in all of the old books that deal with fishing the River Tweed. In *The Northern Angler* (1837), John Kirkbride says, "In the Tweed, a fly with a wing of black turkey feather and a tip of white kills remarkably well." This must surely be the Toppy.

John Younger's book, *River Angling for Salmon and Trout* (1840), lists six patterns for the River Tweed. Although the flies in this book are listed by number and not by name, the second fly is very similar to the Toppy and must be Younger's version of the pattern. He also mentions that some of the colorful Irish patterns were starting to show up on some rivers in Scotland.

In 1843, William Scrope's *Days and Nights of Salmon Fishing on the Tweed* listed the Toppy by name. Scrope also mentioned that it was one of his favorite patterns, a recommendation that helped to make the fly famous.

The Toppy was an early Tweed fly and one of the best patterns of its day, simple in construction and

---

Flies from Edward Fitzgibbon (Ephemera)'s *The Book of the Salmon*, 1850, Veverka

Spey Number 2

Spey Number 3   Spey Number 4

Carron Number 2

Edward Fitzgibbon's *The Book of the Salmon* includes several patterns for the Rivers Spey and Carron. Fitzgibbon was the first to collect flies and record them according to the river they were tied and fished for, the first true fly collector. When this book was written it was still early in the evolution of the classic salmon fly. Salmon flies were starting to change from simple strip-wing flies to flies dressed with more elaborate wings, influenced by Irish tiers. In *The Book of the Salmon* we see that flies for the River Spey were already in use, and the style they were tied in was established. This would date the origin of the Spey pattern to sometime in the early part of the 1800s—and the style still evolves today.

---

somber in color. But big changes were on the horizon, and simple, drab flies would soon share salmon rivers with much more elaborate, colorful dressings.

THE VICTORIANS

As the Victorian era began, salmon flies started to change, and many older, regional flies were replaced by the new, gaudy patterns we regard as the full-dress classics. Irish tiers led the change from simple flies to more elaborate patterns. These early Irish tiers included Pat McKay, originator of the Parson series, James Rogan and his son Michael, and William Blacker.

The earliest fly that we would recognize as a full-dress classic is the Parson originated by Pat McKay around 1836. He took the simple, somber patterns and changed the colors to brilliant yellows and oranges. By adding exotic materials, mainly golden pheasant, McKay made flies that looked more like jewels than fishing lures.

James and Michael Rogan also tied colorful patterns. They felt that brighter patterns would attract more salmon (and more salmon fishermen). It seems that there was always some competition among fly tiers to produce better-looking or more elaborate patterns. With the use of brighter, more brilliant colors and exotic materials, flies changed drastically. In time, many of the older, simpler patterns were replaced. Throughout all

these changes, however, the original Spey and Dee patterns remained essentially the same.

As fly fishing for salmon grew in popularity during the mid-1800s, fly tiers developed a lot of new patterns. Many books about salmon fishing were published during this time, and some contained extensive lists of fly patterns grouped according to the rivers for which the flies had been developed.

To follow the history of the Spey and Dee flies, we can look to the work of anglers and authors whom we can call the first fly collectors, writers such as Fitzgibbon, Francis Francis, Knox, Kelson, Pryce-Tannatt, and Taverner. All of them had a keen interest in salmon flies, and their books contain the history of many patterns.

Victorian salmon-fishing books mention that most Spey patterns were tied by Speyside gillies. At the time, most of these gillies could not read or write, and it fell to well-educated fly fishermen who wrote books to record the fly patterns of the day. Angling writers originated some flies and recorded many others, but they probably also overlooked some of the most important tiers of the time, gillies whose contributions never became part of the written history. We'll never really know, of course.

Edward Fitzgibbon wrote under the name Ephemera. He published *The Book of the Salmon* in 1850. Fitzgibbon was the first man to make the effort to collect local patterns, noting in his book that, "The Salmon of every River in the Empire have favorite flies, some widely differing in size and colour."

The Book of the Salmon included descriptions of flies listed according to the rivers for which they were tied, and it contained fly plates and interesting tying techniques. The illustrations provided contemporary tiers with a correct idea of the colors, shapes, and sizes of salmon flies. It's a comprehensive collection, ranging from early, simple strip-wing flies to the most colorful and elaborate patterns of the time. The book contains thirteen patterns by William Blacker. A Mr. Forrest, of Kelso, dressed all the standard flies for all the rivers of Scotland.

Fitzgibbon describes the standard method for winging Tweed flies: "Each wing, made of a strip of turkey tail, was attached individually. They are therefore fully divided and project over and by the hook, like slightly opened blades of a pair of scissors." Fitzgibbon mentions that most Tweed flies were tied in this manner.

Spey, Dee, and Eagle Patterns by Mr. Brown of Aberdeen from Francis Francis's *A Book on Angling*, 1867

Spey Dog, Veverka

| Tartan (speckled bustard wing), Veverka | Gled Wing (mottled bustard wing), Veverka |

Gray Eagle, Brand

| Yellow Eagle, Brand | Gled Wing (florican bustard wing), Veverka |

Tartan (mottled bustard wing), Veverka

Francis Francis states, "The Spey flies are very curious productions to look at, it being customary to dress them the reverse way of the hackle, and to send the twist or tinsel the opposite way of the hackle." Francis describes the Dee flies as peculiar, too—the flies are usually large but slenderly dressed with heron's hackles of the largest size and wings of two slips of swallow-tailed gled. No head, as it is thought to cause a ripple, while the sharp head of a Dee fly cuts the water with a smooth, even gliding motion opening and shutting its wing with a most lifelike appearance.

The Spey Dog is dressed large for spring, preferably on long-shanked Dee hooks. The hackle is a large black feather with light dun tips, taken from the side of a scotch cock's tail. Francis describes the Tartan as a strange-looking fly and rather troublesome to dress. The Gled Wing, or Red Wing, as it was termed, was the most useful and may have been the first Dee fly developed.

Concerning Eagle patterns, Francis states, "We might liken some flies to shrimps or prawns, and others to butterflies and Dragon-flies, the Eagle completely knocks all such possibilities on the head, as it is like nothing on, over, or under the earth or water that I know of." The Gray and Yellow Eagle were the first Eagle patterns, originated by Mr. Brown of Aberdeen, who is credited with many styles of flies developed for the Rivers Spey, Don, and Dee, as well as many of the low-water patterns for the Dee, including the Blue Charm, Jockie, and Silver Blue. He was also the originator of the Phantom Minnow, an early lure used for salmon.

Many of the flies in his book were listed by numbers instead of names, a common practice among authors of that time. He included seven patterns for the River Spey; as far as I know, this is the first mention of Spey flies. These patterns were developed before Fitzgibbon's time, but his book was the first to list them.

The pattern listed as Number 2 had a body of puce silk ribbed with gold and silver tinsel and a yellowish green silk thread. The body hackle was a "pendant

feather" from a brown cock's tail. Each wing consisted of fibers from a large, brown, spotted feather from a turkey's tail. The wings laid along the top of the hook, and the hook was "exceedingly long in the shank." Fitzgibbon mentions that this is an old, standard Spey fly for spring fishing. How old we don't know, but his book was published in 1850, so it's likely that the first Spey flies were tied sometime in the early 1800s. Judging by the body color, materials, and the manner of its dressing, this could be the fly that evolved into the pattern we now know as the Purple King.

Pattern Number 3 was the same dressing as Number 2, but the wings were made of brown (bronze) mallard. Number 4 had the same wings, with a body of cinnamon-brown floss ribbed with tinsel.

The flies that Fitzgibbon listed for the River Spey exhibited many of the distinguishing features that Spey flies are known for, such as multiple tinsel ribs and the use of silk as a rib material. The body hackles were pendant feathers from a brown cock's tail (a Spey cock), and the wings were strips of bronze mallard tied low along the top of the hook. And he mentions that the hooks had longer shanks.

The patterns Fitzgibbon described are the earliest of the variety known as Spey flies. This series of flies had features and materials not mentioned in earlier books dealing with salmon-fly construction.

Different tiers often used different materials to create essentially the same fly, and Fitzgibbon mentions that there was no one dressing for certain Spey flies. Some flies, furthermore, were tied with different body colors according to the season.

That last practice was related in the classic salmon-fly book published in 1867 by Francis Francis, *A Book on Angling*. It contains chapters on flies, materials, and the salmon rivers for which various patterns were developed. This book included all types and styles of flies, from early, simple patterns to the most complex patterns of the time. In his chapter on salmon flies, Francis says, "I have been many years collecting this list of flies, of the majority of which I have brought patterns away from the rivers themselves, so that they are descriptions of the actual flies used on the rivers by the habitués thereof."

Francis Francis (1822–1886) was left an inheritance under the stipulation that he adopt his grandfather's name. From time of his inheritance on, he devoted himself to the sporting life, mostly fishing and

---

River Don Flies from Francis Francis's *A Book on Angling*, 1867, Whorwood

Fly Number 1

Fly Number 2   Fly Number 4

Fly Number 3   Fly Number 5

Fly Number 6

Flies used on the Don, such as small sizes of the Tartan, are similar to Dee flies but tied on smaller hooks, according to Francis Francis. His book includes six patterns specifically dressed for the Don, which were originated by Mr. Brown of Aberdeen. Brown owned a tackle shop on the Dee, and he originated many of the early Dee, Eagle, and low-water patterns. Francis mentions that Brown was an expert tier and dressed flies like few others.

---

writing about it. He was a trout and salmon angler of rare ability, and the editor of the influential British magazine *The Field*. Francis also raised fish; some of his hatchery's fertilized brown-trout eggs were shipped to New Zealand, where they became the basis of that country's trout fishery.

Francis Francis was one of the first true fly collectors, genuinely interested in fly patterns and their histories. He collected information about salmon rivers and the flies and techniques used to catch salmon. Since he kept in contact with many people who lived along, fished in, and tied flies for famous salmon rivers, his information can be trusted. Although he tied flies, he did not consider himself an expert tier. Rather, as James Babb has said, "Francis Francis was not an innovator, but a connoisseur of techniques gleaned from the cutting-edge anglers of his day."

A Book on Angling sheds light on some of the Spey and Dee fly tiers of the time. Francis mentions that the Dee is a "pattern river," powerful and not easy to fish, but perhaps one of the clearest rivers in Scotland. "The flies used are peculiar . . . usually large, but slenderly dressed . . . and were described as strange creations," he said of Dee flies. He noted that "The wings should be thin of substance and fine in fiber, to give them play in the water . . . and tied on in the Dee fashion, the head should be small as possible, as a large head causes a

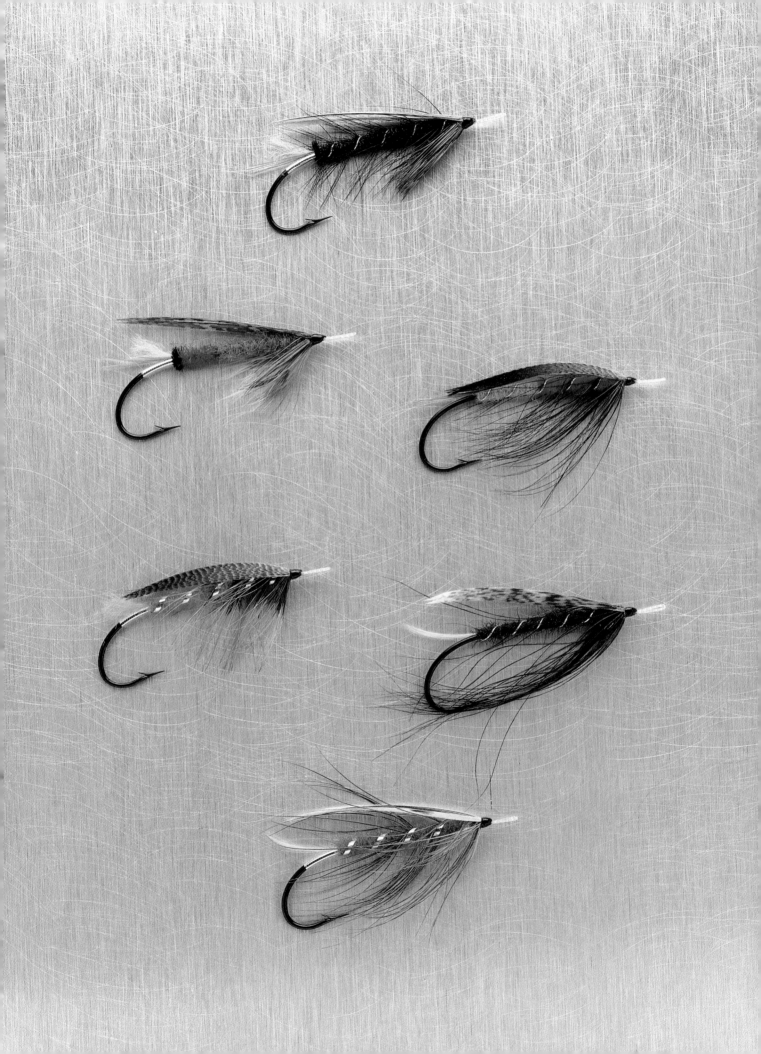

ripple . . . while a small head cuts the water with a smooth even gliding motion, opening and shutting the wings with a most lifelike appearance."

He mentions the earliest Dee pattern, the Gled Wing, sometimes called the Red Wing, which was named after the material used for the wing. This is the pattern that many Dee flies would be fashioned after. Francis notes that this pattern was one of "Mr. Brown's from Aberdeen . . . a man that can dress flies like few others."

Brown owned and operated a tackle shop on the Dee and was credited with creating many of its early patterns. He was the inventor of the Phantom Minnow and many of the summer patterns fished on the Dee, low-water flies such as the Jockie, Logie, and Jeannie. The River Don patterns, which are much like Dee flies but tied in smaller sizes, are also credited to Brown. He originated the Grey Eagle and Yellow Eagle, patterns that were fished in the high, off-color water of early spring. The body hackles were tied with marabou-like feathers taken from the shin of a golden eagle.

Another tier mentioned by Francis Francis was William Murdoch of *The Fishing Gazette*. He is credited as the originator of the Dunt, Catcher, Peacock, and Dodger patterns, all tied in the Dee fashion.

For the River Beauly, Francis mentions that "there is a singular fly used . . . which they term the 'Snow Fly,' and it is used there as long as there is any snow water on the river." He received the fly from "Snowie" of Inverness, and described it as being dressed on a big, long-shanked hook like those used for River Tay flies.

The Tay flies were dressed on the largest of hooks. Francis noted that "all Tay flies have undergone a thorough revolution . . . all the plain wings are gone, the long strips of turkey are gone . . . and mixed wings with Jungle Cock, Wood Duck and toppings, reign." Tay flies were similar to Dee flies in their use of long, black heron feathers for body hackles, but the wings of Tay patterns were more complex.

Francis Francis goes on to describe the Spey patterns, noting that the flies are "very curious productions to look at." He describes the Spey Dog, "dressed on large hooks for spring fishing . . . a body of black Pig's wool, broad silver tinsel rib, over this a hackle taken from the side of a Scotch Cock's tail." The wings were golden pheasant tail with bronze mallard over the pheasant.

Dee Flies by William Murdoch from *The Fishing Gazette*, 1895
Francis Francis's *A Book on Angling*, 1867
George Kelson's *The Salmon Fly*, 1895

Dodger (bustard tail wing), Veverka

Peacock, Veverka   Model Gray Heron, Veverka

Dunt (Waddington shank),   Dunt, Gobin
Veverka

Red Wing or Red Wing Heron,
Veverka

William Murdoch wrote about flies used for spring fishing on the Dee for *The Fishing Gazette*. His most famous Dee fly is the Dunt, recorded in George Kelson's *The Salmon Fly*, but Francis Francis also included several of Murdoch's patterns in *A Book on Angling*. Murdoch states in *The Salmon Fly*, "There is not a better all-around fly of the plain sort than the Dunt put upon the Dee in Spring or Autumn."

Born in 1851, William Murdoch was a well-known personality on Dee side and an authority on natural history and birds and animals of all kinds. He was also recognized as an authority on life and habits of salmon and knew the River Dee from its mouth to its source. He wrote a book called *More Light on Salmon* that describes what a Dee salmon sees, hears, and dies from on it's journey from the North Sea to Cairngorms. He held the position of chief bank teller, and when he retired moved to Banchory, where he won the friendship of many of the Dee anglers and gillies. He also formed the Dee-side Field Club. Murdoch was a major authority on salmon flies and wrote many articles about them. He died on November 29, 1925.

He included some Spey flies he received from Mr. C. Grant of Aberlour, the Purple King and the Green King. According to Grant, the special cock hackles were found only on flies tied for the River Spey, and the birds were "bred for sake of their feathers." The colors of both the Purple and Green King were changed according to the season; as the summer advanced, both flies were tied with bodies that contained more red, and both were given hackles that had more of a reddish hue. For the body of the Purple King, Grant specified Berlin-wool dubbing in purple, stone red, and scarlet. The Green King's body was made of green Berlin wool along with stone red, yellow, a little orange, and scarlet wool.

Francis Francis felt that John Phillips of Dublin made the best hooks. To this day, of course, many fly-tying authors have strong opinions on hooks for salmon flies.

We can see that by 1867 many patterns had been developed and established and that each river had its own set of flies. A particular river's flies were sometimes distinguished by color, but more often the noteworthy feature was the manner or style in which they were tied. Spey and Dee patterns were distinguished by their long, mobile hackles, either Spey-cock or heron feathers, and the way in which their wings were set. Thanks to Francis Francis, we know the names of two of the early Spey and Dee fly tiers, Mr. Brown of Aberdeen and Mr. C. Grant of Aberlour.

In 1872, A. E. Knox's *Autumns on the Spey* was published. It dealt strictly with salmon fishing on the River Spey. Knox's book contains mostly stories about the River Spey, but it also has a chapter about the flies that were developed and used there. Knox states, "Spey flies are simple and unassuming both in composition and appearance . . . yet are tied with as much skill and care as are the more complicated patterns." He mentions that they are not tied to represent an insect, but are taken by salmon for some of the numerous varieties of crustaceans—prawns, shrimp, and so on. While standing on a bridge over the river, he studied the motion of a Spey fly in the water, noting how its undulating movements exactly resembled those of a living shrimp or prawn.

Of the Spey style itself, Knox says, "the subdued tone and simplicity of Spey flies show a family resemblance, but with a little practice they may easily be distinguished from one another, however trifling and insignificant these minute differences may appear to the uninitiated, to the eyes of an experienced fisherman they are of considerable importance, and when Salmon are shy, their success is frequently due upon these virtues. Size of flies vary through-out the season, in spring they are enormous compared with the smaller sizes used in summer."

Knox mentions that the list of sixteen Spey flies contained in his book "are descriptions taken from specimens that were tied by that accomplished artist, Shanks of Craigellachie."

Knox is the first author to divide Spey flies into smaller groups or classes. He placed each of the sixteen dressings in his book in one of four groups, the Kings, Herons, Reeachs, and Speals. The sophistication of flies and the men who wrote about them was steadily increasing. But the best was yet to come.

Original Spey Flies from A. E. Knox's *Autumns on the Spey*, 1872, Veverka

Gold Speal	Silver Speal	Gold Reeach
Silver Reeach	Gold Green Fly	Silver Green Reeach
Gold Green Reeach	Silver Green Fly	Purple King
Green King	Black King	Gold Purple Fly (Gold Purpy)
Culdrain	Gold Heron	Carron Fly
	Black Heron	

Arthur Edwards Knox's *Autumns on the Spey* includes a chapter with dressings for sixteen original Spey flies. Knox tells that when he stood on the Spey Bridge and watched the pulsating action of a Spey fly under the water, he concluded that it must represent a shrimp. Spey flies had an underwater movement that was unsurpassed by any other style of fly.

The flies in Knox's book are descriptions from specimens tied by the accomplished artist John Shanks of Craigellachie. Little is known of Shanks, but he is noted in George Kelson's book *The Salmon Fly* as the originator of the Miss Grant Spey fly. One could speculate that John Shanks also originated the most famous of all Spey flies—the Lady Caroline. It is documented that Shanks named the Spey flies he dressed after sporting women of the time, and the Miss Grant Spey pattern included a tail in the dressing, as did the Lady Caroline, a unique feature for a Spey fly dressing. Most, or should I say all, were dressed without tails except for the two patterns that were named for important women of the time—the Lady Caroline and the Miss Grant.

KELSON'S CONTRIBUTIONS

By the late nineteenth century, many of the plain and simple standard or local patterns had been replaced by the more elaborate and complex patterns we call the full-dress classics. This is when George Kelson showed up on the salmon-fly scene.

George M. Kelson (1836–1920) was relatively unknown until he started writing articles for *The Fishing Gazette* in May 1884. His articles created quite a stir at the time, and many of his fellow anglers urged him to write a book. *The Salmon Fly* was published in 1895, at the peak of the golden age of the Atlantic-salmon fly, and, among salmon anglers, it was the most important book of the time. Kelson's book brought order to the classification of salmon flies and the techniques of their dressing.

His extraordinary fly-tying talent and his articles revealed some new and revolutionary methods of winging a salmon fly. Kelson felt that all the materials in a wing should show, and that it was important to attach them in a certain order to produce a wing that was more opaque and that had a beautiful structure.

Kelson also felt that tying one's own flies enhances the pleasure of salmon fishing, stressing that a tier should take into consideration symmetry, proportion, mobility, and color harmony. His descriptions of feathers and various portions of flies indicate that he was an uncommonly observant student of fly tying. He mentions that tinsel enriches the effect produced by a fly's colors, that black ostrich herl helps to define and complement other colors, that the tag is a very important component of a fly, since it is the first part that a salmon sees. Besides knowing his fly-tying stuff, he was a great angler who kept up with all the latest tackle. And he was a flamboyant personality.

At the time, strip-wing flies as used on the River Dee were in vogue. In his descriptions of materials for Spey and Dee patterns, Kelson mentions that Spey-cock and eagle hackles were expensive, and that he preferred hackles from light-colored pheasants and feathers from the breast of the common bittern to Spey-cock hackles. He sometimes replaced heron hackles with feathers from a crowned pigeon, though he did say that cinnamon heron and Nankeen night heron feathers were the most popular hackles, and that *Demigretta gulanisis* (African black heron) had the best black hackles.

He felt that when fishing a fly with a long hackle, the less action the angler applies, the better. When selecting a long hackle, Kelson noted, a tier should pick the one with the most life or mobility, and he should then let the hackle work with the current. He stated that the golden pheasant "is subordinate to none in salmon fly materials by virtue of its crests." Kelson knew materials like no one before him.

Kelson's chapter on fly patterns contains hundreds of flies and covers all styles. He designed many flies and included many others that were in use at the time. They range from simple grub patterns to many Spey and Dee flies to the most elaborate full-dress classics. Kelson himself used very few patterns when he fished, and he regarded assembling the numerous patterns described in his book as serving a historical purpose.

He also included the patterns of John Traherne, an Irishman with wide salmon-fishing experience. Kelson

Flies Originated by George Kelson, from *The Salmon Fly*, 1895

Captain Walton, Veverka	Black Dog, Burden
Ike Dean, Rossman	Highland Gem, Harrang
Black Dog (Francis Francis), Harrang	Silver Ardea, Harrang

George Kelson fished many rivers for salmon and was credited with catching over 3,000 salmon in his lifetime. He originated many patterns in several styles—grubs, shrimp, Spey, Eagle—and many full-dressed classic patterns. When he fished, he used a limited number of patterns; he considered his book of hundreds of patterns a historic account of the salmon flies of his time, the Victorian era. Some of his Spey-type patterns included complex full-dressed style wings. Flies tied in this style were used on the Tay, and many were called Tay flies.

The Captain Walton was used on the Rivers Spey, Dee, and Beauly. The Black Dog was an old standard of Kelson's father, a useful fly in high water, and a good fly for the Spey, as was the Highland Gem. The Ike Dean was introduced by Kelson's father on the Lochy and was one of the first of the fancy flies. The Silver Ardea is the only standard fly with long hackles over a silver body. When tied with a black silk body, it is called the Black Ardea.

described Traherne as the "Master of Infinite Elaboration," noting that his fly dressings "are the most intricate and brilliant." Traherne's patterns were lavishly dressed, tied with elaborate body veilings and wings of the rarest feathers. But his patterns were not just flies with lots of feathers; they were well thought out, their colors and balance merging to form some of the most intricate classics to come out of the Victorian era.

Among the Dee patterns that Kelson included was the Akroyd, a fly originated by Charles Akroyd in 1878. It was an old Dee standard, often described as the "Poor Man's Jock Scott." Kelson also mentions the Double-Winged Akroyd "introduced by Mr. Garden of Aberdeen . . . a good fly in early season when the water is mixed with snow." Garden was also the originator of the Balmoral, Gardner, and Glentana patterns.

The Glentana was a Dee fly tied to look like the earlier Gled Wing pattern. By the time of *The Salmon Fly*'s publication, gleds had become extinct. Kelson says, "Among the Scotch flies the 'Gled Wing,' otherwise remembered as the Glentana Gled, named from the Hawk that supplied the material for the wing is gone from the Dee-side, and when it died the fly died

too, and there is no imitation of the attractive wing feather that has proved of equal."

He also included the Dunt originated by Mr. W. Murdoch, saying that "there is no better all-around fly on the Dee in Spring and Autumn." *The Salmon Fly* also contained some patterns from a tier named Mr. Turnbull; these had long throat hackles and wings with a more complex construction, much like those on married-wing classics.

Kelson also listed the Black Dog, an old standard of his father, "useful in high water on the Spey." He gave himself credit as its originator. This is not the same pattern mentioned by Mackintosh in 1808. Many fly tiers and writers have speculated on the real origin of the Black Dog described in *The Salmon Fly*, but I'm inclined to believe that it was indeed Kelson's pattern. It is very similar to other patterns that Kelson tied, such as the Floodtide. Both contained Amherst pheasant in their wings, a relatively uncommon material at the time except on patterns that Kelson originated. Kelson mentions that his friend Mr. George Horne of Hereford raised golden and Amherst pheasants. Other Kelson patterns that used Amherst pheasant in their wings are the Highland Gem, Pearl, and Queen of Spring.

The chapter on fly patterns contains the Green King, Black King, and Purple King, all standard patterns on the Spey. Kelson noted that he preferred the Green Queen, which used crowned pigeon for the body hackle, to the Green King. *The Salmon Fly* was the first book to list such now-famous Spey flies as the Lady Caroline and the Dallas created by John Dallas.

Also described were three "modern" Spey flies by Major Grant, an authority on fly fishing for salmon in the Spey and the owner of a castle on the river. Major Grant invented the Glen Grant, Glen Grant's Fancy, and Mrs. Grant patterns. Kelson included a fourth pattern in the group, the Miss Grant, which is credited to Shanks, the same tier mentioned in Knox's book, *Autumns on the Spey*.

Kelson originated several new Eagle patterns. The Floodtide, Golden Eagle, and Quilled Eagle are his inventions.

Kelson was called the "grand old man of salmon fishing" and "the high priest of the salmon fly," but he was also a controversial figure who had strong opinions. Still, his book was the salmon-fly bible of its time. Kelson's writings on flies and materials shows us that he

Dee Flies by William Garden of Aberdeen from George Kelson's *The Salmon Fly*, 1895, Veverka

Glentana (zebra turkey wing)

Double Akroyd

Balmoral

Gardener (argus pheasant wing)

William Garden is known for his traditional Dee Flies. He worked in Invernesshire, then Aberdeen, where he opened and operated a gun and tackle shop. He was known throughout Britain as an authority on angling and shooting matters. He died on March 29, 1906, at age sixty.

The Glentana is taken from the old Dee fly the Gled Wing. When the hawk feather for the wing of the Gled Wing went out of use because the bird died out, the material was changed to cinnamon turkey. Kelson considered the Gardener one of Garden's best Dee patterns and the Balmoral a favorite fly on the Dee. The Double White-Winged Akroyd was used in high water. The Double Akroyd pattern above is my version, two consecutive patterns tied on one long-shanked hook.

was a dedicated student of fishing and fly tying, one who drew lessons from experience, and *The Salmon Fly* is, among many other things, an important chapter in the history of Spey flies.

DR. PRYCE-TANNATT

The next major book after Kelson's was *How to Dress Salmon Flies*, published in 1914. Its author, Dr. Thomas Edwin Pryce-Tannatt (1881–1965) was an Englishman who gave up medicine at the age of thirty-one to devote his life to angling. He accepted the appointment of Inspector of Salmon Fisheries in 1912 and with this job made many friends on the rivers that he helped to improve. By the time of his retirement in 1946, he was a welcome guest on many rivers throughout the country. In his later years, he hung up his rods and filled his days with his second interest, gardening.

Pryce-Tannatt's approach to fly dressing can be determined from a passage in his book: "There is an indescribable something about a fly dressed by an expert amateur, who is a practical salmon fisherman, which the fly dressed by a non-angling professional not infrequently lacks. I have heard this peculiar quality

rather neatly referred to as 'soul.' A precise explanation of what is meant by 'soul' is one of the impossibilities. The term is incomprehensible to the uninitiated, but is completely understood by the experienced man."

All the patterns in his book were tied by him, though he admitted he was not an expert. He had at one time watched a professional, Mr. William McNicol, tie flies, and stated that in that brief time he had learned more than if he had read books or relied on his own experience.

In his section on materials for Spey flies, Pryce-Tannatt describes Spey-cock hackles as "a peculiarity which must be regarded as an exception, both in character and in the manner in which they are put on. Spey flies are peculiar looking, the shortness of the wings, and the unusual manner in which they are put on, produce a sort of hump-backed effect, which looks rather wicked. The hackles are long and very mobile, both Gray and Black Heron hackles are used but the typical hackle is from the lateral tail feathers from a certain breed of domestic fowl, known as the Spey Cock. Not easy to procure, their colors ranging from metallic bronzy black, plain brown and freckled brown and cinnamon. The hackles lack translucence but are very mobile in character." He mentions that he is indebted to William Brown of Aberdeen for sending him flies tied by Speyside gillies, and that "there is no constant dressing of any Spey fly."

He stated, "Dee strip-wing flies, are a very distinct group, being peculiar in their appearance, and somewhat limited in their seasonal and geographical application." Pryce-Tannatt noted that they originated on the "Queen of Salmon Rivers, The Aberdeenshire Dee," and are among the oldest types of patterns still surviving. Dee flies were used for early spring fishing when the water is cold. They were dressed on large hooks and tied sparse so that they would sink better and come within range of salmon lying close to the bottom. Like other writers, Pryce-Tannatt noted that these flies possess an attractive feature in the great mobility of their hackles and wings, which gives them a very lifelike appearance in the water. The characteristic features of Dee flies are their slender dressings and the unique style of their wings.

Pryce-Tannatt's list of Spey and Dee patterns contains all the standards that were included in earlier books, with the addition of a few new patterns, the Avon Eagle, Jock O' Dee, and the Moonlight.

Mr. Turnbull's Patterns from George Kelson's *The Salmon Fly*, 1895

Pitcroy Fancy, Malloy

Wilson, Harrang

Niagara, Veverka

Ethel, Veverka

These patterns were originated by Mr. Turnbull and included in George Kelson's *The Salmon Fly*. The Pitcroy Fancy was considered a modern Spey pattern and the Wilson, named after Mr. Wilson of Moffat, a superb killer on most rivers. The Ethel was a good fly on the River Usk, a killing fly in peat- or porter-colored water.

Pryce-Tannatt had a flair for expressing his ideas and describing flies. His book remains a treasured classic among modern-day salmon-fly tiers.

ERIC TAVERNER
Eric Taverner's book, *Salmon Fishing*, was published in 1931. Like the authors before him, Taverner was a student of fly tying and a collector of patterns. His book chronicles all the previous salmon-fishing books, with bits of information collected after the dust settled from the busy Victorian era.

Discussing Spey flies, he mentions, "The Spey is a River of great power and is said to have caused the creation of a special type of fly . . . with a long mobile hackle which give in heavy water of moderate flow an appearance of life unapproached by any other style of fly." He further stated that the appearance and action of a Spey fly made him think that "it is dressed in the most rational way yet achieved of simulating life struggling beneath the surface of the water."

He mentions the Dee strip-winged flies and "their characteristic method of winging, a tradition that is attributed to the Aberdeenshire Dee, being an attractive fly by virtue of their shape as well as by their translucency and slimness of their dressing."

Taverner was a keen student of salmon flies and their virtues. His descriptions of fly patterns and their styles were accurate and sufficiently detailed so as almost to draw a mental picture for the reader.

Perhaps the best piece of information that Taverner included was the mention of Ernest Crosfield

(1833–1905), an Englishman who had fished all over England, Scotland, and Iceland. He was the premier fly tier of his day and a great fisherman. His flies were fashioned after those of the great Irish fly tier Michael Rogan of Ballyshannon. Many days on the water gave Crosfield great insight into the habits of salmon and the type of fly that worked best in a given circumstance.

Crosfield's patterns exhibited economy of material, intentional translucence, and slimness of dressing. He felt that such a fly would dance in the water and respond to every twist and turn in the current, and he believed that every feather in a salmon fly's wing had a purpose and should fulfill it. His flies were dressed in a manner that would compel the different fibers to show. The wings were tied in a series of bunches so that they sprang from different points, which kept materials from covering those previously attached. He also believed that flies should be translucent, and that with every fiber separated, a fly would produce maximum reflection of light and the best action. Crosfield's theories make sense; natural insects and fish are translucent, and our flies should exhibit the same qualities.

Some of his tying methods included the use of small bunches of wing materials with a collar added to the middle of the wing; this cut down on head size. He also used silk floss to tie a fly, producing an underlying body color that made for a brilliant fly.

Crosfield tied and fished Spey flies, but he is best known for his Black Silk and Brockweir patterns. A pattern that is still used today, the Crosfield, was originated by his brother Shetney for fishing in Iceland.

Crosfield never wrote a book, and we're lucky that Taverner recorded some of his thoughts on salmon-fly

Ernest Crosfield

Spey Flies from George Kelson's *The Salmon Fly*, 1895, Veverka

Red King

Lady Caroline

Rough Grouse

Gold Riach

Several Spey flies are included in George Kelson's book. The Gold Riach was originated by Mr. Riach. The Red King was an old standard Spey pattern, and the Rough Grouse, a pattern that Kelson originated, was a splendid fly on the Spey in dull wet weather. Kelson's book listed the Lady Caroline for the first time but left no clue to who originated it. A later book by John Buckland and Arthur Oglesby, *A Guide to Salmon Flies*, mentions that the Lady Caroline was named after Lady Caroline Gordon-Lenox, daughter of the then Duke of Richmond and Gordon at Gordon Castle.

---

tying. He did write an article, "Notes on Tying Salmon Flies," under the name of the "Poacher" for *Salmon and Trout* magazine.

ACROSS THE OCEAN

With Taverner's book, we can close the door on the Victorian era of salmon-fly tying. We can see that an amazing number of fly patterns were created and recorded from the mid-1800s to the early 1900s. They started as very simple patterns: tail, body, hackle, and a set of wings. From those simple dressings, salmon flies evolved into more elaborate patterns with jointed bodies veiled with brilliant feathers, complex married wings, cheeks of exotic feathers, and toppings of golden pheasant. Throughout all these changes, however, Spey and Dee patterns remained the same.

After salmon flies crossed the ocean to North America, they were transformed back into less complicated patterns, the hairwings. As the years passed, exotic feathers became increasingly rare and expensive; eventually, many feathers became illegal to possess in the United States. Fly tiers tend to use whatever is available, and so hairwing salmon flies grew in popularity. Ira Gruber, John Cosseboom, and J. Clovis Arsanalt were among the noteworthy North American tiers.

This is not to say that the classics vanished. On the American side of the Atlantic, Charlie Defeo, Preston Jennings, and several others tied some of the classic

patterns. Many tiers in Great Britain and Europe, where rare and exotic materials were still legally available, continued to make traditional full-dress salmon flies.

The next important salmon-fly book was *Atlantic Salmon Flies and Fishing*, by Joseph D. Bates, published in 1970. Bates brought to light the work of contemporary fly tiers such as Megan Boyd, Colin Simpson, and Bellarmino Martinez. He included all types of salmon flies—hairwings, classics, and Spey patterns—along with a lot of advice on salmon fishing and a vast amount of information on the flies and their histories. Among other things, Bates explained the change from classics to hairwings.

Like many authors before him, Bates was a student of the salmon fly. He collected all types of flies, but had a real soft spot for the classic salmon patterns. Besides a great appreciation of the tiers and their flies, Bates had a deep interest in the history of the patterns.

Earlier in his life, Bates had traveled to Maine to fish for brook trout and had studied the streamer flies of Carrie Stevens and many other tiers of that area. (They appear in his book on streamers.) Then he got the salmon bug and turned his attention to the flies used for them. Salmon flies became his passion, one that did not end until Bates passed away in 1989.

Bates collected thousands of salmon-fly patterns throughout his long life. His vast collection contained flies from all periods—antique patterns, Victorian classics, and modern-day dressings. Bates kept the salmon-fly fires burning at a time when most fly fishers were interested in other styles of flies.

A SPEY-FLY RENAISSANCE

By the 1970s, Spey and Dee patterns were far from the minds of salmon anglers, at least in North America. Most Canadian and American fishermen tied the simple hairwing patterns for salmon and enjoyed great results. Among most salmon-fly tiers on this side of the Atlantic, the old, graceful Spey and Dee flies were historical curiosities—or entirely unknown.

In a far corner of the Pacific Northwest, however, a fly tier was working on a series of flies for winter steelhead. He searched all the salmon-fly books of the past, looking for a style of fly that would catch the steelhead that ran up the rivers of the Olympic Peninsula. Some of these books described a type of old fly used for salmon fishing in the spring and fall, when the water was cold and often stained or dirty, conditions much

---

Grant Spey Flies from George Kelson's *The Salmon Fly*, 1895

Glen Grant, Whorwood

Glen Grant's Fancy, Scoville

Mrs. Grant, Scoville

Miss Grant, Veverka

The Grants owned a castle on one of the best stretches of the River Spey. They were experts on the flies and salmon of the Spey. Major Grant is credited in *The Salmon Fly* as the originator of the Grant series of Spey patterns, although the Miss Grant was credited to Shanks. Major Grant was also credited with the classic pattern the Green Highlander.

---

like those faced by a winter steelhead angler. These, of course, were the Spey and Dee patterns.

This tier worked alone, perfecting his techniques and slowly converting the original Spey and Dee styles to flies more suitable for steelhead fishing. He was Syd Glasso of Forks, Washington. The fly-tying world first heard of him in 1976, with the publication of *Steelhead Fly Fishing and Flies*, by Trey Combs.

Steelhead Fly Fishing and Flies recounted the early history of steelhead fishing and described the flies used for these fish. Combs covered all of the great original steelhead-fly tiers: Haig-Brown, Prey, Bradner, Mcleod, Drain, Glasso, Johnson, and Lemire. The color plates showed all the important steelhead flies, including those from the early days of the sport, and black-and-white photos by Ralph Wahl portrayed the major figures of steelhead-fishing history.

The color plates included ten flies that Syd Glasso had tied. One could easily see that Glasso was in a class by himself. His flies were tied sparsely, in bright colors, and with long, flowing hackles, low-set wings, and very tiny, neat heads. They had a look and style that was unequaled by any others from the past to the present day. These patterns would be Syd Glasso's contribution to steelheading. They influenced the work of many tiers who came after him, including me.

Unfortunately for the rest of us, Glasso never wrote a book about his fly-tying methods. The only thing Glasso wrote about steelhead fishing was an article for "The Creel," the bulletin of the Fly Fishers Club of Oregon. In it, he mentioned the rivers that he fished on the Olympic Peninsula—the Bogachiel, Sol Duc, Queets,

and Hoh. It's interesting to note that Glasso named a series of flies after one of the rivers he fished, the Sol Duc. This series included the Sol Duc, Sol Duc Dark, and Sol Duc Spey. By naming flies after the river for which they were tied, Glasso followed the tradition of the fly fishers who created the first Spey flies. And Glasso proved that this style worked as well for steelhead as it did for Atlantic salmon: in 1959, he placed fifth in the annual *Field & Stream* fishing contest with an 18-pound, 12-ounce steelhead caught on a Sol Duc in the fly's namesake river. At the time, the Olympic Peninsula was noted for the Northwest's finest winter steelhead fishing.

In that article, published in 1970, Glasso said that he had been fishing and tying Spey flies for twenty years. The piece also mentioned Dick Wentworth, Glasso's fishing companion and a most accomplished angler and fly tier in his own right. Dick is credited with the Quillayute pattern. Glasso had a great influence on many fly tiers who lived and fished in the Pacific Northwest.

Pat Crane was another friend who fished and tied flies with Syd Glasso. Crane is said to have been very particular about the hooks and materials that he used for his Spey flies, which rivaled Glasso's in beauty. Whenever he caught a steelhead, Crane followed a unique personal tradition: he would release the fish and then, with a pair of cutters, clip the hook behind the barb in a tribute to the fish.

Glasso loved Spey flies for some very practical reasons: they were easy to tie (for him, anyway), they looked seductive in the water, and the fish took them solidly. That was enough for him.

Syd Glasso and his white Porsche

Eagle Flies from George Kelson's
***The Salmon Fly*, 1895, and**
J. H. Hale's *How to Tie Salmon Flies*, 1892

Floodtide, Brand

Quilled Eagle, Brand	Yellow Eagle (Halladale), Rossman
Golden Eagle, Veverka	Brown Eagle, Veverka
Nightshade, Veverka	

George Kelson included several new Eagle patterns in *The Salmon Fly*, most of which were similar to Dee patterns in their dressings. The only difference was the use of a marabou-like hackle from an eagle. Eagle patterns were considered the most mobile flies and were used in high, cold, and sometimes off-color water conditions. They can be tied in any number of color combinations today with turkey marabou, either in its natural mottled brown or white dyed yellow, red, and purple.

The Floodtide and the Quilled Eagle are Eagle patterns with very complex wings. Kelson mentions that he rarely fishes any other Eagle pattern but the Quilled Eagle and sometimes dresses it with a yellow hackle instead of gray. The Floodtide was one of the best standards "on the top of a flood." The Nightshade is a good late evening fly. The Halladale Yellow Eagle was mentioned in Major J. H. Hale's *How to Tie Salmon Flies*, 1892, and in J. J. Hardy's *Salmon Fishing*, 1907.

In his article for "The Creel," Glasso also mentioned regretting the vanity that causes an angler to kill a steelhead. "Must I prove that I've caught something?" he wrote. "It's ridiculous to become sentimental over a fish, and yet those desperate, all-out fights at the end of a leader do deserve something better than a final blow on the head."

When Syd Glasso died at the age of seventy-seven on September 6, 1983, steelheading lost its most respected and accomplished fly angler. He was called a pioneer steelhead fly fisher and a fly tier extraordinaire, a man of character and integrity. He drove a white Porsche and fished with cane rods, classic salmon reels, and the most beautiful of all fly styles, the Spey. Glasso also tied full-dress classic salmon flies that are among the most beautiful and symmetrical ever crafted. His flies had a flow and a character that are hard to explain but are obvious when you see one.

Steelhead Fly Fishing and Flies covered other Spey-fly tiers and their steelhead flies, notably Walt Johnson and his Red Shrimp pattern. Harry Lemire,

another steelhead angler whose work Combs included in his book, wasn't tying Spey flies at the time, but his flies showed an influence from Atlantic-salmon patterns; Lemire's Golden Edge Orange is a good example. These days, Lemire ties many of the original Spey and Dee patterns without the use of a vise.

Poul Jorgensen's *Salmon Flies* was published in 1978. This is the book that rekindled interest in salmon-fly tying in the United States. The cover showed a full-dress Durham Ranger that caught the attention of fly tiers. Many started tying salmon flies for the first time, using the step-by-step instructions in Jorgensen's book. *Salmon Flies* dealt entirely with tying, and it covered all the different styles: low-water patterns, classics, hairwings, drys, and, of course, Spey and Dee flies. Both an expert tier and instructor, Jorgensen introduced many people to salmon flies.

Interest in salmon-fly tying grew steadily over the next decade. An increasingly large community of salmon-fly tiers created a growing demand for good materials. Some of the old materials began to show up in fly shops, and replacements were found for many materials that were no longer available. Salmon-fly tying was on the brink of a full-blown renaissance.

Joseph Bates finished his final work, *The Art of the Atlantic Salmon Fly*, in 1987. In that book, which showed the work of the best salmon-fly tiers of the day, Bates described collecting salmon flies as "an obsession that seduced him," and celebrated "the flies' ancient history . . . their intricate beauty, and the complexities of their construction." As he covered the history of salmon fishing, salmon-fly tying, and fly patterns, Bates also shed light on some of the authors who had come before him. And, of course, he furnished a wealth of tying information; each photo of a fly was accompanied by the recipe and a paragraph about the pattern's history and use. The color plates in *The Art of the Atlantic Salmon Fly* showed a number of full-dress classic patterns tied by Syd Glasso. This was the first time that Glasso's exquisite full-dress flies were depicted in a book.

At the time, many new practitioners were taking up the art of tying salmon flies. Quite a few of these new tiers differed from those of the past, in that they did not fish for salmon. Most fished for trout, but some did not fish at all. They simply loved the beauty of salmon flies and the challenge of tying them. It's a trend that continues to this day.

Flies from Dr. Thomas Edwin Pryce-Tannatt's *How to Dress Salmon Flies*, 1914

Gray Heron, Veverka

Jock O' Dee, Veverka   Carron, Veverka

Avon Eagle, Brand

Moonlight (white wing),   Purple King, Veverka
Veverka

Sir Richard (Waddington shank), Veverka

Dr. Thomas Edwin Pryce-Tannatt's *How to Dress Salmon Flies* includes several new Spey and Dee patterns along with some of the original patterns. Pryce-Tannatt was an expert fly tier—he dressed all the flies that appeared in his book, and they were very neat and well proportioned. He changed or altered some of the original patterns to his liking, adding materials and developing techniques to suit. Several of his original flies are included in the plates of Eric Taverner's 1942 book, *Fly Tying for Salmon*.

The Jock O' Dee and the Gray Heron must have been a take off from the Jock Scott because they display the same color pattern. Pryce Tannatt's dressing for the Purple King and the Carron vary from previous Spey-fly dressings—both had a silk rib, on the Purple King it is lavender or red, and on the Carron it is scarlet. The Moonlight is an exception to the Spey and Dee style with its blue chatterer veils. When the Sir Richard is tied in large sizes, Pryce-Tannatt instructs that the body hackle should be changed to a large black heron hackle. The Avon Eagle has a whole feather wing, consisting of a pair of golden pheasant sword feathers (red spear-shaped feathers from the side of the tail) and sides of jungle cock and topped with several golden pheasant crests.

The publication of *The Art of the Atlantic Salmon Fly* coincided with the beginning of what we might call a golden age of salmon-fly tying in North America. Many tiers on both coasts became serious students of the full-dress classics. Spey and Dee flies had a strong following. Not since the Victorian era had the world seen so many talented, devoted salmon-fly tiers.

With all this activity, it was only natural that more books would follow. Judith Dunham's *The Art of the Trout Fly*, published in 1988, was a revolutionary look at flies, one in which standard fishing flies were presented in ways that showed off their beauty. That book changed the way in which flies were viewed and photographed. She followed it in 1991 with *The Atlantic Salmon Fly*, which contained the work of many tiers from Britain, Europe, Canada, and North America.

Salmon-fly tying was already heating up in this country, but Judith's book fed the fire. All sorts of wild and exotic flies began to pour out of vises.

Another great book published at this time is Mikael Frodin's *Classic Salmon Flies: The History and Patterns*. It covers all types of salmon flies, including many of the Spey and Dee patterns.

Elaborate, exotic, full-dress patterns were getting most of the ink, but Spey and Dee flies had a steadily growing fan club. Some contemporary tiers were tinkering with the look of Spey and Dee flies, tying them with more complex wings and body veils. In a sense, these changes repeated those that had happened a century earlier, when standard salmon patterns became steadily more elaborate.

Deke Meyer's *Advanced Fly Fishing for Steelhead*, published in 1992, contains a chapter on steelhead Spey flies and their evolution from Atlantic-salmon patterns, an evolution that began in the vise of Syd Glasso. Meyer mentions Walt Johnson and some of his newer Spey patterns, such as the Deep Purple Spey and the Golden Spey. Johnson, one of the last surviving steelhead pioneers, fished with Glasso and saw firsthand how effective Spey patterns were on steelhead. Glasso's work had a big influence on Johnson's tying, but Johnson has also developed many Spey patterns of his own. He wrote an article titled "An Affair with Lady Caroline" for the October 1982 issue of *Flyfishing* magazine, in which he described the Spey flies he ties.

Meyer's book also showcases new Spey and Spey-style patterns for steelhead by Dave McNeese, Joe Howell, Bill Chinn, Alec Jackson, and me. This is the first book to contain the Mr. Glasso Spey fly by Dick Wentworth, a dressing that had appeared in the February 1988 issue of *Flyfishing* in an article by Alec Jackson called "Steelhead Flies Enter Their Victorian Era."

In his account of Spey-fly history and their journey from Scotland to America's Pacific Northwest, Meyer mentions that the first angler to fish a Spey fly for steelhead was Roderick Haig-Brown. One of the twentieth century's finest angling writers, Haig-Brown was born and raised in England, where he fished for salmon. In the 1920s, after moving to British Columbia, he fished for steelhead with Atlantic-salmon flies. In his book *The Western Angler* (1939), Haig-Brown wrote that he used, among others, the Lady Caroline, a Spey fly. Back then, he couldn't have known that a later generation of Pacific Northwest fly tiers would adopt this handsome

Pacific Northwest Steelhead Flies

Black and Red Spey, Mark Sagester	Signal Light Spey, Kaufmann

Sea-Run Cutthroat Coachman, Syd Glasso

Green Butt Spider, Stidham

Coal Car Marabou Spey, Kaufmann	Cockatoo Spey, Chinn

Orange Heron, Crane

Freight Train Spey, Kaufmann	Tri-Spade, Jackson	Low and Clear Spider, Canfield
	Skunk, Haas	Spade, Jackson
Green Butt Spider, Sherman	Midnight Spey, Noble	
	Summer Spey, Stidham	Purple Peril, Haas
Steelhead Marabou, Aid		Purple Heron, Stovall

The Northwest has a deep tradition of tying of steelhead flies, many in the Spey style. The early tiers included Jim Pray, Peter Schwab, Ed Haas, and Ken Mcleod. Early steelhead flies were simple in construction but bold in color. In time steelhead flies became highly refined, and patterns were developed for specific river systems, much like the early Atlantic-salmon patterns. The first Spey-fly tiers included Syd Glasso, Pat Crane, Dick Wentworth, Walt Johnson, and Mark Canfield. Other tiers from the Pacific Northwest who tied with an Atlantic salmon–fly flair were Wes Drain and Harry Lemire. Many other tiers continue to be inspired to tie flies in this tradition.

style of fly for their own steelhead angling, or that they would eventually help to make these beautiful flies part of the salmon-fly renaissance that shows no sign of slowing down.

The history tells us that Spey and Dee flies began as local patterns for the salmon in specific rivers in Scotland, simple flies tied to meet particular conditions. They are among the oldest salmon flies and have, since their origin, been noted for their appearance and unique action. During the second half of the nineteenth century, as most Atlantic-salmon patterns became increasingly complicated and ornate, Spey flies remained largely unchanged. By the middle of the twentieth century, most North American salmon anglers were concentrating on hairwing patterns, and Spey flies had become relatively obscure dressings on

this side of the Atlantic. As interest in tying salmon flies blossomed in the 1980s and '90s, the eye-catching, full-dress Victorian patterns often overshadowed the less colorful Spey and Dee flies.

On the West Coast of North America, however, fly fishers had discovered that these old Atlantic-salmon flies caught Pacific steelhead very well. Syd Glasso and a handful of other Northwestern fly tiers mastered the Spey and Dee styles and began converting salmon flies into steelhead flies.

These days, there are probably more fly tiers than ever crafting Spey flies, Dee flies, and patterns derived from them. The essence of the Spey style remains the same: a body of silk and fur; a long, mobile body hackle; a set of low-set wings; and a small, neat head. To many of us, these are the most elegant and graceful of all flies.

Walt Johnson Steelhead Speys

Royal Spey

Spectral Spider   Red Shrimp

Deep Purple Spey

Shimmering Iridescent Spey

Walt Johnson was one of the last true pioneer steelhead fly fishermen and tiers from the Northwest. He was there from the beginning of the steelhead fly-fishing boom, fished in its heyday, and enjoyed its golden years. It saddens me to think that Walt did not see the completion of this book (he died before its publication). Walt's flies are inspired by Syd Glasso's flies. Johnson's first fly was the Red Shrimp, a fly designed to trigger a response from wild steelhead fresh from the ocean.

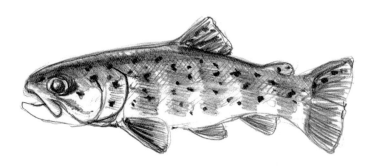

CHAPTER 2

Materials

WHEN I STARTED THIS CHAPTER, I WANTED ONLY to familiarize you with materials used for Spey and Dee flies. As I went along, though, I also explained some of the things I've noticed about feathers used on all types of salmon patterns. Some patterns in the Spey-fly category have very elaborate wings, and most of the materials described in this chapter will come into use on one fly or another. It also occurred to me that someone interested in tying Spey patterns is probably also interested in other styles of salmon flies and their materials. It's hard to describe a feather and not mention its applications, so I put down all that I have learned about each feather.

Before we examine specific materials, let's look at the general components of a Spey fly. First on the list is one of the various styles of return-eye or blind-eye salmon hooks that have shanks slightly longer than average. The hook is the frame of a fly, and materials should be selected and tied on to accent the shape and balance of the hook. With experience, you will notice that a certain style or length of hook naturally lends itself to a specific fly pattern. Low-water patterns, for instance, look best on fine-wire, return-eye hooks; the fine hook accents the slim dressing. Hairwing patterns always look better tied on double hooks; a double seems to balance the pattern better than a single hook does. Full-dress feather-wing patterns look better on big, wide-gapped hooks, while low, married-wing patterns look better on smaller-gapped hooks.

Spey and Dee patterns use long-shanked hooks that accent the long, wispy materials. Dee flies were originally tied on large Limerick hooks sometimes called long Dees or simply Dee hooks. Many low-water hooks have slightly longer shanks and fit in this category.

A hook's size is very important. When you select a hook for a particular pattern, consider the materials you will tie to it. Many materials come only in certain lengths and will look best only on certain hooks. Each pattern seems to work best on a small range of hook sizes; some flies look good on larger hooks, while others fit better on smaller hooks.

Size 1 hooks are perfect for steelhead Speys. Salmon Spey flies look best when tied on size 2/0 hooks, give or take a little. If the hook is much larger than that, finding bronze-mallard wing material of the right length becomes a problem. Dee patterns can be tied on the largest hooks, since their materials are long enough. The married-wing classics are best tied on sizes 2/0 to 5/0 hooks; anything larger, and you run into problems finding materials for the wings. I like to dress my married-wing flies on hooks with slightly longer shanks so the wings have a low, sleek, racy appearance.

Today, there are many hooks suitable for Spey and Dee patterns. Not too many years ago, hooks for these flies were rather scarce. Thanks to growing demand, hook companies are making more models designed for these styles.

Most of the original Spey patterns didn't have tails. The only original Spey patterns with tails are the Lady Caroline and the Miss Grant. Dee patterns had tails, and many had veils to accent the tails. The tails of Dee patterns consisted of golden-pheasant crests, often with veils made of tippets or red body feathers from a golden pheasant. Some of the early Dee patterns had tails made with the red feathers from the body of a golden pheasant. Some modern-day steelhead Speys have tails of golden-pheasant crests dyed in fluorescent colors.

Tail materials should be chosen carefully. The correct length is very important, particularly on a pattern that uses golden-pheasant crest for the tail, in the wing, and for a topping. Its tail sets the style of a fly because it dictates the length and the height of the wing. By the time you realize that a tail is too short or too long, you will have tied much of the rest of the fly, and you won't be able to correct the mistake. So, take your time and try to picture the complete fly in your mind before attaching the tail material. Use only feathers that have perfectly straight stems. Study flies made by good tiers, and try to learn from your mistakes. With experience, you'll learn to judge materials for tails and toppings.

The original Dee patterns had tips and tags made of tinsel and various colors of silk. As a rule, Spey flies didn't have tags, though many had bright materials in the rear quarter of the body, which served as a tag of sorts. Many steelhead Speys have tips and tags of tinsel and fluorescent silk.

The bodies of the original Spey and Dee patterns were tied with various materials—Berlin wool, pig's wool, mohair, and seal fur. Those materials are still used today, along with new synthetic dubbings. Dee-fly bodies were made with several sections of brilliantly colored seal fur dyed yellow, red, blue, orange, claret, and green. Spey patterns had somber bodies—olive, brown, green, and deep purple—usually made of several shades of wool blended together.

Body materials should be sparse. That makes for a more attractive fly that sinks well. Heavily dubbed bodies trap air and sink much slower. The most sparsely dubbed flies are the steelhead Speys, which are tied with flat, waxed floss with seal fur dubbed onto the floss for the front portion of the body.

All of these patterns are ribbed with various tinsels. On some of the original Spey patterns, different colors of silk were also used as ribs. Many of the old Spey patterns had ribs that crisscrossed the hackles; these counterwound ribs kept the hackle stems from coming loose when cut by a fish's teeth. Dee patterns were ribbed with the broadest tinsels. The fibers of the seal fur made a veil over the tinsel, giving the body an inner glow in the water.

The body hackles of Spey and Dee patterns were of some type of long-fibered feather chosen for its mobility in the water. In the case of Spey patterns, the most obvious feature was the body hackle taken from a Spey cock. A Spey-cock hackle was a feather from the side of the tail of a rooster that was raised along the River Spey and bred for its hackles. They were very rare and are now believed to be extinct. Some of the Spey patterns also used heron hackles.

Dee patterns used black or gray heron hackles of the largest size. The flies were big, and they required the longest hackles. Some Dee patterns used a chicken feather for the body hackle and a long heron hackle for the throat hackle.

Eagle patterns were, not surprisingly, tied with hackles from eagles, either in their natural color or dyed yellow. The hackles were taken from the shin of the bird. They were marabou-like in texture and very mobile in the water.

The original Steelhead Speys were tied with gray and black heron hackles. A modern substitute is a hackle from a blue-eared pheasant, either natural or dyed black. Many of the modern patterns are tied with hackles dyed bright orange, purple, or yellow.

Body hackles should be tied on so that all the fibers flow toward the rear of the fly. Heavily hackled flies look good in a shadow box, but flies for fishing should be tied on the sparse side.

All Spey and Dee patterns have some type of throat or collar. Most of these were made of duck flank feathers, though guinea fowl and golden-pheasant body feathers were commonly used. Most of the original Spey patterns were tied with collars of teal flank; indeed, this was a distinguishing feature. Dee patterns had extralong throat hackles made of various duck flank feathers and sometimes heron hackle.

I always look for the longest feathers when selecting a throat material. The length of the throat accents the long body hackle. Try to keep the throat hackles as sparse as possible; for that matter, keep body hackles sparse, too. Sparsely dressed flies swim or track better than heavily dressed ones.

The wings of early Spey flies were tied with two strips of bronze mallard. This was another traditional feature. The wings were tied on the shoulders of the fly, and they were never longer than the hook bend. Dee flies used long slips of turkey or goose quill, tied on in a special manner that gave them a scissors action in the water. The earliest Dee patterns used gled for the wing. Gled was from a bird of prey (a type of hawk), and its color, markings, and soft texture made it the best choice for wings. When this material was no longer available, tiers switched to cinnamon turkey tail. The color was similar, but the action of the material in the water was not the same. Many anglers felt that Dee flies never fished the same after gled went out of use.

Some Dee-like patterns, such as the Black Dog and Floodtide, had very complex wings. They were similar to other Dee patterns in that they had long body hackles, but were winged in the full-dress or married-winged style. Many of the flies tied for the River Tay were of this style. Their wings contained sections of bustard and dyed swan quills, with cheeks of jungle cock and toppings of golden-pheasant crests. Many modern Spey patterns also have jungle-cock cheeks, though the original flies did not.

Contemporary steelhead Speys have wings made of various materials. Golden-pheasant body feathers, hackle tips, and strips of goose quill dyed in bright steelhead colors are all used. The wings are low and sleek, tenting or veiling the body of the fly.

The heads of Spey and Dee patterns are always made as small as possible. This is mentioned in the earliest descriptions of these flies, and a small, neat head remains an important part of these styles.

The original Spey and Dee patterns were real fishing flies. Their shape leads many to believe that they were first tied to represent a shrimp or prawn. The body hackles worked in a very seductive manner and resembled the legs of a prawn. Spey and Dee flies are among the oldest salmon flies, and they remained unchanged even as most other salmon flies became more ornate and complicated during the late nineteenth century. I suspect that Spey and Dee flies stayed the same because they worked very well.

I like Spey and Dee flies to have a flowing appearance, with all the materials flowing toward the rear of the hook. This gives the Spey and Dee patterns the graceful look that they are known for. Ideally, the materials will look like they're underwater while the hook is still in the vise. A finished fly should have a swept-back look, like one that has been fished and has had its materials pressed back by the current.

Some fly tiers like to give salmon flies high wings. But when a high-winged fly is subjected to the pressure of a river's current, it doesn't stay high-winged very long. On a full-dress fly, the tail and wing might no longer match after the fly gets wet. This is another reason to match your materials to the hook you are using. The hook is the foundation of a fly; feathers should be selected and attached so that they match the shape and balance of the hook. I always consider what water and current will do to the texture and shape of my flies.

With experience, you can tie flies that look the same after they are fished as they did when they first came out of the vise.

GENERAL OBSERVATIONS

Tying salmon flies takes desire, passion, practice, and good materials. Practice is essential; the more flies you tie, the better you get. You learn how different materials act when you tie them on a hook, and in time you can overcome any obstacle. Knowing in advance how a certain material will act under thread pressure is something that comes only with practice and the repeated use of a certain material.

Each style of fly—the Speys and Dees, classics, low-water patterns, and hairwings—has its own look and will take time to master. Tying all the different styles of salmon flies will give you knowledge about a wide array of materials and tying techniques. All other types of flies are much easier to tie after you spend some time tying salmon flies. It helps to watch other tiers and learn their techniques; you may see something on their flies that you like and you can incorporate into your own.

Materials are fifty percent of fly tying. The other fifty percent is the various techniques used to tie them on a fly. You cannot tie quality flies with inferior materials. This, too, is a learning experience, discovering how to find the best of the best when selecting materials to tie your flies. No one can teach you this. One tier can show you certain qualities to look for, but the more you handle materials, the more you will notice subtle differences from one piece of material to the next. When I buy materials I will look at the stock available, choose what I feel are the best three items of the bunch, and then decide among them. If they all look good, I'll take them all. I do the same when selecting certain materials for a fly I am tying. I'll prepare a few choices, and then use the feather or feathers that will look best on that fly.

Make sure that materials are clean, with no broken or curled tips on the fibers. Look for good markings on feathers, such as fine mottling, bold bars, and spots or splashes of color that will accent your flies and make them stand out from the rest. Look for unique feathers, those that differ from others of the same type. These are the feathers that tie great flies.

Try to have a few different sources of materials. Many outfits that sell salmon-fly materials dye them the same nominal colors, but the results are actually many different shades of those colors. When blended or tied on together, these different shades will give your flies a brilliant, multicolored appearance. It's best to buy materials that you can pick through, as opposed to ordering them by mail. I have at times ordered materials through the mail and have fared well, but many times you don't get what you expected.

Again, experience is your teacher. As you select materials and tie with them, you will learn what to look for. Among the things you will learn to consider are color, shape, length, and texture.

Color

Many salmon flies are tied in very bright colors, and for them we select materials that have rich, brilliant hues. Dyed materials must display even, vivid, clean colors. Natural, undyed materials should show good color and a luster that only nature can create.

Natural materials have colors and patterns that cannot be duplicated. Many feathers have colors that consist of different shades blending into a main color, sometimes with the extra attraction of iridescence. We cannot dye feathers to match or copy nature. Equally unique are the different color patterns displayed on natural feathers. Look for feathers that have an interesting or bold pattern. This is one of the features that separate good materials from exquisite ones. Feathers that display unique colors and markings make your flies different and memorable.

Shape

Here, we consider not only the overall shape of our completed flies, but also the different shapes of the individual feathers on each fly. Differently shaped feathers lend themselves to specific applications. Feathers for body hackles should have a taper. Wing feathers with tapered tips are more graceful than squared-ended feathers and help to give a fly flowing lines. Feathers used as body veils are more squared at the tips so that they mark off a section of the body. Chatterer and kingfisher feathers are an example. Both have good color, but the tip of a kingfisher feather is square, as opposed to the chatterer's pointed or tapered tip. The latter feature makes for a more flowing appearance, which you might want on some flies. On others, you might prefer the distinct edge of a kingfisher veil. Think about the

effect you want, and then find feathers with the right shapes to create it.

Some tiers choose jungle cock necks according to the color of the nails. I choose my necks by the shape of the feathers. I prefer necks that have long, narrow feathers and eyes that make a fly look more sleek. I also prefer to tie jungle cock slightly longer and lower than most tiers do, as this gives the fly a racy look. It all boils down to personal preference and making your flies different.

Size and Length

Change the length of one feather in a fly, and the pattern has a whole new look. This is really noticeable on Spey and Dee patterns. Many tiers use body hackles with fibers that just reach the back of the hook, while others use hackles with fibers that extend a fair distance past the bend. Depending on the length of the hackle, the same pattern can have two different looks. It's the same with hooks. Using a hook with a longer shank changes the style of a pattern; it gives the fly a stretched-out look.

The size or length of feathers must be taken into account when tying large patterns. Feathers only come in certain lengths, and you must have the right length for a given hook size. On big flies, the most important thing is the length of the wing material you have. The hackles must be long enough to fill out the body of a large fly. On large patterns that include a topping, the length of that component must also be taken into account. Do this before you start tying, or you might construct nearly all of a big, handsome fly before finding out that you don't have a crest long enough to make the topping. Lay out all the materials before you start tying feathers to the hook.

Texture

This aspect of feathers and other materials is very important. To some extent, all feathers are soft, but some are more rigid than others and are used for different applications. Soft texture really matters when you tie mixed-wing or married-wing patterns. The softer the texture of each material, the better the results. You'll also find softer materials easier to shape.

Softer materials also display more action in the water, as shown by the wings on Dee patterns. The textures of feathers used for body hackles and collars makes a difference. Flies for fishing in slow currents should have softer materials than flies that will be fished in a strong, faster current. Many tiers use a stiff body hackle and a soft collar or throat; this makes for a pulsating action in the softer collar material.

Rigid or stiff feathers are usually hard to work with. They should be reserved for applications that call for that quality, such as providing structure to a fly's wing.

Technique

Salmon-fly tying involves learning and using many techniques. Preparing feathers—sizing them, and sometimes reshaping them so they tie on more easily—makes the tying process go smoother and produces better, more streamlined flies. Tails, body and throat hackles, and feathers used for wings must be prepared in certain ways before they can be tied in place. Among the other techniques a tier needs to master are attaching tails so they lie straight; making bodies with dubbing, silk, or tinsel; attaching and winding ribs; making body hackles and throats; and, most important, making wings with various types of feathers.

These methods are learned by practice. The more you tie, the better you get. Fly-tying books can help you to learn certain techniques, but watching a good tier can help even more. Observing another tier's methods can save you a lot of time that you would otherwise have to spend trying to figure out things on your own.

State of Mind

Attitude matters when you tie flies. You must be relaxed when you sit down at the vise. When I'm not in the right frame of mind when I start, my efforts are fruitless.

There are times when you reach a certain stage of a fly and no matter what you do, it just goes wrong. When that happens, get up from your vise and come back to it later. Sometimes, a brief time away will get rid of the jitters, and when you take up where you left off, the area that was causing you trouble will come together with one easy turn of the thread.

When you're in the groove, you'll know it. Working with good hooks and materials will inspire you to tie flies that you'll keep as examples of your skill.

Tools

A good rotating vise, quality scissors, a dubbing needle, flat-nosed pliers, a whip-finish tool, a thread bobbin, and a bobbin threader are the basic tools you need.

A rotating vise is very handy for tying salmon flies. You can view all sides of the fly and position the fly at the best angle for each operation.

You want scissors that have sharp blades with fine tips. The tungsten-tipped scissors used for eye surgery are the best, letting you cut feathers and other materials quickly, cleanly, and accurately. Don't go the cheap route; buy the best scissors you can afford. Scissors are your most-used tool, and a good pair makes tying easier.

A thread bobbin is a tool that lets you place each turn of thread exactly where you want. A bobbin threader makes it easier to change colors or rethread the bobbin after breaking the tying thread.

Your dubbing needle is used to separate fibers and finish your flies with head cement. It's basically a needle that can go where your fingers can't—a simple tool, but very helpful.

Flat-nosed pliers come in handy for flattening the stems of feathers and fitting them so that they tie in easily and lie straight.

Your whip-finish tool finishes the heads of your flies. A loop of fine monofilament will accomplish the same thing. Wind the tying thread over the two strands of mono, with the loop end extending out past the eye of the hook. Make the seven turns of thread, following the shape of the fly's head. Place a finger on the head of the fly to keep the turns of thread from unwinding, cut the thread, slip the end of the thread through the monofilament loop, and gently pull the loop toward the back of the head. This is the same method used to tie off a guide wrap on a rod. I like this trick because it gives me good control over the wraps that form the whip finish.

A clean and uncluttered background is also important. Many tiers use a white or light gray piece of cardboard that lets them see a clear silhouette of the fly. This helps in judging the sizes of materials and the overall look of the fly.

THREAD

I tie all my salmon and steelhead flies with Danville's Flymaster 6/0 thread. White, black, and red are the colors used most often on salmon flies. Some steelhead flies call for hot orange, purple, and claret thread.

Try to keep your thread flat, or untwisted. As you make each wrap of thread on a fly, you also put a twist in the thread. The twist builds up, and from time to time you must spin the bobbin (or simply let it hang for a minute) to get rid of it. Your thread should be flat and untwisted when you tie in materials and finish off a fly's head. Twisted thread tends to make fine, hollow-stemmed feathers misbehave. If you periodically remove the twist from your thread, you will have less trouble with many materials, and you will also create less bulk on the hook.

To a large degree, the quality of your flies depends on how well you handle the thread. When fly tiers talk about thread control, they mean the ability to put each wrap exactly where it should be and with precisely the right amount of pressure. Like all other fly-tying skills, this sort of control comes with time and experience.

You can accomplish many things with your thread, but you cannot correct mistakes by making more wraps. This is one of the hardest things to learn. When you see that something is going wrong, don't try to fix the problem with additional wraps of thread. Undo the wraps you've already made and then correct the problem.

HEAD CEMENT

There is only one head cement to use on salmon flies, and that's Cellire, a clear, thin lacquer. Depending on the size of a head, three to five coats are required. Cellire dries to a clear, hard finish with a brilliant gloss. I've tried other head finishes, but none equals Cellire. It comes in several colors, too, but I always use clear. Some tiers use colored head lacquers (if a pattern calls for a red head, for instance), but I find that colored lacquer oozes back onto the fibers and spoils the fly's appearance. If a fly needs a red head, use red thread and coat it with clear Cellire.

On certain steps, I'll add head cement to the base of a feather to stiffen or reinforce it. When tying in wings, I'll add a drop of head cement to the tie-in area. It helps to keep the fibers in the correct position and makes for a sturdier wing.

HOOKS

The hook is the foundation of a fly, and materials should be selected and attached so that they compliment the size, shape, and proportions of the hook. A hook's style determines the style of the fly tied on it. Every tier has his own preferences, but good tiers agree that subtle differences in the diameter of the wire, length of the point, height of the barb, and shape of the bend all matter.

Return-Eye Salmon Hooks

Antique long Dee dbl.	2/0 Partridge, Elver, Veverka
7/0 Partridge 1/0 Partridge CS10	2/0 3/0
2 Partridge low-water, Silver Spectre, Veverka	4 Kate, Mcullough
2 Partridge, down-eye Golden Shrimp, Veverka	2 Muddy Iris, Warren
7/0 Partridge, General Practitioner, Veverka	2 Galec Supreme 2 Mustad 2 Partridge (antique)
2 Bob Veverka's Classic Salmon Hook	1 Partridge low water (old)
2 Wilson Dry Fly	1/0 Allcock (old)
2 Unknown	2 Allcock (old)
6, 45mm treble Waddington Shank	
3/0 Alec Jackson Spey Fly Hook	1/0, 4 Dave Mcneese

The hook is the base of a fly, so the fly should be tied in a manner that is in harmony with the style of the hook to accent and balance the hook. A different style of hook will change the style of the fly you are tying.

Many contemporary hooks come close to the ideal Spey-fly hook, but the perfect hook is rare. The perfect hook for steelhead Speys would be a size 1 hook with a slightly longer shank, slender point, and barb with a small, fine, low-pitched eye. For Dee patterns, long-shank hooks made by Partridge work well. Various new and old styles of hooks that can be used for Spey patterns are the Alec Jackson Spey Fly Hook, Bob Veverka's Classic Salmon Hook, Dave McNeese's Salmon Irons, Partridge, and the old-style Allcock, Wilson, and Willis hooks.

I prefer a hook made of very fine wire. The shapes of the point, barb, and bend might seem like trivial concerns, but small differences mean a lot to a trained eye. To me, small flies look best on hooks that have short points and small barbs. Dee patterns, on the other hand, look best on hooks with long points and flared barbs; this style of hook accents the long, wispy hackles of a Dee fly. It's all a question of balance, symmetry, and personal taste. Small things can make all the difference.

A hook's bend, shape, and proportions will change the overall look of a pattern. These changes are particularly noticeable on the more complex flies that have married wings and toppings, because a hook's style determines the height and length of the tails and wing.

The length of the shank has a big influence on the shape and proportions of a fly. Flies tied on long-shanked hooks have long, low wings, whereas those on shorter hooks have shorter, higher wings. The relative dimensions of the gap and shank determine the length and height of a salmon fly's wing.

Spey flies should be tied on hooks that have straight shanks. Some new hooks have very radical, fancy bends. On one of these hooks, the shank drops very quickly into the bend; or, to look at it differently, the bend starts very early, about three quarters of the way back on the shank. A hook of this style does not lend itself to flies that have low, body-hugging wings; the wings appear to be sticking up. Spey-fly wings should be low and swept back, an effect that can be achieved only on a hook with a straight shank.

I feel that the most important feature of a hook is the eye. The wire diameter and the eye's overall size and pitch are critical. An eye made of fine wire makes for a smaller, neater head. A low pitch—that is, a shallow upward angle—gives a fly a sleeker, more streamlined look.

Hooks for Spey and Dee flies have always been hard to find. When I first started tying these flies, there were not many suitable hooks on the market. Most looped-eye hooks lacked the features needed for Spey flies, such as a slightly longer shank, the right bend, and a fine eye with a low pitch. Some of the earlier Partridge low-water hooks worked for Speys, but they were hard to find. If you were lucky, you might have found some older hooks at an antique-tackle show or in an old fly-tying collection.

Blind-eye hooks were just coming back into use when I started to tie salmon flies. One way to find old blind-eye hooks was to buy antique flies; you could strip off the old materials and use the hooks. Naturally, tiers did this only with antique flies that were in bad condition. Antique flies in good shape should be protected and studied.

Today, we have available to us a number of hooks that can be used to tie Spey and Dee patterns and all the other styles of salmon flies.

Partridge has been making hooks for a long time and offers several return-eye and blind-eye hooks in Dee-fly lengths. The Heritage Bartleet model has an extra-long shank for tying blind-eye Dee flies. A traditional-length blind-eye hook (Code CS10/3) is intended

Blind-Eye Salmon Hooks

Heritage, Pryce-Tannatt, long point

3/0	6/0 forged bend (antique)
4/0	1 1/2 Alec Jackson
5/0	2/0 Phillips long Dee (antique)
6/0	2/0 dbl. Partridge, Jim Curry's Red Shrimp, Veverka
Long Dee dbl. (antique)	Partridge long shank
Ron Reinhold Droughtwater Dee, Gled Wing, Veverka	6/0 Eugene Sunday

Heritage, Harrison Bartleet, long shank

6/0	7/0	8/0

Today a number of companies and individuals supply hooks for Spey and Dee flies. Each tier has his own preference, and each style of fly has a series of hooks that fit that style and accent its overall look; for example, Spey and Dee flies tied with long wispy hackles look best on a long-shank hook.

Hook making is an art form. Each hook maker leaves his mark by the way he forms a hook bend, files the point, and cuts the barb. The tempering of the steel wire is crucial. Most important is the finish of a hook: japanned black, which when done properly is a shiny dark black smooth finish, much like black enamel. The process and ingredients are a well-guarded secret only learned by experience and experimenting.

The shape of a hook bend, the point of the hook, and the barb are very detailed, and by varying these and the length of the shank, the style of the hook changes drastically.

Phillips long Dee hooks are very rare, as are any of the original hooks made by Phillips, whose hooks were mentioned in several early books. Phillips was an artist when it came to hook making—his styles were elegant, and he paid great attention to fine details that made his hooks stand out from the rest.

for classic married-wing flies. Partridge has a number of eyed hooks for salmon and steelhead flies. The CS10 Bartleet and the heavier-wire CS10/2 can be used for fishing or display patterns. The Code N Single Low-Water hook is a good model for Spey flies, as is the 01 Single Wilson hook.

The Bob Veverka Classic Salmon Hook is made by Daiichi in gold, blue, and black finishes, and in sizes 2, 4, 6, and 8. This hook was designed to imitate the classic hooks of long ago. It's made of fine wire, with a

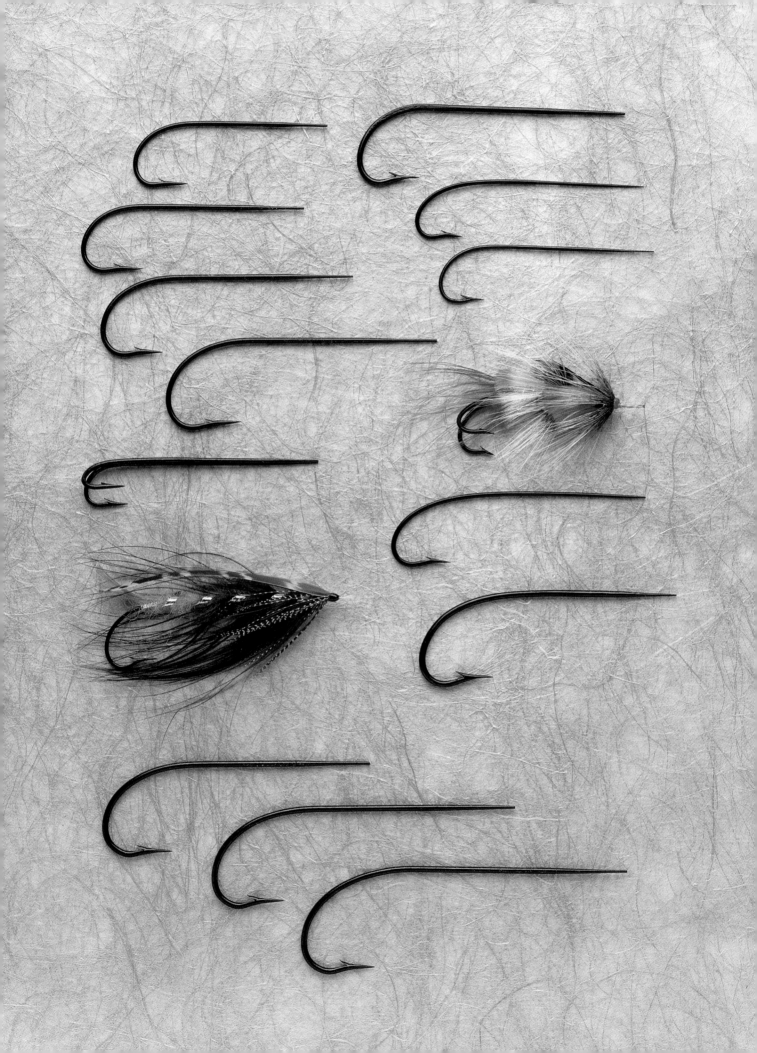

slightly longer shank and a very small, neat, tapered eye. The pitch of the eye is very slight, which makes for a streamlined silhouette. When I first showed these hooks to Alec Jackson, he said that he hadn't seen a hook made with such a fine eye in the last fifty years. I only wish that I had these in sizes 1 and 1/0 for Spey flies. The sizes available are good for small, sparse Speys, low-water flies, dry flies, and reduced feather-wings.

The Alec Jackson Spey Fly Hook, also from Daiichi, is available in several colors and in sizes 3/0, 1/0, 1½, 3, 5, and 7. Many contemporary steelhead-fly tiers use this hook. Alec also has a blind-eye hook designed for Spey and Dee patterns.

Heritage Hooks, owned and operated by Phil Castleman, carries a line of relatively inexpensive blind-eye hooks for classic salmon flies and Spey patterns. Sizes range from 1/0 to 8/0 in several styles with long and short shanks.

Ron Reinhold handmade hooks offers a series of classic blind-eye hooks made in old styles—Phillips, Bartleet, and Pryce-Tannatt—along with several custom-designed models. Ron combines methods from the Victorian era with a touch of modern ingenuity. All of his hooks are handmade from scratch. Ron designed and built his machines, and he hand-files the points. He uses wire that matches the diameter of antique hooks but is stronger and more consistent. His hooks are electrically heat-treated to obtain a consistent temper. The black finish is the same true japanned finish used on hooks a century ago. Ron promises that you won't find a better finish anywhere.

Ron strives to make the most elegant hook available. Barbs are long and guttered. Points are polished, and their tips are slightly honed. Shanks are perfectly tapered. Ron finishes the points in hollow, harpoon, and round styles, each subtly different.

Ron will also refinish old hooks and is always in the market for examples of original antique hooks. He has hooks in styles and sizes for any antique or contemporary pattern.

Eugene Sunday has been making hooks by hand for a number of years. I consider him the grandfather of the custom, handmade, salmon-hook business in America. Gene is a real artist, and his hooks have a genuine flair. His precise, finely tapered shanks blend into finely tapered eyes at one end and barbs with fine grooves and masterfully filed points on the other. I have tied a num-

Ron Reinhold Custom Handmade Blind-Eye Salmon Hooks

Wm. Bartleet	Noble DS
4/0 long shank	2/0 Dee
5/0 long shank	2/0 long Dee
5/0 very long shank	3/0 Dee
Noble S	**Long Dee, Noble DS**
5/0 1XL	3/0 long Dee
	4/0 Dee
6/0 1XL	4/0 long Dee
	5/0 long Dee

T. E. Pryce-Tannatt
2¼ inch
2½ inch

Droughtwater Dee
3/0, ¾ long shank
4/0, ½ long shank
4/0, ¾ long shank

Specially styled hooks with long shanks and Limerick bends were originally used to tie Spey and Dee patterns. During my career as a fly tier, the antique blind-eye hooks were always hard to find, but today there are a few tiers such as Ron Reinhold and Eugene Sunday who make custom or handmade hooks. During the early 1980s there was a resurgence in the art of tying classic salmon flies, and blind-eye hooks with twisted gut loop eyes came back into use, not so much for the fishing purposes as to closely duplicate the classic salmon flies.

Ron Reinhold can make any style of hook from scratch. He selects the wire, grinds the point, and cuts the barb, and then hand-bends it to shape and finishes it with a black finish that matches the look of the old hooks.

ber of flies on Gene's hooks; many of the Dee patterns in this book are tied on his custom-made hooks.

Antique hooks are very rare. Any salmon-fly hooks from the late 1800s are almost impossible to find, and long-shank Dee hooks are even rarer. Most of my old hooks have come from antique flies that were in bad condition.

You will almost never find full boxes of antique hooks; at least I never have. Usually, you will come across partial boxes or, more often, single hooks here and there. Perhaps my best find was a bag of seventy-seven blind-eye, long-Dee hooks from Harry Darbees's

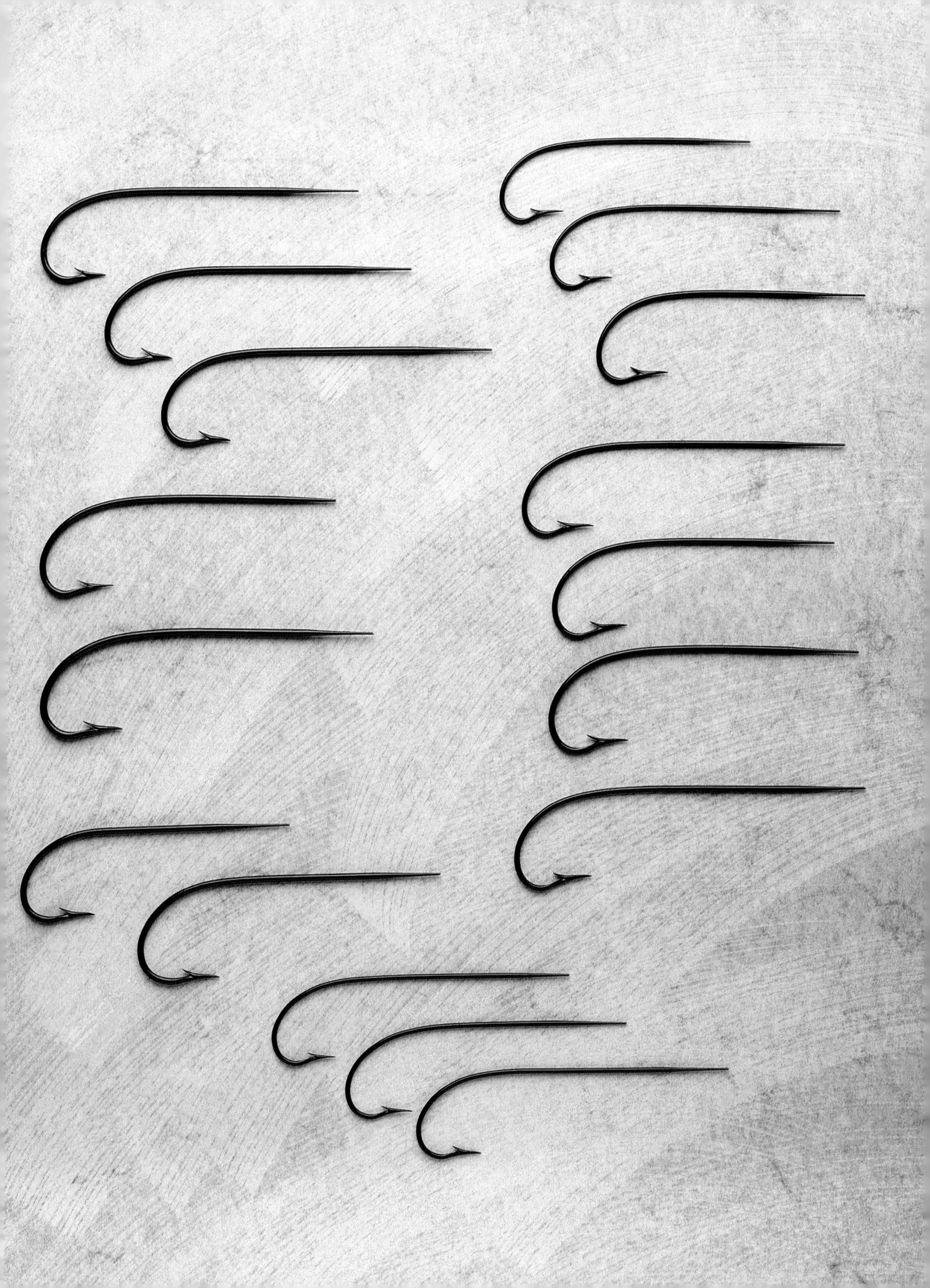

collection of old hooks. The length of the shanks was perfect and the wire was the finest I had ever seen, with handsome bends and fine points and barbs. I tied a number of flies on those hooks, from Dee patterns to low, swept-wing classics.

From time to time a few boxes of old Partridge, Allcock, or Willis return-eye hooks turn up, and these can be used for your finest steelhead Spey patterns. Most steelhead Speys are tied in sizes 2, 1, and 1/0. Size 1 is the perfect size, since most materials used in steelhead flies fit this size hook best.

Willis hooks are very rare and some of the finest salmon hooks ever made. Sometimes they show up in an old fly tier's materials collection. I had some that Mike Martinek sent me a number of years back, and used most for the steelhead Speys that I tied for Trey Combs's book *Steelhead*. They were some of the finest return-eye hooks that I ever had the pleasure to tie flies on. Made of very fine wire, they had even finer eyes, graceful bends, small barbs, and fine, short points.

Allcock hooks are rare, but some turn up from time to time. Allcock made a number of styles of salmon hooks. The nicest ones I ever tied on were from a group of return-eye hooks that Walt Johnson sent me. They were finely made of heavy wire and had slightly longer shanks. The wire at the bend was slightly heavier than the shank, which made for a beautifully keeled fly with most of the weight in the bend of the hook.

Partridge hooks have been around for a long time. If you can find some that were made in the mid-1900s, you will have some very fine hooks for Spey flies. For certain patterns, old Partridge low-water hooks are fine, as are the size 2 Wilson Dry Fly hooks.

Waddington shanks are sometimes used for Spey and Dee patterns. Some of the Dee patterns take on a special look when tied on Waddington shanks and tipped with dressed treble hooks. I've tied a number of Dee patterns on these and included some in the color plates.

BODY MATERIALS

Classic salmon flies had bodies made of tinsel, silk, and various dubbing materials. On most, the body was ribbed with some type of tinsel.

The bodies of the original Spey patterns were made of wool or mohair. Wool bodies consisted of several colors blended together to produce one dominant hue.

Syd Glasso Steelhead Spey Flies
from Trey Combs's *Steelhead Fishing and Flies*, 1976
Joseph Bates, Jr.'s, *The Art of the Classic Salmon Fly*, 1989
Trey Combs's *Steelhead*, 1991
Joseph Bates, Jr., and
Pamela Bates Richards's
Fishing Atlantic Salmon, 1996

Quillayute, Wentworth	Black Heron (hackle-tip wing), Stovall	Polar Shrimp (goose-quill wing), Burden
Courtesan, Veverka	Mr. Glasso, Wentworth	Polar Shrimp (hackle-tip wing), Veverka
Brown Heron, Glasso	Orange Heron, Glasso	Sol Duc, Veverka
Gold Heron, Veverka	Black Heron (strip wing), Veverka	Sol Duc Spey, Veverka
Silver Heron, Veverka		Sol Duc Dark, Veverka

Syd Glasso was the first to convert the original Spey flies to steelhead flies for use on the rivers of the Pacific Northwest. He started a true American fly heritage with his finely tied steelhead Speys, inspiring many other tiers with a style that is still carried on today. Glasso's flies were tied sparsely in hot colors with the finest hooks and materials. His flies had flowing lines, were finely ribbed and hackled with long wispy heron hackles, and were always tied symmetrically to the hook, which made them stand out from the rest. Throat hackles were of the most finely penciled teal flank, and the wings were precisely set, low and swept back. His flies were always finished with his trademark small, neat, perfectly formed heads.

Most Spey-fly bodies were shades of olive, green, or brown mixed with a little yellow or red. Purple was also a standard color; it was made by blending several colors of Berlin wool.

The early Dee patterns used mohair or pig's wool for the body material. In time, fly tiers decided that seal fur was the best, most translucent fiber for dubbing salmon-fly bodies.

Hot-colored or fluorescent floss and seal-fur dubbing are used in the bodies of steelhead Spey flies.

Developed many years ago by Syd Glasso, this feature is widely used today. Black, orange, and purple are some of the most important colors for steelhead flies. Many patterns incorporate purple; it's as dark as black, but still shows a hint of color.

These days, many synthetic dubbing materials are used on salmon flies. They come in a wide array of colors and in blends of different shades. Because they are translucent, many synthetics are good substitutes for seal fur and other original materials. An added feature is their ease of use.

Wool

The original Spey flies had bodies made of wool. The material was known as Berlin wool, and each color was a mixture of several different colors. Olive, green, brown, yellow, red, and purple were blended or mixed in various amounts to arrive at a certain color for a given Spey pattern.

The early Spey patterns described in A. E. Knox's book *Autumns on the Spey* had bodies of mixed wool. Many of the dubbing blends included red wool in varying amounts. As the season progressed, tiers increased the amount of red in their dubbings.

On patterns such as the Kings, Reeaches, Speals, and Herons, I still use wool to dress the bodies. I feel that it maintains the traditional look of the flies. Wool absorbs water like a sponge, so it's a natural choice for Spey-fly bodies. Although wool yarn is easy to wrap around a hook, the original Spey patterns were tied with various mixtures of wool that were applied as dubbing materials.

Mohair

The first Dee patterns used mohair for the body material. Mohair is a soft, semitranslucent hair that blends well and dyes easily. It's very smooth and slippery, and at times it can be a hassle to dub on your tying thread. But mohair has a very soft texture, enough fiber length to be used for body veils and wings, and a very seductive, flowing action in the water. It doesn't have quite the translucence that seal fur does, and most Dee-fly tiers eventually switched to seal.

Mohair was also used for patterns that had manes of hair as wings, such as the Owensmore. It was also used as a tail material on some of the old patterns and as the collar on the Beauly Snow Fly.

Body Materials

Seal fur, red, purple

SLF synthetic fiber, red, purple, orange, yellow

Dazzle Dub, purple, black with gold accent

Mohair, orange, natural (white)

Tinsel, oval gold and silver, flat and embossed

Flashback Shrimp, Selig (mohair blend)

Jock Scott, floss wing, treble, Veverka

Lagartun 12 strand silk

Japanese silk

African goat, blue, highlander green, orange, red

The earliest flies had various types of fur dubbed and wound on the hook shank to form the body of the fly. Salmon flies used furs that displayed a translucent effect. Mohair or pig's wool (fur clipped from the ears of a pig) was used on the earliest salmon patterns, but by the time George Kelson wrote *The Salmon Fly* in the late 1800s, seal fur replaced mohair and pig's wool as the best translucent fur. Today many materials are used for the bodies of Spey and Dee flies, including wool, mohair, African goat, seal fur, and synthetic blends of dubbing.

Wool or silk floss is also used for salmon-fly bodies. Most salmon flies have tags that are tied with silk, and bodies on many salmon patterns are tied with various colors of silk. A new concept, silk-wing flies, uses strands of silk for the colors in the wing of a fly veiled with some type of duck flank feather roof or overwing.

Tinsel is used for salmon-fly tips and body ribbings. It adds flash to flies that are attractors and, in the case of Spey flies, provides a shield to protect fragile hackle stems. Spey flies were also tied with tinsel wound over the hackle to protect them from salmon teeth—this way, if teeth bit a body hackle stem, the rib would hold the hackle in place and keep the fly in working condition. A Spey fly with a broken or cut body hackle is useless.

Seal Fur

The standard body material on salmon flies tied in the late 1800s, seal fur is a highly lustrous, translucent fur that displays brilliant color when dyed. It has coarse, almost glassy guard hairs and very fine underfur. The guard hairs provide the translucence, and the coarser a seal-fur blend is, the more translucent. The fine underfur, however, is much easier to dub on your tying thread.

Seal fur takes dye very well. On Dee flies, the colors used most often are yellow, blue, red, claret, and green.

Orange and purple are the most popular colors for steelhead Speys.

Polar-bear dubbing is similar to seal fur, and many steelhead-fly tiers used to use polar bear fur in place of seal. Today, there are many synthetics that rival the translucence and appearance of seal fur.

Pig's Wool

Pig's wool was used on some of the early salmon flies, before seal fur came into use. Kelson mentioned that it is the most brilliant of all dyed materials. The best fur is taken from under the ears of a pig. This material is rarely used these days, simply because it is very rarely available. Most patterns that have pig's-wool bodies are very early flies such as those mentioned by Fitzgibbon and Francis Francis.

African Goat

This is a natural hair used today as a seal-fur substitute. African goat hair is very soft and lustrous, and it has a fair degree of translucence. It comes in a wide array of salmon-fly colors and is readily available.

African goat dubbing has a very soft, slick texture. Some tiers find it difficult to use. When tying with African goat, gently loosen the fibers before you start to twist the material on your thread. When you make your first turn of thread, make sure that the end of the dubbing is trapped against the hook. With each additional turn of dubbed thread, give the thread a slight twist to keep the material from unraveling.

African-goat dubbing is very similar to mohair in texture and appearance. When it's used on large Dee flies, the fibers can be picked out so that they veil the broad tinsel rib, creating a desirable halo effect like that of the original patterns.

Synthetic Living Fibre

Developed by Davy Wotton, this is a blend of synthetic fibers that rivals the appearance of seal fur. It is highly translucent and comes in blends that combine several colors to arrive at one main color. Synthetic Living Fibre, or SLF, is available in all the salmon and steelhead colors, and it's a very easy material to dub on your thread.

I've used all of the above materials. It's hard to say which one I like best, because each has its own attributes and applications. I always felt that natural dubbing was superior to any of the synthetic fibers, but in recent

---

Early Salmon-Fly Patterns from Francis Francis's *A Book on Angling*, 1867

Beauly Snow Fly (Waddington shank), Veverka

Lord James Murray, Nolte

White Wing (Waddington shank), Veverka

Crane, Rossman

Wasp, Veverka

Dun Wing, Nolte

Francis Francis includes many patterns in *A Book on Angling* and lists them according to the rivers they are dressed for. He included many of the original patterns that were tied for the Dee, Spey, Tay, and Tweed and all the Rivers of Scotland and Ireland. He knew many of the tiers that dressed flies for a specific river and checked with authorities on the flies he wrote about, so we know his information is accurate. Francis states in his chapter on salmon flies, "I have been many years collecting this list of flies, of the majority of which I have brought patterns away from the rivers themselves, so that they are descriptions of the actual flies used on the rivers by the habitues thereof."

Francis writes that there is but one singular fly used on the River Beauly, called the Snow Fly, and as long as there is any snow water on the river that fly kills well, indeed far better than any other. The Beauly Snow fly was originated by Mr. Snowie of Inverness.

The spring flies for the Tay are the largest size of flies, and the Lord James Murray is one of the flies used on the Tay that underwent a thorough revolution from a plain strip-wing fly to a mixed-wing pattern. Other patterns that were swept up in this revolution are the Black Dog and the Wasp patterns. The Crane is an Irish pattern, dressed on large hooks and used in rapid and high water, which Francis Francis received from a fisherman on the Suir.

The Dun wing is an old Scottish pattern and a capital fly on the Tweed, as is the White Wing, a fly that was fished in the evening. James Wright, who tied the White Wing, would later go on to originate some of the classic salmon patterns: the Doctor and Ranger series and the Silver Gray and Thunder and Lightning. Wright was considered the finest fly tier practicing on the Tweed at the time.

---

years some beautiful synthetic dubbings, such as SLF, have become available. It's good to learn how to use the entire range of body materials.

Silk

Used for tags and bodies on salmon flies, silk comes in a wide range of colors and diameters for various applications. Many of the early Spey patterns had silk ribs, some of which were wound through the hackles.

You can use silk instead of the tying thread when you dub a body. Twisting the dubbing onto a strand of silk the same color makes for a very bright body. Dubbing materials stick to silk better than they do to nylon tying thread, which helps when you tie with difficult materials. Rogan and then Crosfield used this method.

Some of the finest silk that I have used comes from Lagartun, a French company. It is a twelve-strand floss of the highest quality, very smooth and dyed in all the colors used on salmon flies. Using all twelve strands works well to make bodies on larger patterns. Separating the strands produces material for tags or the bodies of small flies.

Japanese silk is also used for tying salmon flies. This material comes in the widest array of colors, with shades ranging from one end of the spectrum to the other. I find that it works well for tags and the bodies of small salmon flies. It's very thin, which makes it useful on small, slender flies and for very fine tags. To make the body of a large fly, you have to double Japanese silk a few times to build up enough diameter, and that makes it hard to work with. More often than not, you will fray some of the fibers and end up with a fly that has a fuzzy body. Japanese silk has many uses, but it's not the best body material on big salmon flies.

Silk is also available in various colors in single strands, useful on small flies and for making tags. A salmon fly's tag should be fine and smooth, and a single strand of silk works best for this application.

White silk is important if you want to form a tapered underbody. All colors show up best against white, and many tiers use white thread or fine floss as an underbody so that a fly doesn't change colors when it gets wet. Others paint the shanks of their hooks white to get the same effect. Some steelhead-fly tiers wrap body materials over silver tinsel, which produces a body with an inner glow.

Silk can also be used to make wings. Strands of silk are doubled over the tying thread and tied in one on top of another to form a bright, multicolored wing.

Fluorescent Rayon Floss
Its brilliant, hot colors make fluorescent rayon floss a popular material for tags and bodies of steelhead flies. It's available in several colors. Orange and red seem to be the most popular among steelhead anglers; on salmon flies, chartreuse is among the favorite colors. It comes on spools, like thread, and it's fine enough that

you can put it in a bobbin and use it to tie most of a fly, switching to normal thread when you reach the head. Using this material in a bobbin lets you create flies with beautiful, slim bodies. Many steelhead Spey patterns have bodies that are half fluorescent floss and half seal fur. The tier will make the rear half of the body with the bright, single-strand floss, and then dub seal fur on the floss to make the front section of the body. It makes for a slender, very bright body. You can also use fluorescent single-strand floss as the dubbing thread on a salmon fly that calls for seal fur; match the color of the floss to that of the seal, and you'll end up with a brilliant fly.

Tinsel
Tinsel is used to make ribs on most salmon flies and to make entire bodies on some patterns. It comes in flat and oval varieties and in several sizes of each. Flat tinsel is available smooth or embossed. Silver, gold, and copper are the most common colors on salmon flies, though tinsels are also available in red, green, and blue.

Most tinsel-bodied flies have ribs of oval tinsel, and almost all other body types (such as dubbed fur or silk) use a rib of flat or oval tinsel and sometimes both. Flat tinsel is most commonly used to make entire bodies, but oval tinsel is used on a few patterns for the body or a section of the body.

When I use flat tinsel for the body of a fly, I always double-wrap it, attaching the tinsel at the front of the fly, wrapping it rearward, and then wrapping forward to make a double layer. When a fly's body is made of oval tinsel, the material is tied in at the butt of the fly and wound forward to form the body.

Flat tinsel is available in fine, medium, and large sizes. Fine is used for tips and tags on salmon flies, medium is used for bodies and ribs on small patterns, and large is used for the bodies of big patterns and the ribs on the largest salmon flies. Most of the original Dee patterns were tied with ribs of the very broad tinsel. Many of the original Spey patterns had several ribs of flat and oval tinsel.

Fine oval tinsel is used for tips on salmon flies. Medium oval tinsel is used for the sections of a body or as a rib on small patterns. Large oval tinsel is used for the rib on large patterns and on flies with heavily dubbed bodies. Many salmon patterns have ribs made with both flat and oval tinsel. This double rib provides more light reflection, and the oval tinsel reinforces and protects the stem of the body hackle. When both flat and oval tinsel are used, the flat is wound first, and then the oval is wound tightly behind the flat tinsel.

There are two types of flat tinsels used for salmon flies: the original metal tinsels and the modern Mylar tinsel. When you make a body with flat metal tinsel, you must wrap the material so that each turn lies edge to edge with the previous turn—no overlapping. Since it's more flexible, flat Mylar tinsel can be wrapped with a slight overlap. This produces a tiny, uniform spiral that reflects light from different angles.

Flat Mylar tinsel is nice to work with. It comes with a gold finish on one side and silver on the other. It never tarnishes, as some real tinsels do, and it's durable.

One of the hazards of metal tinsel is that it has a tendency to cut your thread. But even though they cut thread and tarnish, metal tinsels still have a place in salmon-fly tying. There is something about the color that's different from plastic; if you look at a fly tied with metal tinsel and one with Mylar, you will see a slight difference. And metal tinsel adds weight to a fly, which might be a reason in itself to use it. I like to use real copper tinsel on some of my flies; copper gives a pattern a different look, sometimes the one that brings the grab.

All the oval tinsels I use are real metal. I have spools in extra fine, for tips and tags; fine, for tags that are made entirely of tinsel; medium fine, for ribs on small bodies; and medium and large, for ribs on various patterns. Many old patterns call for "twist," which is three strands of fine oval tinsel twisted together. I find this material too bulky for tags and use it only to make ribs on large flies with heavily dubbed bodies of seal fur or the like.

Obviously, tinsel adds flash to flies. Many years ago, fly fishers noticed that gold tinsel worked better at certain times of day or in a particular season, and that silver likewise had its times and seasons. I've noticed this in my own fishing; in some places and at certain times, the fish prefer silver to gold or vice versa.

Besides adding flash to a fly, oval tinsel also provides some protection to a body hackle. A hackle stem wound along the rear edge of an oval-tinsel rib is shielded, at least partly, from the teeth of a fish.

FEATHERS

The feathers used on salmon flies come from a wide array of birds—pheasants, ducks, turkeys, chickens, and many other land and water birds. Feathers and pieces of feathers are used for tails, body hackles, throats and collars, body veils, and, of course, all types of wings. The underwing, main wing, wing veils and sides, cheeks, and toppings are tied with various types of feathers, each unique in its purpose. Without feathers, we wouldn't tie flies.

Fly tiers devote a lot of thought to feathers and their uses, evaluating such attributes as color, markings, size, shape, texture, structure, and mobility in the water. We have substitutes for some natural materials, but for feathers there is no replacement. The early salmon-fly tiers were remarkably ingenious in their use of feathers, as you will realize once you've tied a fair number of salmon flies. Each type of feather has unique properties, and each fits into the puzzle that makes up a salmon pattern.

I've always been interested in birds, and throughout my life I've studied, raised, and at one time hunted many types. For a number of years I raised various pheasants, ducks, quail, partridge, and grouse. In the process I learned about bird behavior and collected many types of feathers for fly tying. I had different types of pens and tried to furnish them with some of the things that birds would have in nature, such as trees, bushes, perches, sand or dusting boxes, and some type of natural cover to which my birds could retreat when they felt uneasy. I fed them natural grains and greens to maintain the quality of their feathers. The dust boxes contained sand so that my birds could take dust baths and keep their feathers clean and in tip-top shape.

I never planned to raise chickens, until one day I came home and found a number of them hanging around my pheasant and quail pens. They had escaped from a neighbor's property and wandered to my place. I fed them from time to time, but mostly let them fend for themselves. At night they would roost in the long-needle pines around my house. In the spring they hatched some eggs. I never handled the offspring, which grew up to act like no domestic chickens I'd ever seen. The roosters were wild and cackled all spring. From time to time I would thin the flock and collect all sorts of wild-looking hackles. A fly tier who has room to keep a few chickens will find that his time and effort are well spent.

I learned a lot about birds by raising them. They are very interesting to watch, as each type has its own personality and funny traits, and its own breeding displays and calls. A fly tier can never have too many feathers or know too much about them.

CHICKEN HACKLES

Chicken feathers are used mainly for body and throat hackles on salmon patterns. A few salmon flies, such as the Black Dog, use chicken hackles as an underwing material. Some steelhead flies have hackle-tip wings.

Both cock and hen feathers are used. Cock hackles are stiffer; hen hackles are very soft and are used as throat or collar material. On many salmon flies, cock hackles are used for the body hackles and hen hackles are used as throat material. This produces a fly with a pulsating action.

Natural hackles come in a wide range of colors. Badger and furnace hackles, either in their natural colors or dyed, are called for in many salmon and steelhead patterns. So are grizzly hackles. When dyed, these two-toned feathers create a color pattern that's varied and broken up.

White hackles are dyed the many different colors needed to tie salmon flies; yellow, orange, red, green, and blue are often called for. Natural black hackles, as opposed to dyed-black feathers, often display an iridescence that adds a nice accent to a fly.

When a chicken feather is used as a body hackle, its shape is very important. The fibers should increase in length from the tail end of the body up to the throat; this gives the body a tapered appearance. Only experience will teach you the skill of choosing a hackle with the right size and shape to dress a certain salmon pattern, though it helps to study the flies of good tiers.

Most salmon patterns call for a rooster feathers for their body hackles. On many of my flies, though, I use hen hackles because they have a nicer taper in their fibers. I prefer the taper and the slightly swept-back tips of the fibers on hen hackles; they add to the appearance of a fly with low, swept-back wings. The problem is finding hen hackles that are big enough. A typical hen neck has only a few feathers large enough to use as body hackles on salmon flies. Most of the feathers work better as throats and collars on small classic and hairwing flies. All throats and collars should be tied with soft hen hackles rather than stiffer rooster hackles.

On some patterns, rooster feathers are used for the body hackles and hen hackles are used for the throat. This makes for a fly with a pulsating action. Many anglers switch between flies made with softer or stiffer

---

Spey Feathers

Crown pigeon

Purple hen neck   Brown-eared pheasant, dyed yellow, orange

Orange Heron, Veverka   Turkey marabou, orange, purple, natural mottled   Swan feather

Tippett G P, Veverka

Green Heron, Veverka   Brown-eared pheasant hackle

Blue-eared pheasant hackle, dyed black, natural gray   Silver pheasant crest   Schlappen, brown and black

Bleached goose quill, dyed black

The mobile body hackles that display great action in the water define the Spey and Dee style. The original Spey hackles were taken from the side of the rooster's tail (pendant feathers). These roosters, believed to be extinct today, were a special breed of chicken raised along the River Spey.

Dee flies were tied with long gray and black heron hackles. Now pheasant rump hackles, which have long and wispy fibers, are used. Various breeds of pheasants have feathers that match the original materials used to tie the body hackles on Spey and Dee flies.

Some modern substitutes for heron include blue-eared pheasant, natural gray and dyed black; brown-eared pheasant, natural brown, and buff white off the saddle, dyed yellow and orange; bleached goose quill, natural white and dyed black; silver pheasant crests; schlappen; marabou, dyed orange; and natural mottled turkey marabou.

---

hackles according to the type of water they're fishing. In slow water, a fly with a softer hackle will have a very subtle action. In fast currents, a pattern tied with stiff rooster hackles will keep its shape.

When using a cock hackle for a body hackle, I usually fold the feather and wind it on. If I'm using a hen feather for the body hackle, I strip one side before attaching the feather to the hook. Hen hackles have more web than cock hackles do, and have a tendency to mat together; stripping one side of a hen feather makes for a sparser, cleaner body hackle. When used for a collar or throat, a hen hackle is folded and then wrapped.

For wings or underwings, I use rooster hackles. They have stiffer stems and fibers, and they make for a

well-defined wing. They also have the right shape, long and straight with a tapered tip.

For a number of years now, the best necks for salmon-fly tying are Chinese necks. They have feathers in the right sizes and shapes for salmon flies, and they come in natural colors (including badger and furnace) and all the necessary dyed colors. The smallest hackles on a Chinese neck can be used for fine hackle-tip wings on steelhead Speys and similar flies. The larger feathers work as body hackles and as underwings on classic salmon patterns. At the top of a Chinese neck, you will find some soft, long-fibered feathers that make beautiful body hackles and throats on Spey patterns.

The original Spey-fly hackles were feathers from the sides of the tail of a Spey cock, a type of chicken that's now extinct. Similar feathers, at least in size and texture, are sold under the generic name of schlappen. These are available in natural colors and dyed. They'll work as body hackles on most Spey flies, and they're as close to the original material as can be obtained. The hackles used on the original Spey patterns were natural black and various shades of brown; some had gray tips on the fibers.

The best way to get the side-tail feathers for tying authentic Spey patterns would be to raise some chickens and from time to time collect the feathers from the sides of their tail. With the right breed of chicken, you could come close to the original material.

Chicken hackles are sold strung (feathers of the same size sewn together at the butt ends), on necks (a patch of skin from the bird's head and neck), and on full skins. Strung hackles are generally used for wings on streamer flies, but they also have some uses on salmon flies. A package of strung furnace or badger hackles usually contains some feathers with interesting colors or markings.

Necks and skins are good ways to buy hackles. A neck has feathers in a huge range of sizes, and each feather has a mirror-image double that matches it in size, shape, and curvature. A complete skin provides you with a wide array of differently shaped and colored feathers to tie with.

PHEASANT FEATHERS

Pheasants supply some of the most important feathers used on salmon flies. Feathers from various pheasants provide us with materials for tails and tail veils, body veils, body hackles, throats, collars, wing components, and toppings.

The golden pheasant tops the list. Its unique crests are the most important feather in salmon-fly tying; no other feather has the same shape and color. On many salmon flies, tails and toppings made with golden-pheasant crests serve as both frames and accents for the wings. Also important to fly tiers are the golden pheasant's tippets, body hackles, and tail feathers. Nearly every feather from a golden pheasant is used on one salmon fly or another.

Among the other pheasants that furnish salmon-fly materials are the Lady Amherst (tippets, crests, and tails), Impeyan (its metallic, iridescent feathers are used for cheeks), ring-necked (rump hackles, tails, and white feathers from around the neck), and blue-, brown-, and white-eared pheasants, whose long-fibered hackles are used for body hackles and throats on Spey and Dee patterns. Other pheasants with interesting feathers used by contemporary fly tiers include the various breeds of peacock pheasants. Although plumage from these birds is not called for in old salmon-fly patterns, the eyed tail feathers of peacock pheasants are used on some modern flies.

At one time I raised many of the exotic pheasants, in the process gaining a world of knowledge about the different species and their feathers. I had golden, Lady Amherst, copper, Elliott's, silver, blue-eared, and several other species of pheasants. Some of my older pairs of birds hatched their own eggs and raised the young in their pens. A number of my golden pheasants were almost wild and had never been touched by human hands.

I had one male golden pheasant that I would let out of his pen every spring. He would stay around all summer, displaying to the females in my pens. He'd also eat all of my flowers. His color was outstanding, and his feathers showed a brilliance that the plumage of the pen-reared birds lacked. With autumn's first snowfall, I'd find him standing outside his pen. I would let him in and he would stay there for the winter. I'll never forget the sight of that magnificent bird flying through the pines around my house.

I collected many feathers from my flock and enjoyed having them around. Their different calls and springtime mating displays were interesting and exciting. It was a lot of hard work but well worth the effort.

Lady Amherst Pheasant

The Lady Amherst pheasant is used for its tail feathers and tippets. The tail feathers are a beautiful white with iridescent, wavy black bars. The fibers of the tail are used for wing sections on married-wing flies such as the Black Dog and Floodtide. Many of the flies Kelson originated utilized Lady Amherst tail in their wings. The tippet feathers are white with black bars and are used as wings on some classic patterns.

The classic married-wing patterns were tied with six sections in each wing, usually three different colors of dyed goose and three sections of natural fibers such as bustard, peacock, golden pheasant, or Amherst pheasant. The wings contain twelve sections in all, six on each side. On a fly that has Lady Amherst pheasant in its wing, that section consists of just three fibers from a tail feather.

The best feature of the Lady Amherst's tail is the length of the fibers. They are long enough to use on the largest flies. Some tiers use Lady Amherst tail as a substitute for peacock-wing sections. The two feathers have similar color patterns, but the Lady Amherst fibers are longer. This helps on a fly such as a very large (size 5/0 or bigger) Jock Scott, for which it's very hard to find peacock-wing fibers long enough.

Amherst tail fibers are longer than those of golden pheasants. Lady Amherst pheasants can be cross-bred with golden pheasants in the hope that the tail feathers of the offspring will have the coloration of golden pheasants with the fiber length of the Amhersts. These birds are referred to as three-quarter goldens. But this is not a common practice among breeders of ornamental pheasants; most breeders try to keep the two species separate.

Lady Amherst tail fibers are very delicate and brittle. If you're not careful when marrying them to other fibers, they start to separate at the tips, and it's very difficult to get them back together. When you use Lady Amherst tail fibers in a married wing, try to get the materials to marry with a single delicate swipe of your fingertips. Repeated attempts to marry Amherst tail fibers with another material will only make the tips of the fibers separate farther apart. When that happens, it's best to cut a new section of tail fibers and try again.

Tail sections can be dyed and used for horns on salmon flies. When dyed, these fibers retain their black bars and specks, and they make very attractive horns on some salmon patterns. Dyed Amherst tail fibers give a very buggy look to large, butterfly-like creations. The fibers are usually long enough to use as horns on even the largest flies.

Horns of natural or dyed Amherst tail fibers add a wasplike look to some Spey and Dee patterns. Why more Spey patterns don't have horns is a mystery to me. Horns add a nice accent to patterns such the Sweep, Nitehawk Spey, and the Ghost series. The horns have their own lively action in the water.

When selecting Amherst tail feathers, look for a complete set of center tail feathers that match in colors and markings. Try to find feathers that are bright white with bold barring. Amherst tails are sold in pairs. One feather is used for the left side of a wing section and the other for the right side.

Check to see that the fibers are completely married, joined from base to tips. A few sections, of course, will have splits, but most of the feather should consist of perfectly married fibers. As tail feathers get old and dry out, they become brittle and sometimes impossible to marry. Steaming tail feathers seems to soften and add a little moisture to the fibers, making them easier to tie with.

When you tie with Lady Amherst tail, try to cut sections that have the same length and the same pattern of markings. This way, the left and right wings of the fly will match in shape and markings; each part of each wing will mirror its counterpart in the other wing.

Lady Amherst tippets are white with black bars. They are used for the main wings on some classic feather-wing salmon flies. The Lady Amherst and the Evening Star are examples of classic patterns on which the main wings are made of entire tippet feathers from Amherst pheasants.

The hollow stems of Amherst tippets are often delicate. I usually crimp them with a pair of flat-nosed pliers to make them easier to tie on straight and firmly. As with the tail fibers, too much fussing with Amherst tippets can ruin them. The tippets are not used on Dee and Spey flies, though they could be dyed and used for tail veils.

Lady Amherst crests are not often called for on salmon flies, though Syd Glasso used them for the tail and topping of his Sol Duc Dark steelhead fly. Amherst crests are wine-red in color, with darker tips and a very slight curve in each feather. This is an important feature in crests used for tails and toppings on small, low-winged patterns such as steelhead Speys. These feathers are the right length and shape for such flies, and that's probably why Glasso used them. On many steelhead flies, Amherst crests are used as a topping to compress the wings down and keep them low along the body of the fly.

Golden Pheasant

Kelson summed it up when he said that for salmon-fly tying, no bird is more important than the golden pheasant. "The golden pheasant is subordinate to none," he said. "It has attained the highest pitch of popularity among fly dressers, mainly by virtue of its crests." Feathers from this bird used on salmon flies include the tail, the red body feathers, tippets, and, most important, the crests, which are called toppings on classic Atlantic-salmon patterns.

Golden pheasant crests cannot be replaced. They are often the most important feathers or features on a salmon fly. Used for tails and toppings, golden pheasant crests create the shape that we associate with salmon flies. Nicely shaped, bright, lustrous, and glistening crests add to the beauty of your flies. A sweeping, turned-up tail and flowing crest create a frame that cannot be made with any other material. Without these exquisite feathers, we simply would not have salmon flies as we know them.

When I choose crests for salmon flies, I concentrate more on shape than on color. All crests should have a very lustrous, clean, golden color. Some tiers choose only crests that have bright orange tips. At one time I did the same, but I've found that shape is more important than color. For a low-winged pattern, you need crests that have a slight curve that will encase the wing. For high-winged flies or those that use entire feathers for their wings, you need crests with drastic curves, almost hook-like in appearance. You need the same shape for wings that consists of five or six toppings tied one on top of another to form a shower of crests. This type of wing is found on the Sun Fly series, the Chatterer, for example. In this style of wing, all the crests should come from the same head so that they match exactly in shape and color.

I select certain crests just for tails, the shape being the most important feature. Some head sections have many feathers with the shape that I prefer for tails, and

Dee Flies from George Kelson's *The Salmon Fly*, 1895

Killer, Rossman

Tri-Color (argus wing), Veverka

Claret-Brown, Rossman

Green Queen (Waddington shank), Veverka

White-Winged Akroyd, Veverka

Perhaps the most famous of all the old Dee patterns is featured in George Kelson's *The Salmon Fly*: the Akroyd, also called the Poor Man's Jock Scott. William Blacklaws, a fishing tackle maker who originated the Beaconsfield, helped Charles Akroyd publicize his namesake pattern, and the first Akroyds used golden pheasant crest as a hackle, which was then changed to a common yellow hackle.

The Green Queen is one of Kelson's own patterns, and he preferred it to the Green King in bright weather and water. The Claret-Brown is also one of his patterns. The Tri-Color and the Killer are similar in their dressing: When the fly is tied with a red breast feather from a golden pheasant and white wings, it is known as the Killer, but with a teal throat and turkey wing, it is called the Tri-Color.

I'll buy them for that reason. The tail of a fly is very important, and you should make tails with the best crests you have. A crest used for a tail must have a straight stem so that the tail is perfectly in line with the hook shank when viewed from above.

The tail sets the shape, length, and height of a salmon fly's wing. A tail's length varies according to the size and style of the hook, and its shape varies with the style of wing. If you're not careful when selecting a crest for the tail, you might tie most of the fly and then realize, when it's time to make the wings, that the tail is too long or short to match the wing materials or the hook style. You can finish the fly, but it will look out of balance. Everyone makes this mistake; the main thing is to learn from it.

With salmon flies, you always have to keep in mind how the section you are working on will blend with the steps that preceded it and those that will follow. When each component accents or blends into those before and after it, the fly takes on a flowing appearance. It looks like it's all of a piece. In many ways, tying a

salmon fly is like assembling a puzzle. All the pieces have to fit.

A tail or topping should be sized to fit the fly you are tying. You don't want to strip off so many of the fibers that you make the feather wispy and flimsy. When you use a crest feather as a tail, you will have to strip off some fibers at the tie-in area. A topping, however, should be selected so that you can tie it on by the small tab that attached the feather to the skin. This tab is flexible and aligned with the center of the feather, and it makes an easy tie-in spot. When you attach a crest by this little tab on the end of the stem, the feather's natural shape will fit the shape of the wings. Some tiers take a long crest and size it down by stripping off fibers, and then crimp the stem at the tie-in spot. This should be done only when you can't find a crest that's the proper size.

A golden pheasant's head bears hundreds of crests, from tiny feathers for the smallest tails to four-inch-long toppings. The feathers down the center of the skin are the best. They are the straightest; their stems and fibers are in line with their bases. A feather from the side of the head has a tab or base that is not aligned with the rest of the stem. That's how nature makes them. If you tie one of these on a fly, the crest will angle to one side. Sometimes, these feathers can be stripped at the base, crimped with flat-nosed pliers, and used for tails and toppings. But the best salmon flies require crests from the top or center of the head.

Always try to find toppings that are straight from base to tip. Many tiers try to straighten crooked crests by wetting them and laying them on a curved surface. This usually doesn't work; after a while, crests straightened this way go back to their original state. Lightly steaming a crest will bring it to its best shape, but don't overdo it.

You can use the smallest crest feathers, those found at the base of the crests and tippets, as a toucan substitute for body veils. I use them for body veils on the Steelhead Sunset and Golden Argus Spey. They also work for tails and toppings on Sol Duc–style flies. A head usually has only two pairs of these unique feathers.

Golden pheasant crests were used as body hackles on a few of the original Dee patterns. The first Akroyds were hackled with golden pheasant crests wound over yellow seal fur; later tiers changed to a yellow chicken hackle. The Gardener pattern, tied by William Garden,

also used a crest as a body hackle. Crests are not easily wrapped as body hackles. They have very brittle, wiry stems, and I believe that's why they went out of use. It's a great idea though. What other feather could provide more attraction and reflect light better? Dyed, a crest feather would make a brilliant body hackle.

There are two types of golden pheasant crests: good ones and bad ones. Don't waste time on the bad ones.

Tippets are the feathers that follow the crests. Found on the neck of a golden pheasant, they are orange with black bars. Entire tippet feathers are used in pairs to make wings on some patterns and underwings on some married-wing flies. Individual fibers are used for the base of mixed-wing salmon flies. Some Atlantic-salmon patterns have tippets as tail veils, while others call for them as wing or side veils. Several of the original Dee patterns used tippet fibers for tail veils. A few patterns have cheeks made with small tippet feathers.

When you use entire tippets to make wings, match the size of the feathers to the size of the hook so that you can tie them in by the little tabs on the stems, just as you would a crest. If you can't find the proper size for a feather-wing pattern, then start with larger tippets, strip some fibers off the base of each feather, and crimp the stems at the tie-in point. On properly sized wings, the black bars line up with the butt of the fly.

Used whole as underwings on married-wing patterns, tippets reinforce the main wings. This style of wing is tied with a pair of tippets as the underwing and then two matched, married wings on the outside of the tippet feathers. When a married wing is in place and ready to be tied on, the underwing will help to keep the married sections from crimping or pinching over to one side when you apply thread pressure. This is a common problem on complicated flies; if not held correctly, the far wing has a tendency to crimp or cave in and in time will come apart.

In a mixed wing, strands of tippet add support and serve as a base for the next part of the wing. Many of the original salmon patterns called for an underwing of fibers from a golden pheasant tippet. Typically, a recipe says something like, "Golden pheasant tippet in strands." That means individual fibers, not a whole feather.

Most steelhead-fly tiers and some salmon-fly tiers dye their tippets hot orange. This gives them a more brilliant and contrasting color. Tippets are also used in the wing of the General Practitioner prawn pattern, from which many steelhead prawn patterns evolved.

The red body feathers of a golden pheasant are used for wings and tails and are wrapped to make collars on many salmon and steelhead flies. These feathers have a beautiful, natural rich red color.

When used for a collar or throat, a body feather is folded. The feathers come in a wide range of sizes; you can find some that will hackle small flies, and others that will work on big, classic patterns such as the Shannon. When wound on as collars, they have a very spiky look. Red body feathers dyed purple and black are used for throats and wing material on various steelhead Spey patterns.

Some tiers find these feathers a bit short for making collars. True, the stems aren't very long, but there's usually enough length for two good turns. If necessary, you can wrap two collars to fill out the throat on a larger pattern.

The Lady Caroline fly utilizes golden pheasant body feathers for its tail and collar. The tail is made up of individual fibers, and the collar is a body feather folded and wrapped. With its olive-brown body, gray heron body hackle, and bronze-mallard wing, the Lady Caroline is a very somber pattern. The red tail and collar add a bit of color; when viewed in the afternoon light, they create a sparkling image.

When they're used as wings on salmon flies, matched pairs of body feathers are tied in just like the tippet wings on the Ranger series. These feathers can also be used as underwings on patterns like the Gordon, if you don't have sword feathers from the tail. Steelhead flies that have wings made of red body feathers include the Sol Duc series by Syd Glasso. When tying wings on this style of fly, use the smallest and narrowest feathers you can find. The stems of small feathers are tricky to tie in properly, and it might take a few attempts to get them right.

The earliest Dee patterns had tails of golden pheasant body feathers tied flat. They are tied on the same way to make the top wing of a General Practitioner.

Tail feathers from golden pheasants supply parts of many married-wing classic flies. These feathers are a rich dark brown color with dark, wavy bars. The fibers are long enough to tie flies up to size 5/0. Many married-wing patterns use tail fibers from a golden pheasant in the top sections of their wings.

Always select the two center feathers from any type of pheasant tail. They have the longest fibers and the best markings.

Golden pheasant tail is not the easiest material to marry to other feathers. It has a tendency to separate at the tips when handled, a problem that only gets worse when you try to correct it. When marrying another feather section to golden pheasant tail, get the job done with one gentle swipe of your fingertips.

Old, dried-out tail feathers are particularly hard to work with. It's best to use fresh, perfectly clean tails. For many years, I had my own flock of golden pheasants. I had fresh tails every spring, and that's how I noticed the difference between new and old feathers. Sections from the fresh feathers were much easier to marry to other feathers in a wing. Old quills can sometimes be brought back to life by steaming them; this adds a little moisture to the fibers and makes them softer, a little less brittle, and easier to work with.

Golden pheasant tail is not commonly used in strips to make a whole wing. The only Spey pattern that uses it for the main wing is the Miss Grant. If you want to tie flies that use strips of golden pheasant tail as their wings, find feathers that have the darkest, boldest markings and fibers that are married all the way to their tips. Golden pheasant tail is tied in on edge; if it's tied flat, the fibers will separate.

The sides of the tail have red feathers called sword feathers, which are used for the underwing of the Gordon fly. They are bright, shiny red in color, and each one is shaped like a sword.

Silver Pheasant

Few classic salmon flies call for feathers from silver pheasants. For Spey-fly tiers, the most important feathers are the crests, which are a substitute for black heron. The largest crests have long, iridescent black fibers and make good throats on Spey flies. Although the stems are very short, you can get a few turns, enough for a throat or collar on a sparse fly. On larger or more heavily dressed flies, you can apply two crests. These feathers work well for the collars on the Sol Duc style, which originally had throats made of black heron. The stems of silver pheasant crests are too short for the feathers to work as body hackles.

The shorter crests, those two inches or less in length, make beautiful wings on salmon or steelhead patterns. You stack them and tie them on as you would if you were tying a hairwing fly. These small crest feathers slick down in the water and move very well. They have an iridescent hue not found in hair; they're nature's version of Flashabou. Examples of patterns that can use this type of wing include the Nighthawk, Sweep, and the Black Bear series.

Some of the body feathers of the silver pheasant can be dyed and used for throat hackles. They have a bright white background with fine black penciling, and they take dye well. When wound as collars, these feathers produce a speckled appearance. Some popular dyed colors include orange, purple, green, and blue, all in hot or fluorescent hues.

Traditional Atlantic-salmon patterns rarely call for silver pheasant feathers. A fly of American origin, the classic New England streamer, uses the body feathers as cheeks, most notably on the Gray Ghost and similar flies tied by Carrie Stevens. Some streamer flies also use the crests as wing toppings that simulate the iridescent color of baitfish.

Ring-Necked Pheasant

Among the useful feathers provided by ring-necked pheasants are the tails, rump hackles, and the small, white neck feathers that give the bird its name. The long-fibered, rusty brown rump feathers can be used to make body and collar hackles on Spey flies. Some of the early steelhead Spey patterns used them. The rump hackles have long fibers, but fairly short stems; when you use one as a body hackle, don't plan on getting more than two to three wraps out of it.

Ringneck rump hackles are best used as Spey-fly collar material, folded and wound. The fibers are very delicate, and most hackles have some fibers with broken tips. Try to avoid using feathers with broken fibers; they make a fly look shabby.

The best rump hackles come from old, wild cock birds. Most wild ringnecks don't get to old age, but a bird in its second year will have beautiful hackles. A lot of the skins for sale in shops are from pen-raised birds whose feathers don't match the colors and quality of plumage from their wild cousins. The varied diet of wild birds improves their feather. If you plan to tie Spey flies with ringneck rump hackles, you need feathers from a healthy, wild bird.

Rump hackles can be dyed and used for the collars on steelhead Spey flies. You can buy skins dyed purple, orange, green, or black, all of which show iridescent tones that accent the colors.

Tail feathers from male and female ringnecks furnish material for tying simple strip-wing patterns such as the March Brown, a good general-purpose fly. I prefer the hen's tail for March Brown wing sections; it has a buff color and the fibers have more web, a good quality in a material used for simple strip-wing flies. It makes for a more durable wing that's less likely to split apart.

The small white neck feathers of the cock bird can be dyed various colors and used for tail and body veils. In the right colors, the neck feathers can work as substitutes for Indian crow and toucan.

Blue-Eared (Manchurian) Pheasant

This bird's hackles are must-haves for Spey-fly tiers, because they are good replacements for the heron hackles that are illegal to own. The body, neck, back, belly, and rump all have long-fibered feathers that can be used for body hackles and throats on Spey and Dee patterns.

These slate-gray hackles come in a range of sizes for both small and large patterns. The feathers from the neck down to the rump are on the spiky side, and these are the hackles used on most flies in the 2 to 5/0 size range. The largest hackles are from the rump of the bird; some have very long fibers. Save these for your best and largest Dee patterns. Dyed black, these hackles work well on old Dee patterns such as the Akroyd and Balmoral, or any other fly that calls for long, black heron hackle. Under the tail, each skin has several dark gray to almost iridescent black hackles that can be used on large Spey flies that need long, black hackles. Hackles taken from the flanks of the bird have a softer texture than those from the neck, shoulders, and rump.

The only problem with hackles from blue-eared pheasants is that the stems are short, which means that the feathers must be tied in at the center of the fly. Some of the largest feathers have longer, thinner stems that can be tied in farther back on the body of a fly. Except for their stem length, blue-eared pheasant hackles are excellent heron substitutes; only a trained eye can tell the difference between these hackles and the real thing.

You can sometimes buy these hackles packaged by the dozen, but they are more often sold on a complete skin. Packaged feathers are usually all the same size, but they're a good way to buy dyed hackles. They are available in yellow, black, and several other important colors. If you buy a skin, you have all the different sizes and can tie hundreds of flies. Look for large skins that bear all the different sizes of hackles in good numbers, and check to make sure that the hackles don't have broken or frayed tips. Look for a skin with nice, long rump feathers, since these are the most important and the fewest in number.

When I raised blue-eared pheasants, I would from time to time collect the molted feathers, and I always had a good supply of hackles. Pen-raised blue-ears are big and even-tempered and very useful to someone who ties Spey flies.

Brown-Eared Pheasant

Brown-eared pheasants also furnish body and throat hackles for Spey and Dee flies. A skin bears three types of feathers we can use. The body hackles are a rich, dark, shiny brown, and they can be used to hackle patterns such as the Lady Caroline and Gold Reeach.

The feathers on the back and rump of the bird are a chalky white color. I usually dye the white rump feathers orange, yellow, or purple and use them for body hackles or collars on my steelhead Spey patterns.

Under the tail area of the bird, you will find some feathers that make good replacements for eagle hackles; they can be used for imitation eagle hackles. These hackles are chalky white with gray splashes, very webby and marabou-like in appearance, much like the eagle hackles used on some antique patterns. In their natural color or dyed yellow, they are the best substitute I've found for eagle hackles.

White-Eared Pheasant

White-eared pheasant hackles are rare finds. This bird is the largest of the "eared" pheasants, and its feathers have the longest fibers. The body feathers are used for throat and body hackles on Spey and Dee patterns. All the hackles are white, and they can be dyed any salmon-fly color you need. I usually dye them hot orange, yellow, purple, and black, and employ them as body hackles on some of the more colorful Spey and Dee patterns.

WATER BIRDS

The original Spey and Dee flies used a number of feathers from water birds. For the most part, this plumage is a thing of the past. Some water birds are endangered or threatened species, and many others are simply illegal to kill and possess. Fly tiers have found substitutes for water-bird feathers that are no longer available. I mention the following feathers only because they are historically interesting, and I do not advise fly tiers to attempt to obtain them.

Coot

This was used as a substitute for gray heron on small Spey flies. Coot is very close to heron in texture and color. It is very webby and has good mobility in the water.

Heron

Heron feathers are currently illegal to possess in the U.S. That poses a problem, because many of the original Spey and Dee patterns call for body hackles and throats made of gray or black heron feathers. Indeed, heron is the material that gave the original Spey and Dee flies their long, graceful, flowing appearance.

Herons are big birds, and their largest hackles are long enough for the biggest Dee patterns. The spiky fibers do not mat or clump when wet; each fiber remains separate from all the others, and each has its own action in the water. That's why the early Spey-fly tiers used heron hackles on their flies.

The colors most commonly used were gray, black, and purple (actually a reddish brown). Black heron hackles have a soft texture, almost like marabou. The gray hackles are more spiky, with very little web. When used as body hackles, gray heron feathers were stripped on one side to keep the fly sparse. Sparse patterns sink faster and swim better than heavily dressed flies.

Some of the old Spey patterns had wings made with strips from the wing quills. Body and throat hackles, however, were the primary use of heron feathers.

It's too bad that this material is no longer available. Herons are far from endangered, and their numbers have been growing for a long time. I like to see them on the water and I'm glad that someone had the sense to create legislation protecting them, but still, it would be nice to be able to tie a few Spey and Dee flies with this unique, original material.

Years ago, hats were commonly adorned with feathers from herons and other water birds. The birds were hunted for their plumage, until they were nearly wiped out by the plume hunters. That's what led to their protection.

Fly tiers have found a number of substitutes for heron hackles, including feathers from the various eared pheasants. Among the oldest heron replacements is crowned pigeon, which is very similar to gray heron in color and fiber length, though its texture is softer. Kelson mentioned that he used crowned pigeon on certain patterns instead of heron. It is, however, rarely found for sale or in materials collections. I've used it a few times, but not enough to form an opinion on its value to a Spey-fly tier. A complete skin probably has a number of useful feathers.

RAPTORS
Gled and Kite
Gled, also known as kites, were hawklike birds that furnished the wing material on the original Dee flies. Strips of gled feathers had a reddish brown background with darker bars. More important, however, was the material's soft texture and its action or movement in the water. The earliest descriptions of Dee patterns mention wings made of gled, and many anglers of the time felt that the material had no equal.

This raptor, however, became extinct fairly early in the history of salmon-fly tying. By the time Kelson wrote his book, gled was no longer in use, and indeed no longer available.

Most fly tiers settled on cinnamon-colored turkey as the best substitute. The overall color is close, but turkey strips lack the darker bars that distinguished gled from other materials. Nor does turkey have the same action that made soft, mobile strips of gled such desirable wing materials. A number of writers commented that Dee patterns were never the same after gled became unavailable.

Golden Eagle
Feathers from golden eagles were used as body hackles on the original Eagle patterns. Eagle hackles were very mobile in the water, having an action similar to that of marabou. The hackles came from the shins of the bird and were dyed yellow or used in their natural color. Their beautiful, fluffy body hackles distinguished the old Eagle patterns from all other salmon flies.

Eagle feathers, of course, are no longer available to fly tiers. The modern substitute is turkey marabou. White marabou can be dyed yellow, but even better are turkey marabou feathers in various natural shades of mottled brown. These feathers are almost identical to the original eagle hackles in texture and color.

DUCKS
Duck feathers are very important to Spey- and Dee-fly tiers. They are used for throats and collars on most Spey and Dee patterns. Traditionally, a Spey fly is incomplete without its teal-flank collar. Duck feathers, specifically bronze-mallard feathers, also supply wing material for traditional Spey flies. Various feathers from ducks become tails and tail veils, body and throat hackles, and wings and wing veils on many classic salmon patterns. Teal, wood duck, and bronze mallard are called for on many salmon flies.

I used to raise several types of ducks, and before that I hunted many species—canvasbacks, broadbills, mallard, widgeons, pintails, wood ducks, and teal. After the hunting season, I'd spend hours watching ducks through a spotting scope, studying their habits and plumage. Like any serious hunter, I learned to identify the various species both on the water and on the wing.

Between hunting them and raising them, I got to know a lot about ducks and their feathers. Among the most important things I saw is the difference between a fully matured bird's feathers and those from a juvenile. The best feathers for fly tying always come from older, wild male birds.

Flank feathers from male ducks are the most important to salmon-fly tiers. The smallest feathers at the front of the flank are used for cheeks on streamers and for collars on small salmon flies. Feathers from the middle of the flank are larger and symmetrical, with equally long fibers on both sides of the stem; these make good throats on various sizes of salmon flies. The larger feathers from the top and back of the flank provide material for wings and wing veils. Barred wood-duck and mandarin feathers come from this area. These feathers are not symmetrical; one side has longer, webbier fibers than the other. You need to have a matched pair of feathers—one from the duck's left side, and one from the right—to make wings or veils with them.

Flank feathers are generally sold in packages, either by the dozen or by weight. When bought in bulk, they must be sorted into lefts, rights, and centers, and then paired. It's a lot of work, but you end up with all kinds of usable feathers. About 30 percent of packaged feathers are of no use to a salmon-fly tier.

You can sometimes find full duck skins for sale. Some of the better ones to look for are hooded merganser, gadwall, wood duck, and mandarin duck. Besides the flank feathers, these skins also have other useful plumage. Look for clean, brightly marked feathers. Steaming feathers will make them fuller and easier to use.

When I make a collar with a flank feather, I usually fold the hackle and tie it in by the tip at a spot that lets me wrap the thinnest portion of the stem around the hook. "Folding" a hackle is the process of taking the fibers on one side of the stem and forcing them to the other side. This puts all the fibers on the same side, doubling the density of the hackle and allowing you to wrap a neat, conical collar. Here's the method that I use. With the better, convex side of the feather facing you, hold the tip with your right thumb and index finger. The middle finger of your left hand holds the butt end of the stem against the joint of your left thumb. Then use your left index finger to push the fibers on the left side of the feather behind the stem. As you do that, pinch the stem and the pushed-back fibers between your left thumb and forefinger. Then slide the pinch to the right, folding the fibers behind the stem of the feather. I start this process at the base of the feather and have to repeat it several times to fold all the fibers. It's a technique that comes only with practice.

For a collar on a sparse pattern, I'll strip one side of the flank feather or make only one wrap with a folded feather. When I use a flank feather as a body hackle, I always strip one side. A folded feather makes a body hackle that's too dense, and an overly dense, bushy body hackle can make a fly swim on its side unless it's tied on an exceptionally heavy hook. Keep body hackles on the sparse side, and your flies will swim and track better.

To make a tail, take fibers from the side of a flank feather that has less web. Strip off a number of fibers, fold or roll them together, and tie them on. Look for feathers with bold markings for tails and tail veils.

For wings or wing veils, select material from the side of the feather that has more web and the best markings. Naturally, you need two matched feathers—one from the right side and one from the left—to make wing sections or veils. I usually cut the section of fibers away from the quill, but many other tiers cut a piece of the quill, leaving the section of fibers attached to it. They find that this helps to keep the fibers together as they position the wing and tie it on.

Wings on Spey and Dee flies are tied one side at time. Do the left or far side first, and then tie on the right or near wing. The wings are mounted on the shoulders of the fly. I usually tie them so that the fibers have a swept-up look, but a lot of tiers attach wings so that the tips have a downward curve. Neither way is inherently right or better; it's a question of taste.

When mounting wings made of flank-feather sections, always tie them on at the root or base of the fibers, close to the spot where the fibers were attached to the quill. This is the softest area of the fibers and the easiest to work with. Tying in a wing at the soft spot also makes for a wing that's less likely to split. Of course, you have to use material that's the right length, and that changes according to the size and style of the fly. A flank-feather section is the right length if the tips of the fibers reach the rear of the hook and the roots land at the tie-in area at the front of the fly.

Another style of wing, used on such flies as the Silver Blue and Golden Demon, is called a rolled or folded wing. Here, the flank-feather sections are tied on edge, much like the quill sections used for wings on some wet flies for trout. This creates a bold wing silhouette and a look that's completely different from the low wings of a Spey fly.

To make a rolled or folded wing with a flank feather, I cut a section of fibers approximately four times the desired width of the finished wing. I fold in the outer edges so that they meet in the center of the section, and then fold the section down the middle, ending up with a four-layer wing. It's also possible to use two matched strips of fibers placed back to back.

After checking the length of a folded or rolled wing, hold it on top of the fly and pinch it with your index finger and thumb. Hold the wing in place and take one turn of thread over it. Gently pull the thread down while maintaining your pinch on the wing, and let the front section of the wing compress. Make another three or four wraps with the thread. Don't release your pinch, and check to see that the butts of the fibers are still straight. Take another three or four turns of thread. As you release your pinch, slide your fingers rearward along the top of the wing. If all went well, the wing is straight and low along the fly's body. If the wing doesn't have the look you want, take it off and try again. Sometimes the process goes easier the second time, because the fibers have already been compressed. If the wing still doesn't turn out right, the problem might be with the material. Make up a new wing and try again.

Like wing strips, the wing veils on full-dress patterns come from matched pairs of flank feathers. Like Spey-fly wings, they are attached one side at a time. The length of wing veils (also called side veils) varies from one tier to the next; some tiers like short veils, while others stretch them out as long as they can. Side veils are usually made of wood duck and pintail married together, though some flies use single strips of wood duck, teal, or pintail.

Gadwall

Some Spey patterns have throats and wings made with flank feathers from this handsome duck. Gadwall flank feathers are similar to teal in color and markings, but they have a grayer background and are not as distinctly and finely barred as teal flank. Syd Glasso used gadwall flank feathers for collars on some of his Spey patterns and for wings on his Brown Heron and Gold Heron variations.

The feathers from the back are used on landlocked-salmon streamers such as Joe's Smelt and the Counterfeiter. Long, narrow feathers with tapered points and very fine markings are tied in flat on top of the hook to make streamer wings. These feathers are very rare and should be saved for your finest streamer patterns. The smaller, curved feathers from the back are used for cheeks on streamers such as the Counterfeiter, a landlocked-salmon streamer of my own design.

Hooded Merganser

Hooded mergansers supply Spey-fly tiers with two important materials: the brown, barred flank feathers and the jet-black feathers from the back of the duck. The flank feathers have a rich, rusty brown background with very distinctive dark brown barring. The stems on these feathers are very thin and the fibers are long, making them very valuable for throats and collars on various salmon patterns.

The flank feathers are highly sought for throats on Spey flies; they make nice variations on the Gold Reeach, Gold Heron, and Brown Heron. The fibers are so long that these feathers can be used on the largest Dee patterns. Flies with claret-colored bodies look

---

Duck Feathers

Bronze-mallard quill		Pair of barred wood duck
Egyptian goose	Golden pheasant red body feather	Barred mandarin
Lemon wood duck	Counterfeiter landlocked-salmon streamer	
	Yellow Badger landlocked-salmon streamer	Blue-winged teal
	Nighthawk	Mallard flank
European widgeon	Hooded merganser	Teal	Gadwall
	American widgeon	Guinea fowl	Vulturine
Elver	Shoveler	Teal	Teal, dyed purple
Turkey hackle		Common guinea fowl

Duck feathers are used for all styles of flies, from classic Catskill dry-fly wings and nymph tails and collars, to landlocked-salmon streamer cheeks, and in many types of applications in tying salmon flies. Duck feathers are used for tails and tail veils, throat hackles, collars, and wing materials on Spey and Dee flies. Spey flies are distinguished by their collar of finely penciled teal flank feather. Other collar materials include guinea fowl hackles, in their natural state and dyed kingfisher blue for salmon flies, and dyed hot red and orange for steelhead flies. The wings on the original Spey flies were tied with two slips of bronze-mallard quills.

---

especially good with throats made from the reddish brown flank feathers. The old Glentana pattern is an example; its color scheme is accented by a collar of hooded merganser.

The smaller flank feathers can be used for throats on small Atlantic-salmon patterns or cheek feathers on landlocked-salmon streamers. They make beautiful cheeks on this style of fly, and I use them on my Yellow Badger streamer pattern.

The jet-black feathers located on the back and shoulders of the duck are a substitute for black heron on flies such as the Sol Duc Spey series. They also make good body hackles on some of the old Spey patterns originally tied with black Spey cock feathers.

Hooded merganser is rarely used on classic, full-dress salmon flies. In fact, one rarely sees a skin or feathers for sale. Over the past thirty years, I have had two skins, one from a merganser I shot and one that belonged to a fly-tying collection I bought at an antique-tackle show.

The hooded merganser is one of my favorite ducks to see in the wild. It is a striking bird on the water, with its black head, pronounced white hood, contrasting brown side feathers, and black chest with white bars. Its slender beak looks more like a weapon than a bill, uniquely shaped for catching and holding small fish. Generally, hooded mergansers are found on small backwater ponds much like those frequented by wood ducks. Fast on the wing, they are often seen flying low over the water, snaking up a channel, river, or estuary.

Red-Breasted Merganser

Red-breasted merganser flank feathers resemble those from teal, but they display a broader barring pattern. Softer than teal flank, they make nice collar material. Dyed hot orange and purple, they make handsome collars on steelhead Spey patterns.

This material is hardly ever available in fly shops or catalogs. The best way to acquire red-breasted merganser feathers is to hunt ducks or have a friend who hunts and doesn't mind collecting feathers for you.

Mallard

Mallards furnish some of the most important feathers to Spey-fly tiers. Bronze-mallard shoulder feathers have mottled brown fibers with gray roots. Some are dark brown, while others are more bronze in color with varying degrees of penciling. They are used in strips for Spey-fly wings and for roofs on built-wing salmon flies. All the original Spey patterns used bronze-mallard strips for their wings.

To make the wings of a Spey fly, you will need a matched pair of bronze-mallard feathers, one from each side of the bird. Take two sections or slips that are the same length and width and have similar patterns and coloring. This style of winging is done one side at a time and on the shoulders of the fly. Each wing should be tied in at the gray area that was attached to the quill. Since it's soft and ties in easily, this part of the fiber keeps the wing sections from splitting, a common problem with bronze mallard. Pryce-Tannatt mentioned that

the finished wings should look like an upside-down boat hull, and that describes it nicely.

On classic patterns, bronze mallard is used for roofs. Two sections from matched feathers are tied on so that they cover the top of the main wing, acting as a roof for the wing. I attach these sections one at a time, similar to the way I tie on Spey-fly wings, except that each half of a roof is tied on the shoulder and top edge of the main wing. This procedure can be very frustrating. Many tiers have trouble with bronze-mallard roofs, and some leave them off altogether. The trick is to find a pair of feathers that fit the length of the fly and have a natural curve that matches the shape of the fly's wing. Packaged feathers are flat and lack the natural curve, but you can steam them to restore the curve. When sized and fitted properly, roof sections will tie on quite easily. As I've noted before, tying a salmon fly is putting a puzzle together, and the job goes much easier if the pieces fit. Use feathers' natural shapes to your advantage.

Bronze mallard is also used as a rolled wing. Patterns that have wings of this style are the Golden Demon and the Thunder and Lightning. Many Spey flies can also be tied with this type of wing. To make a rolled wing, start with a section of feather four times as wide as the desired width of the finished wing. Hold the section with the good side facing away from you, and fold the two outer edges in so that they meet in the middle. Then take the section and close it like a book; now you have four sections or strips making up one wing. Wings of this style are tied on edge and display a bold silhouette.

Mallard flanks are used as collars on some flies, but they lack the clear, dark penciling pattern that teal has. Gray flank feathers are used for collars on the series of flies called Spiders. Some of the largest flank feathers have fibers sufficiently long to use as a body hackle or a very long throat. They can also be dyed various colors and used for throats and collars. Smaller flank feathers can be dyed or used in their natural color for cheeks; several landlocked-salmon streamers and saltwater patterns use them this way.

Mandarin Duck

Mandarin is very similar in color and pattern to our wood duck. It has a more reddish or cinnamon background, and the barred feathers have a finer white bar at the tip. This is a beautiful duck in the wild, and the only one that rivals the brilliantly colored wood duck.

Mandarin has two important features that make it my choice over wood duck: longer fibers and finer, more distinctive markings. Many tiers prize it for making the side veils on Black Dogs. Mandarin's only drawback is that it is rarer than wood duck.

The barred feathers are used in sections as wings or side veils. Some salmon patterns use it for tail veils, and barred mandarin makes an attractive accent when used in this manner. The unbarred flank feathers are used for collars on Spey patterns, and the smaller flank feathers are used for cheeks on landlocked-salmon patterns.

Northern Shoveler

The northern shoveler is a brightly colored duck with an iridescent green head similar to a mallard's, a white chest, and rich reddish brown flank feathers. Its flank feathers are very useful as throats and collars on Spey and Dee patterns. The flank feathers are a reddish brown color, almost cinnamon, with darker, irregular bars. The fibers are long and very soft. While the stems are fine, they're also very durable, making this one of the easiest duck feathers to use for collars.

Some of the feathers from the back, upper section of the flank are also used for wings. They are used as a whole wing or in strips for Spey-fly wings. When used as a whole wing, they must be used in pairs, a right and a left.

Shoveler duck is rarely used in old salmon-fly patterns, though the original dressing for the Ghost called for strips of shoveler duck for the wing. One classic pattern that comes to mind is the Britannia mentioned by Kelson. It is a full-dress, feather-wing pattern, and the wing is made up of a pair of flank feathers. In *The Book of the Salmon*, published in 1850, Edward Fitzgibbon describes Britannia as one of his favorite patterns.

Pintail

Pintail flank feathers are used mainly for side veils on classic salmon patterns. It is similar to teal in color, with slightly longer, webbier fibers that make it a good choice for delicate veils. The webby fibers also make pintail easy to marry to other feathers. The Jock Scott and many other classic patterns have wing veils made of married strips of wood duck and pintail. Thanks to the length of their fibers, some flank feathers from pintails can be used as collars on very large Dee patterns.

Green-Winged Teal

Green-winged teal flank feathers have very fine penciling on a white background. The crisp markings add character to a pattern whether they're used as wings, tail veils, or throat hackles. Teal flank is the most distinctive barred duck feather used for throats on salmon flies. The original Spey flies always had throats of teal flank, and a fly was deemed unfinished without one.

These feathers have many uses. For use as collar material, a teal flank is folded and tied in by the tip. When used as a body hackle, the feather is stripped on one side. Sections from matched feathers can serve as side veils on wings; most often, the teal strips are married to strips of wood duck for this purpose. Some flies have tail veils made of teal flank with extradistinct barring. The largest flank feathers can furnish strips for the wings of some Spey fly patterns.

Teal flank is also used on simple strip-wing flies. When used in this manner, a wide section of a feather is folded twice to make a four-layer wing that is attached on edge. The Crosfield and Silver and Blue have this type of wing.

Many species of teal from around the world are useful for fly tying. The North American green-winged teal is the one most often called for, and the one most readily available.

Blue-Winged Teal

Blue-winged teal is not usually used in Spey-fly tying, though it can be. The flank feathers are a tannish color with dark brown spots. They can be used for collars and throats on small Spey patterns. Blue-winged teal also makes a good accent on a fly that has wings made of peacock-quill strips; the colors and patterns go together nicely.

European Widgeon

European widgeon flank feathers have a gray background and irregular dark bars similar to those on teal feathers. The flank feathers are used for throats and collars on Spey and Dee patterns.

American Widgeon

American widgeon is also useful to Spey-fly tiers. The mid-size flank feathers have a reddish brown background and markings similar to those of teal; they work as collars and throats. The largest flank feathers can also be used in strips for wings on Spey patterns such as the Gold Heron and the Brown Heron. American widgeon also works well for making a light-winged Gold Reeach.

Wood Duck

This duck supplies two different types of flank feathers that are useful to fly tiers: the black-and-white barred feathers and the unbarred lemon feathers. Called summer duck in old salmon-fly books, wood duck was used mainly for its barred feathers.

The barred flank feathers are used as tail veils, wings, or wing veils. As a wing veil, wood duck is usually married to teal or pintail flank, as on the Jock Scott and many salmon flies of this style. Its bold black-and-white bars add vertical markings to a wing made up of horizontal elements.

To make a veil for a tail, take slips from matching (left and right) feathers, put them back to back, and tie them on as you would a wing. Among the patterns that use barred wood duck as tail veils are the Green Highlander and the Silver Spectre. For side veils, attach strips one at a time on the sides of the wing.

No other feather displays such a brilliant white as that on barred wood duck. Some feathers have a wide white bar, while others have narrower bands of white in the barred area. I prefer those with narrow white bars, but it's strictly a question of taste. Naturally, barred feathers should be paired with others that are the same size and that have the same markings. Two well-matched feathers look like mirror images of each other, differing only in curvature.

I have used the larger unbarred flank feathers as throat and wing material on my Summer Duck Spey and as a wing veil on the Black Dog. The small unbarred flank feathers make good cheeks on landlock streamers. They are also used on many trout patterns; many Catskill dry flies have wings made of lemon wood duck, as trout-fly tiers call it.

Goose

Goose shoulder feathers, also called nashurias, are substitutes for swan quills. They are used in strips as a main wing or in narrow sections on married-wing patterns. Naturally bright white, goose shoulders can be dyed all the colors used in salmon-fly wings.

I have always liked goose quill better than swan because it is much easier to work with and more readily available. The length is sufficient for a size 5/0 fly. Since its texture is much softer than swan's, goose takes a much nicer shape and marries more easily to other materials. Strips of white shoulder feathers work very well on the White-Winged Akroyd and other Dee patterns that have white wings. I use goose dyed orange and purple for strip wings on some steelhead Spey patterns.

Many of the classic patterns use goose quill for the colored sections or strips in married wings. Various colors of goose quill, usually three sections, are married together and then married to three sections of naturally colored feathers such as bustard, golden pheasant, and peacock wing.

Like other feathers, goose shoulders have to be sorted into matched pairs. Some feathers are considered "centers" because the fibers on both sides of the quill are the same length. These come from the center of the back, and one of these feathers can provide material for both wings on a fly.

Another good use for goose came to me from Steve Gobin. He takes a few fibers from a goose shoulder, twists them around his tying thread, and wraps them to make the butt of a salmon or steelhead fly. This trick produces a bright, neat, very small butt. It's perfect for small salmon patterns, since ostrich herl with short fibers is very rare. Nothing looks worse than a perfectly tied, small (say size 8) salmon pattern with everything in proportion except for a big ostrich-herl butt. Steve's approach solves the problem.

Some of the body feathers from a goose can be bleached to remove some of the web. They are then dyed and used for hackles on Spey patterns.

Swan

Swans are used mainly for their shoulder feathers, which are dyed various salmon-fly colors. Strips of swan made up the colored sections of many classic married-wing flies.

Some of the flank feathers can be used for hackles. Since the fibers are very long and webby, the feathers must be bleached, a process that burns off some of the web. Swan-flank feathers can then be dyed and used as body and throat hackles.

Swan feathers are very rare and seldom used these days. They're also much coarser and harder to use than goose shoulders. Their texture is well suited to making wings on old brook-trout flies such as the Trout Fin.

Egyptian Goose

Egyptian goose flank feathers can serve as a substitute for unbarred wood duck. They are much larger than wood-duck feathers, and their long fibers make them suitable for large flies such as some of the Dee patterns. For instance, Egyptian goose makes a nice collar on a large Glentana.

LAND BIRDS

Marabou Stork

The marabou stork provides soft, fluffy feathers for the hackles of Eagle patterns. Their fibers are much longer than those of turkey marabou. Dyed yellow, marabou-stork feathers are used on the Yellow Eagle pattern.

When using these plumes for body hackles on Eagle patterns, choose feathers that have thin stems. For a sparse pattern, strip one side of the feather; just a few turns of a folded, complete marabou feather can produce an overly heavy hackle.

Guinea Fowl

Many old fly-tying books refer to guinea fowl as gallina. Guinea fowl is mainly used for its black, white-spotted body feathers that become throats and collars on many salmon patterns. Dyed kingfisher blue, guinea fowl serves as a substitute for Eurasian jay. Thanks to its long fibers, this material can be used on larger flies.

Some old salmon patterns required guinea fowl dyed red or yellow. Many steelheaders dye these feathers hot orange, and the black-and-orange pattern makes a striking collar.

Guinea-fowl feathers come in two varieties. Those called single-dot feathers have large, bold white dots, and when wrapped as collars, they create a barred pattern. Single-dot feathers usually have very long fibers that make them suitable for the largest flies. The feathers that have a salt-and-pepper pattern usually have a gray background and shorter fibers; they look best in their natural color. Each type creates its own pattern when wrapped as a collar, and each lends itself to certain patterns.

When I use guinea fowl as a throat hackle, I usually fold the feather and tie it in by the tip. For sparse patterns, I strip one side of the feather.

Some patterns call for strips taken from the tail and wing quills of guinea fowls. This material is hard to find in sufficient lengths. It is most often employed as wing veils, and it adds a unique look to the sides of a wing.

Vulturine Guinea Fowl

Vulturine guinea fowl is much rarer than the common variety. The feathers have the same types of markings as those of common guinea fowl but with a much darker background and bright, contrasting white spots. These are the most distinctively marked of all the guinea-fowl feathers. They are used for collars and throats on Spey and Dee patterns and look best on dark patterns such as the Silver Heron and Black Heron.

These birds have other useful feathers. Some Spey flies can use the electric-blue hackles as collars. These naturally blue feathers also work as hackles on Spring Grub flies and as collar material for the Elver pattern. The long, black, narrow hackles with white centers and blue outer edges are used as wings on Elver-type flies.

Vulturine guinea fowl is a prized skin among salmon-fly tiers. Most of its feathers have uses on some style of salmon fly. A complete skin bears feathers in a wide array of colors and shapes.

Kenyan Crested Guinea Fowl

This bird supplies black feathers with robin's-egg-blue dots. Some tiers use them for collars and throats on contemporary Spey flies. These soft-fibered feathers are a natural substitute for jay, though the fibers are not long enough for larger salmon flies. Feathers vary in size according to their location on the skin. Some of the best and softest hackles come from the flanks under the wings.

Capercaillie Grouse

The largest of the grouse, these birds are an iridescent black with some white patterns in their tails and along the sides of their bodies. The most commonly used feathers are from the tails, which are black at the base and tip, with white splashes throughout the fibers. They make interesting wings on small Spey patterns. The body hackles are not specifically required by any salmon-fly patterns, but they make good throats on flies that need long, soft, black hackles.

Ruffed Grouse

Ruffed grouse furnish one feather useful to Spey-fly tiers, as was brought to my attention by Eugene Sunday. The black feathers from the ruff of the neck can be used for collars and throats on flies that call for black heron. The fibers are long and soft and the stems are fine.

A few patterns used ruffed-grouse body feathers as body or throat hackles. Many of the old patterns call for red grouse, which is the species commonly found in Europe. The red grouse's feathers are indeed a more reddish brown color than those of our ruffed grouse, and they are a material worth having.

OTHER WING MATERIALS

The wings of salmon flies consist of fibers or sections taken from the tail, shoulder, and wing quills of various birds. Most are large birds such as bustards, turkeys, swans, and pheasants. Classic salmon flies have many types of wings, from simple strip wings to the most elaborate married wings.

Traditionally, Dee flies have had wings made with two slips from turkey quills and other large feathers. The tier first prepares two matched slips perfectly alike in size, color, markings, and curvature, and then ties them on one at a time, setting them on the shoulders of the fly so that they lie flat over the body. When viewed from above, Dee-fly wings form a V and look like slightly opened scissor blades. This style of wing gave rise to the name Dee Strip-Wing Flies, as the patterns used to be called. Other types of flies also had strip wings, of course, but the strips were mounted on edge and had a more pronounced silhouette. What made Dee flies unique was the way the wings were attached.

Early Spey flies usually had wings made of two strips of bronze mallard. Later, some tiers created Spey patterns tied with turkey-quill wings.

Full-dress patterns have wings made of several sections of fibers from various quills. The pieces of feathers are married together, and the results are called married-wing flies. Marrying is the process of taking slips from different feathers and attaching them to each other by means of the tiny hooks or barbules along the edges of the fibers. In effect, these little barbules are the original hook-and-look fastener material. By aligning two quill sections and gently preening them with his fingertips, a fly tier can zip them together. Each side of a married wing usually contains three sections of natural materials with mottled patterns, such as speckled bustard,

Wing Materials

Ocellated turkey quill	Wing types:
Speckled bustard	Cutty Sark, teal flank wing, Warren
Florican bustard	Orange Heron, hackle tip wing, Veverka
Cinnamon turkey	Lord Iris, married goose quill wing, Veverka
	Gordon Cummings Spey, bronze-mallard wing, Burden
	Vibrant Orange, goose strip wing, Veverka
	Purple March Brown, pheasant tail wing, Veverka
Goose shoulder, yellow, green	Lady Amherst tippet
Scarlet macaw tail	
Argus quill	
Lady Amherst tail	

Feathers are used to tie all styles of flies, but salmon flies are tied with the widest variety of feathers. Wings on salmon flies range from simple strip wings of the early Spey and Dee flies to the most elaborately complex mix of exotic feathers. Some salmon patterns include dozens of different types of feathers to tie a single fly.

The original Spey flies were tied with two slips of bronze-mallard feathers, gray at the roots and darker brown at the tips. Pryce-Tannatt describes them when tied on like an upside-down side of a boat hull that when done correctly looks rather wicked.

Dee flies are named for their Dee strip wings, tied with two separate sections of turkey quill or other large-feathered birds that would open and close like a pair of scissor blades in the water. Any large-fibered quill will work, but some standards include turkey, bustard, peafowl, argus pheasant, and goose quill.

florican bustard, and golden-pheasant tail, and three brightly colored sections of dyed goose or swan. Each section is made up of only three or four fibers from a quill. Making married wings is not hard, though it requires patience and good feathers.

Argus Pheasant

Argus pheasants have large wing quills that can furnish wing material for any of the Dee or Spey patterns. Sections of the wing quills are also in married wings. The feathers are very soft and marry well to other feathers.

Argus quills have a tan background with large copper and bronze eyes at the base of the fibers (where they attach to the stem) and wavy brown bars and spots at the ends of the fibers. The opposite side of the feather also has very long fibers that can be used for Dee-fly wings. The background is gray fading into a light tan with medium-size brown spots. Few other feathers or quills have usable wing material on both sides of the quill and a different color pattern on each side.

For large flies such as some of the Dee patterns, argus pheasant is my favorite wing material. It ties in easily and has a very sleek look. The fiber length measures from an inch up to four inches, and the color pattern works nicely on Dee flies. Sections from the same areas of a pair of matched quills have the same pattern; they look like mirror images of each other.

This is one wing material that all Dee-fly tiers must have. The quills to look for are taken from the wings. Some are two feet long and shaped like machetes.

Other spotted quills from an argus pheasant can be used for wing material. The two center tail feathers are three to four feet in length and have a nice pattern for wings, though the wing or side feathers are used more often. Some of the body hackles can be used for throats, where they create a beautiful spotted pattern.

Ocellated Turkey

The tails feathers of an ocellated turkey have gray backgrounds with fine, darker bars. At the tips, they turn an iridescent grayish blue and then bronze. Although ocellated turkey is not specifically called for in Spey-fly patterns, strips of the tail feathers would make good wings on, say, a Grey Heron. A fly tier who had a complete skin could probably find many neat feathers to tie flies with.

Speckled Bustard

Bustards are used mainly for their tail and shoulder feathers, fibers from which are important in the construction of married-wing salmon flies. The speckled pattern of these beautiful feathers adds a unique look to a fly's wings. Several different species have the right markings to be considered speckled bustards by fly tiers. The quills range from a sandy buff color to a rich, dark brown with a speckled pattern throughout the fibers.

Speckled bustard was not used on the old Spey flies, but it's a very important material for tying mixed-wing flies like the Black Dog and Floodtide. Some contemporary tiers use strips for Spey- and Dee-fly wings. The fibers are long enough to work on any fly.

Look for pairs of matched tail feathers that have white-tipped fibers. They make eye-catching wings on Spey and Dee patterns. I had a pair of these a number of years back and tied many Spey-fly wings with them.

Bustard quills come as center feathers or paired feathers. Center feathers are nice to have because you only need one to get material for both wings. Paired feathers have only one usable side apiece, which is why a tier needs two matched quills to make wings. Wing material comes from the side with the longer fibers.

Bustard quills have the longest fibers of any feather used in married wings, and bustard's soft texture makes it easy to marry to almost any other material. I find it essential for married-wing patterns. Its soft texture and superior marrying qualities hold wings together like no other material.

The quills are not cheap, but you've got to have them if you are going to tie married-wing salmon flies. Price depends on the size of the quills and the length of the fiber. The color and quality of the feather also figures into the price.

Although they're rarely used, the neck feathers of bustards make nice body hackles or long throats on Spey and Dee patterns. The hackles are white with black specks, and the fibers are very long. Dyed red, yellow, hot orange, and purple, they make handsome body hackles and collars on some Spey patterns.

Florican Bustard

This species of bustard also furnishes material for married-wing salmon flies. Florican-bustard quills have dark brown bars on a reddish tan background. The fibers are very soft and very long; good quills can provide material for the largest salmon flies. Most classic patterns call for both speckled and florican bustard in the makeup of their married wings.

Each side of a florican bustard's tail has several white feathers. If you acquire some of these very rare quills, guard them and only use them on your best and largest married-wing patterns. They can be dyed all the salmon-fly colors and utilized for the colored sections of wings. If you tie large flies, say size 5/0 and up, you will find it very difficult to find swan or goose quills that have sufficiently long fibers. White florican bustard solves this problem.

Peacock Quills

The wing quills of peacocks furnish sections of some salmon-fly wings. Kelson mentions that a peacock has "the plumage of an angel, the voice of a Devil, and the stomach of a thief; but for all that, he is very useful for fly dressers." The creamy, transversely speckled feathers found in the wings brighten up a fly and heighten the effect of mixed wings. Some strip-wing patterns also use sections of peacock quills.

Peacock wing quills have a unique pattern of markings that adds a distinctive look to a married wing. The bottom strip of the Jock Scott's wing consists of peacock, and one cannot help noticing its bright and brilliant appearance.

The only problem with peacock quills is finding feathers with fibers sufficiently long to work on larger flies. Tail feathers usually have longer fibers than peacock wing quills have. When I can't find peacock quills with adequate fiber length, I use Lady Amherst pheasant tail; it has much longer fibers and the color pattern is very similar to that of peacock quill.

Some Dee flies have wings made with strips of peacock quills. An example is the Peacock Dee pattern described by William Murdoch in an article called "Spring Flies for the Dee," published in *The Fishing Gazette* in 1895. Obviously, strip wings made from peacock quills must come from feathers that match in size and the pattern of markings. The wing sections come from the areas of the two feathers that are most nearly identical in pattern.

Peacock Herl

A few salmon flies have wings made completely or partly with peacock herl. This material comes from the eyed feathers of a peacock's tail. The iridescent color of herl, which combines green and bronze with hints of blue, seems naturally attractive to many fish. Attaching a bunch or clump of herl is the most common way to make a wing with this material, though some patterns use just a few strands of herl as part of more complex wings. The Silver Spectre and the Beauly Snow fly are two patterns with wings consisting of bunches of peacock herl.

Peacock herl is also used for bodies. Several strands of herl are twisted around the tying thread and then wrapped around the shank to form the body of the fly. Single strands of herl are sometimes used for butts in much the same way as ostrich herl. Strands from the sword feathers along the sides of the tail are used for tail veils. And some contemporary salmon patterns have throat hackles made of the blue body feathers of a peacock.

Turkeys

Feathers from various species of turkeys have many applications in salmon-fly wings. Wing quills and tail feathers are called for in many of the original salmon patterns. Pieces of turkey quills serve as underwings on many patterns, as sections of married wings, as wings of small strip-wing flies that have the strips mounted on edge, and as the flat wings of Dee patterns.

Turkey quills come in many shades of mottled brown. Tail feathers have fibers long enough for the largest patterns. The one drawback of turkey feathers is that the fibers are thick and rigid where they meet the quill. This makes it difficult to construct flat wings that have a graceful, flowing shape, and this is the reason that I use tail feathers from other birds to make wings on my Dee patterns.

Dyed salmon-fly colors, white turkey tails can provide material for the largest married-wing flies. This comes in handy if you want to tie married-wing patterns on size 5/0 or larger hooks, since finding material for the largest flies is always a problem. Try to find white tail feathers without stress lines. For some reason—their food, perhaps, or inadequate water—white turkey tails almost always have stress lines that will show up as imperfections in the wing of a fly.

Here are some of the uses of various turkey feathers.

White-tipped turkey tail feathers are dark brown with black bars and bright white tips. They are used mainly as underwing material on married-wing patterns such as the Jock Scott. Strips of white-tipped turkey formed the wings on some of the original Dee patterns, such as the Dunt.

For as long as I have been tying, these feathers have been hard to find in good shape. Most either have nicks in the tips or lack bright white tips. Good ones are rare and should be saved for underwings on your finest Jock Scotts and wings on Dunts and Toppys.

Cinnamon tail feathers supplied the wings of many early Dee patterns. Originally, these were used as a substitute for gled. They come in various shades, all of which are useful to Spey- and Dee-fly tiers. Some are a light, almost sandy color, while others have a dark, rich cinnamon color. The most sought-after tail feathers are those with lighter tips or tips that fade into a light dun. These furnished wing material for the original Glentana, Akroyd, and Balmoral Dee patterns.

Cinnamon blue dun tail feathers are mostly cinnamon in color with a light blue-dun accent on the tips. They are highly sought after for the wings on Dee patterns.

Blue dun tail feathers are predominantly dun, though they're sometimes splashed with small specks of black. They are not commonly used, but they could add a unique look to Spey patterns such as the Grey Heron and Silver Heron.

Zebra turkey is similar to peacock wing in color. This must be a mixture of two different turkeys; the feathers are like no others, displaying a unique pattern of markings. Wings made of zebra turkey look great mounted on edge because the bold pattern shows best this way. They can be used on any of the Dee patterns to make a unique fly.

Other types of turkey quills used on various patterns include dun brown, dark speckled, silver gray, and mottled gray with black bars and white tips. Many different types of turkey quills can be used for strip wings on Spey and Dee patterns. These days, many tiers make wings with feathers from hybrids; these display unique markings that accent Spey and Dee patterns.

ACCENTING PLUMAGE

The small feathers used for cheeks and veils on salmon flies generally have brilliant, translucent colors that provide a bit of contrast or enhancement to our flies. Jungle cock, Indian crow, toucan, chatterer, and kingfisher have traditionally been the most common accenting feathers. They cover the three important colors used in tying salmon flies: red, yellow, and blue.

Most accenting feathers are tied in by their stems. The challenge is that different feathers have stems that differ slightly in shape; when thread pressure is applied to them, they react in different ways. Some flare or twist, refusing to lie flat as the thread bears down on them. That's why it's a good idea to study all the different stems and fibers of materials used in the construction of salmon flies. In the process, you get insight into how they are shaped and how they behave under thread pressure. The stems of some feathers need to be custom fitted and shaped before they are tied on a fly. Other stems must be crimped and flattened with a pair of flat-nosed pliers. Still others need to be shaped to form a curve that hugs the wing of a fly. When feathers are prepared properly, one turn of thread should lock them in place.

Tying a salmon fly with veils, cheeks, sides, and toppings is like putting together the pieces of a puzzle. There's a lot going on, and all the pieces must fit together. Materials that are prepared and shaped will tie in with less trouble, lie flat, and require fewer turns of thread.

Jungle Cock

Jungle cocks provide one of the unique feathers used in fly tying. They have no substitute; no other feather even comes close to matching them. The enameled feathers from the neck of a jungle cock are called eyes or nails, and they are used for cheeks on many of the classic salmon patterns. Jungle-cock nails are also used as tail veils and underwings.

These feathers vary in color from almost white to rusty brown. It's good to have several necks that differ in the color, shape, and size of the nails. Some patterns look good with darker nails and some look their best with pale white eyes.

When I choose jungle-cock necks, I look for those that have the fewest feathers with splits. The next most important feature is the shape of the nails. To me, the shape is more important than the color of the nail. I prefer necks with small, narrow nails that complement the shape of a sleek, low-winged fly.

Save feathers that have no splits for display flies. Those that have very minor splits can be repaired by coating the backs of the feathers with glue, and then used for tying fishing flies.

Use the nails that run down the center of the neck in places where you need a straight feather with no curve. These are most commonly used for underwings, as on the Black Dog pattern. Matched feathers from the sides of the neck have a slight curve; the farther from the center of the neck, the more drastic the curve. The drooping feathers used on Dee patterns come from the sides of a neck and have a pronounced natural curve; this curve accents the flies' flowing shape.

When selecting jungle-cock nails for a fly, try to find two that are close to the exact size needed for a certain application. Once you've found two matching feathers, put them together back to back. Lay them gently along the side of the fly to see how much of the feathers you need to use, and then, still holding both feathers, strip off any excess fibers. This way, you will produce two feathers identical in length.

When you use jungle-cock nails for the sides or cheeks of wings, you will usually need to prepare them before tying them on. If you don't prepare the feathers, they will most likely flare when attached to the fly. Take each jungle-cock eye and use a fingernail to put a series of small crimps on the inside of the feather, starting at the base. This produces a small curve in each feather so that it will hug the side of the fly when tied on. When prepared this way, jungle-cock nails will lock in place with your first turn of thread, and they will lie tightly against the body or wing rather than stick out from the sides. They will look like cheeks rather than fins.

Jungle cock adds so much to salmon flies that many patterns wouldn't be worth tying without it. Picture a Jock Scott without it; the fly simply wouldn't be as beautiful.

Chatterer

Chatterer feathers are brilliant electric blue in color. Several species of chatterers provide feathers for salmon flies. These birds range in color from pale or light blue to royal blue. I particularly like chatterer feathers for their shape; they tend to have tapered points that add to the graceful appearance of a salmon fly.

Tail veils, body veils, and cheeks are the primary uses of chatterer feathers. They are not often used on Spey and Dee patterns, though some tiers add tail or body veils made with chatterer feathers. One Dee pattern, the Moonlight, calls for body veils made with feathers from the sides of a chatterer's tail.

Kingfisher

Most kingfisher feathers are brilliant blue, but they also come in a color called purple kingfisher, a royal-blue shade with purple accents or highlights. They are used for the same purposes as chatterer feathers: veils for bodies and tails, and cheeks on the sides of wings. Kingfisher has a brilliant natural color that makes the feathers as important and useful as those from chatterers. Both are rare feathers, but kingfisher is much less expensive. Kingfisher feathers have squared tips, whereas chatterer feathers generally have tapered, pointed tips.

In some cases, kingfisher is easier than chatterer to use for cheeks. Blue kingfisher feathers come from the back and rump, and nearly all of them have straight stems. All of a chatterer's feathers are blue, but those from the sides of the bird typically have curved stems that make them hard to use as cheeks; hit them with a turn of thread and they twist. Chatterer feathers usually work more easily when tied in on edge and used as veils. As on any bird, the feathers with the straightest stems come from the area running from the nape of the neck to the rump.

Indian Crow

These semitranslucent feathers are brilliant red with darker red tips. The tips have a slight crimp and are used mainly for tail and body veils, as on the Popham pattern. Larger Indian crow feathers are used for side veils or wings, as on the Red Sandy. Many patterns employ Indian crow as cheeks, and some Dee flies have tail veils made of these feathers.

The stems lend themselves to being tied in flat, which makes Indian Crow easy to use for body veils on flies like the Popham. It's uncanny how the natural crimp in the tips of the feathers lets them fit around ostrich-herl butts, almost as if the feathers were shaped just for this purpose.

Since Indian crow feathers are rare and expensive, many tiers look for substitutes. Some tiers dye the white feathers from the neck of a ring-necked pheasant, put a crimp in the tips, and then dye just the tips a darker red. I've seen some beautiful substitutes that looked just like the real thing when tied on a fly; the color and crimp matched those of the original to perfection. One thing the substitutes cannot replicate is the structure of the stem and how it ties in. Substitute feathers have semihollow stems, and they tend to twist so that they do not lie straight and flat. This can be very frustrating. Most substitutes also lack the translucence that real Indian crow displays. When hit by light, Indian crow feathers throw off a glow.

As in most cases of substitute materials, nothing comes close to the real thing. The colors and structures of some feathers are unique, which is why tiers used them in the first place.

Toucan

Toucan feathers are used for body veils because of their golden yellow color and translucent fibers. The Jock

Scott and other flies of this style have toucan veils. Several salmon patterns also employ toucan as tail material.

A body veil generally consists of several stacked feathers. How many to use depends on the size of the fly or the desired appearance of the veil. The more feathers used in a veil, the brighter the color. I usually stack the feathers so that the tips are all even; then I determine the length of the veil and strip off excess material from the butts of the feathers. When I tie the veil in place, I try to make the first turn of thread land across the bases of the first few fibers of the feathers, and not across the stems alone. Toucan feathers have a tendency to twist out of alignment when tied in only by the stripped stems.

Toucan feathers are rare and expensive, so many tiers look for a substitute. But a Jock Scott tied with substitute materials for the body veils just doesn't have the glowing hot spot produced by the original materials. As with most replacements, nothing else looks like the real thing. A feather might have the right color, but it lacks the translucent quality of toucan. Still, a tier might not have any choice. Some tiers use hen necks that have been double dyed, that is, a hen patch dyed brilliant yellow and then bright orange. Another material that comes close to toucan is a small feather from the base of a golden pheasant crest; these lie between the crest section and the tippets. When dyed golden yellow, the CDC feathers used on trout flies make a nice substitute for toucan.

Ostrich Herl

Ostrich herl forms the butts of many salmon flies, and this use alone makes it an essential material. Some of the original Dee patterns had ostrich-herl butts, and most of the original Akroyds used it in the center of the body. Herl was also used for heads on some old salmon flies.

When used as a butt or joint to separate the sections of a body, as on the Popham or Jock Scott, ostrich herl adds definition to each section of the body. Look at the hot spot of yellow silk ribbed with fine silver tinsel and veiled with golden toucan feathers on a Jock Scott's body, and you can't help noticing that the ostrich-herl butt serves as a boundary or frame for that section of the fly.

Ostrich herl is also used for bodies. Several strands are twisted onto the tying thread and then wrapped around the hook. The front section of the Ghost pattern is made of herl. Alec Jackson, a great steelhead-fly tier, twists brightly colored herl around tinsel and uses that for the bodies of his unique patterns.

European Jay

The shoulders of the wings from a European jay furnish beautiful blue feathers with dark markings. These feathers fulfill some of the same functions as those from chatterers. Salmon-fly tiers use European jay to make tails, cheeks, veils, and collars on many patterns. Some of the classic patterns have side veils made with a pair of matched feathers. The Ghost pattern's tail is a matched pair of jay feathers set back to back and tied on edge. Two matched, back-to-back feathers mounted on edge make up each section of the body veils in the Traherne series of flies.

Many of the Irish salmon-fly patterns call for throats of European jay. When wrapped as a collar, European jay is stripped on one side. Although it makes a beautiful throat, a jay feather has a very short, thick stem and short fibers. On small patterns, it looks great; no dyed feather comes close to the natural color. On larger flies, however, tiers have to use guinea fowl dyed kingfisher blue.

European jay wings are sold in pairs. One feather must be taken from each wing to make a matched pair. When used for a tail or a body veil, the matched feathers are put back to back and stripped to size. Sometimes it's necessary to flatten the stems with flat-nosed pliers to get the feathers to behave when tied to the hook. The stems are short, heavy, and hollow, and when tied down they have a tendency to twist. When you work with jay feathers, make the first turn of thread with just enough pressure to hold the flattened stems in place. As you add turns of thread, start to move away from the fibers and out onto the stem, making the wraps progressively tighter. This will help alleviate the twisting problem. Add a little glue to the base of the stems and let it dry before the next step.

Macaw

Fibers from the blue-and-gold center-tail feathers of macaws are used for horns on some salmon flies, as are fibers of scarlet macaw. Originally, these fibers were tied to flies to represent the antennae of large insects. Their stinger-like appearance adds a nice touch to some patterns. A pair of horns makes a handsome accent to the topping of a Jock Scott and other flies of this style. I sometimes add a set of horns to a Spey pattern such as the Ghost. Some Dee flies also look good with horns, though adding them is not standard practice.

The most important feathers are those from the center of a tail. These have the longest fibers for horns. Some full-dress patterns call for macaw fibers in their wings. Since macaw is one of the most difficult feathers to marry, using it as a side veil is easier than trying to make it part of the main wing.

Most macaws have brilliant, colorful feathers that have a number of functions on salmon flies. For instance, they can be used as side or cheek feathers. Among my favorites are the wing coverts that are used to tie the Shannon fly. They have the shape of a small banana and are colored a bright yellow with a red stem and blue tip. They help make the Shannon one of the most beautiful classic patterns.

Macaw body feathers are brilliant red, yellow, and various shades of green. They can make cheeks, veils, or collars. Scarlet feathers are the most useful, but they are very rare. Most macaw feathers come from bird breeders who collect molted plumage.

I'd always wondered what part horns play on a fishing fly. Then I made a trip to the Matapedia with Steve Gobin and Mike McCoy. The fishing was slow, so we started experimenting with all types of salmon patterns—hairwings, strip-wing flies, and some full-dress classics tied true to pattern. We couldn't believe the action of the horns; even when most other parts of a fly had little action, the horns were always in motion.

HEADS

The heads that finish our salmon and steelhead flies are our signatures, our own special touches that make our flies different, however slightly, from those of other tiers. Many tiers strive for a certain shape and size when they finish the heads of flies, and a fly's head can be as much of an identifying feature as the style in which a pattern is tied.

I try to finish a fly with a small, neat, wedge-shaped head from which the feathers seem to explode. Accom-

plishing this requires a base that is neat, smooth, and small, with no bulky spots. An eyed hook must have a narrow return wire, and a blind-eye hook should have its shank ground to a needle point.

Many tiers wonder how to make small heads on flies. You have to use the fewest possible turns of thread that will securely attach the materials. All materials should be prepared so that they tie in with one or two wraps of thread. On Spey and Dee patterns, you tie in only two slips for the wings and making a small head isn't very difficult. Old books that describe Spey patterns mention that the heads should be kept small.

When mounting Spey- and Dee-fly wings, attach them one at a time and hold them in position with two or three turns of thread. When you cut off the butt ends, trim them close and try to cut them on an angle so that the head tapers. Make sure that your thread is flat, and shape the head with the least number of wraps. Flattening the butt ends of the wings with your fingernail compresses them and makes for a smaller head.

On classic patterns with complex wings, the method I use is the one employed by Crosfield and then picked up by Syd Glasso. Glasso adapted the technique to the more complex patterns; Crosfield tied simpler patterns with fewer materials. Making a small head on a classic pattern takes lots of concentration and preparation. The underwing and main wing are tied on behind the head area, and then the collar is added over their butt ends. This places the bulk of the main wing behind the head area and in the process cuts down on the size of the finished head. The fibers in the top of the collar are stripped off; those on the sides and bottom are left in place. Feathers added after this are usually the cheeks, topping, and horns. The shapes of these feathers will cover any blank spots behind the head. So, the fly's head holds only a few small feathers, but it looks like it's holding the whole wing. Even with practice, however, this is a hard procedure to master.

It's very important to use a thin head cement. The first coat should disappear into the head and penetrate to the shank of the hook. Most flies require three or four coats of head cement. The last coat should cover any thread wraps and produce a smooth finish.

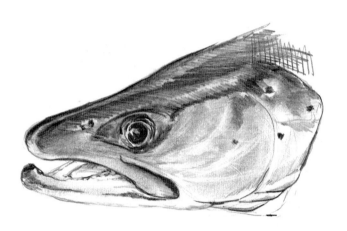

CHAPTER 3

Spey Patterns

SPEY FLIES USE SIMPLE COLORS AND MATERIALS. The originals, developed for the River Spey in northeastern Scotland, had very somber colors. Their unique feature is a long body hackle of Spey cock or heron hackle. Their action in the water is unsurpassed. The original flies were tied to represent shrimp and their movements in the water, according to A. E. Knox's 1872 book, *Autumns on the Spey*.

The original patterns are very old, even for salmon patterns, and they are still used today. They are defined by their wool bodies, ribs of various tinsels, long mobile body hackle, throats of teal, and wings of bronze-mallard strips.

The unique body hackle of Spey cock came from a large chicken raised on the Spey for the sole purpose of their hackles. The hackles were taken from the sides of the tail, and they were usually reddish brown with some dun coloring toward the tips. They were large birds that were bred very little according to written history. They may have consisted of one flock of birds and their offspring, and in time they died out, but I'd like to think that even today one of their descendants is running around a farmyard along the River Spey. Our only remnants of the original material are in some of the antique patterns that ended up in the collections of modern-day salmon fly tiers and collectors.

For contemporary tiers, the modern substitute for Spey cock is schlappen in its natural color or dyed brown, black, or yellow. It is from the same area on the bird as the original, along the sides of its tails. Some of the original Spey patterns called for heron hackles for the body hackle. Many tiers today use a substitute such as the hackles from the eared pheasants, which are similar in color and fiber length. Throughout the book I have recorded the original materials used to tie the early Spey and Dee patterns for historic value only. See

chapter 2 for modern substitute materials to replace the original materials that are not available.

Materials like silks, tinsels, and furs for dubbing are easy to find today. Although the original body material was Berlin wool, many contemporary tiers use different colors of seal fur to dub the bodies. The wool body material on the original patterns was several colors blended together. Black, olive, yellow, red, and purple were combined in various amounts to create one color. Most Spey patterns had bodies of black or shades of olive.

Ribbing on the bodies included several ribs, flat gold and silver tinsel, oval gold and silver tinsel, and many times silk thread. The color of the silk varied depending on the pattern. Some Spey flies made with silk are the Purple King, Culdrain, Dallas, and Carron. The silk rib on some of the early Spey patterns was wound on counterclockwise and over the hackle. Sometimes the oval tinsel was also wound on this way to prevent the hackle from unwinding if a salmon's teeth cut the stem. The tinsel would hold the hackle stem in place, and the fly could still be fished. This is important because a Spey fly with no body hackle is not the same fly.

The throats on the original Spey patterns were tied with teal flank feathers, and tiers felt that a Spey fly was not complete without them. Try to find teal flank that has a fine distinctive pattern that will add to the appearance of the fly. For the wings look for bronze-mallard feathers that display a fine penciling and a rich brown color. When tied on, the wings should never extend past the bend of the hook. Heads were tied with black thread.

You can use return-eye hooks or traditional blind-eye hooks. Sizes range from a size 2 to 3/0 or 4/0. Size is limited; flies smaller than a 2 lose their appeal. Larger

Contemporary Spey Flies

Thunder and Lightning (Waddington shank), Veverka	Copper Speal, Veverka
Golden Pheasant Spey, Warren	After Eight, Warren
Brora, Boyd	Twilight Spey, Waslick
Muddy Waters, Stovall	
Copper Reeach, Veverka	Copper Green Reeach, Veverka

Black Heron, Whorwood

Spey Leader, Selig

Today many talented fly tiers are practicing the art of dressing salmon flies. Many new Spey patterns are devised each year, and most hold true to the basic Spey design and style with unique additions that fit certain fishing conditions or a fly tier's fancy. Today many are fishing these Spey flies as well. Long Spey rods for steelhead and Atlantic salmon have hit the scene on the rivers of the Pacific Northwest and throughout Canada.

flies are limited by the bronze-mallard fiber length—long-fiber bronze mallard is hard to find.

Spey fly tiers of the past include Mr. Brown, in Francis Francis's 1867 *A Book on Angling*, and John Shanks as mentioned in A. E. Knox's 1872 book, *Autumns on the Spey*, and later in George Kelson's 1895 book, *The Salmon Fly*. Arthur Knox's book includes all the Kings, Reeaches, Speals, and Herons, and Kelson's adds a few new patterns, most importantly, the Lady Caroline and the patterns originated by the Grant family.

TYING THE LADY CAROLINE

Hook	Size 1/0, 2/0 blind eye
Tail	Red golden pheasant body feather, strands
Body	Olive-brown wool
Ribs	Flat and oval gold tinsel
Body hackle	Gray Spey hackle (blue-eared pheasant hackle)
Throat	Red golden pheasant body hackle
Wings	Two strips of bronze mallard
Head	Black thread

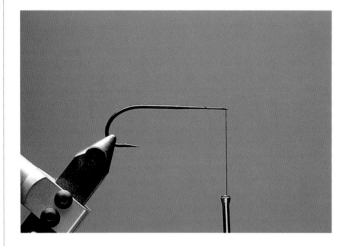

1. Place the hook in your vise so the shank of the hook is on a straight horizontal plane. Start the tying thread on the hook where your gut eye will go and cover an area of about ¹/₂ inch with thread to form a base for your twisted gut.

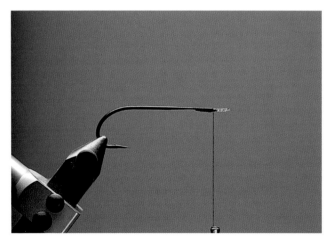

2. Form a loop with the twisted gut and prepare it so the ends that will be tied on the hook shank are flat. Many tiers simply flatten the ends with their teeth, but a better tool is a pair of flat-nosed pliers. Once the gut is prepared, place the flattened ends on the bottom of the shank. Then tie it on the hook with tight turns of thread and cover the entire piece of gut. Try to keep it as smooth as possible, and when finished, make sure there are no bumps.

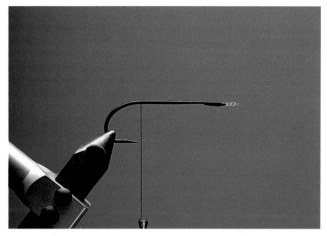

3. Wind your thread toward the back of the hook in tight turns to form a base of thread on the shank of the hook. Stop when your thread reaches the area on the shank that is in line with the point.

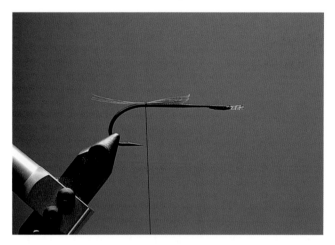

4. Take a golden pheasant's red body feather, strip off several fibers, and tie it in for the tail.

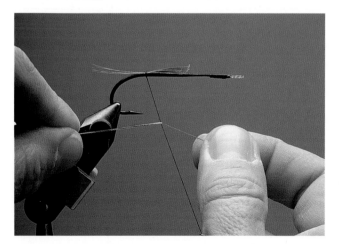

5. Lay the strand of oval gold tinsel on top of your tying thread.

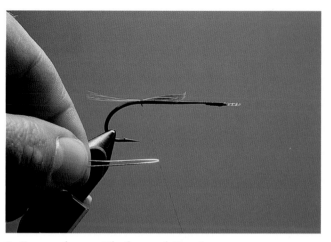

6. Form a loop with the oval tinsel.

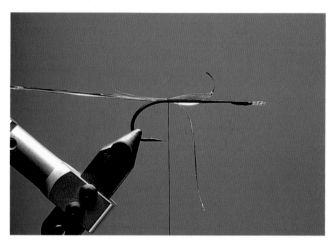

7. Tie it in on the back side of the hook, and then do the same with the strand of flat gold tinsel.

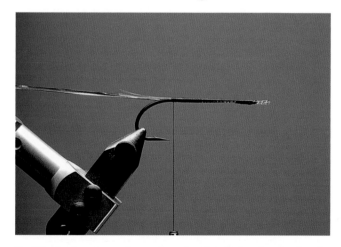

8. Wind the thread up the shank of the hook, in the process tying down the loose ends of tinsel. Try to make the underbody as smooth as possible. This pattern has a dubbed fur body, so any small bumps or rough spots in the body will be covered. On patterns that have a silk or tinsel body, the bodies should be perfectly flat and smooth or bumps will show on the body.

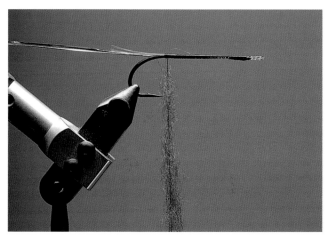

9. With your thread at the back of the hook just above the point of the hook, twist the fur dubbing on the tying thread, forming a uniform length of dubbing on the thread.

10. Wind the dubbing to the center of the hook.

11. Prepare the body hackle by folding it, and then tie it in at the center of the fly by the tip of the hackle with the fibers flowing toward the back of the hook.

12. Proceed with the dubbing toward the eye of the hook. Stop dubbing just behind the eye of the hook, leaving enough room for the next tie-in steps. (Experience will teach you how much is enough.)

13. Start with the strand of flat gold tinsel and make five turns. The third turn of flat tinsel should be placed just in front of the body hackle stem. When done you should have five turns of tinsel, evenly spaced. Each rib will be wound on separately.

14. When you reach the tie-in area just behind the eye of the hook, tie it off.

15. Make five turns of oval gold tinsel just behind but not touching the flat gold tinsel, and tie it off once you reach the tie-in area.

16. Take the body hackle by the butt end of the stem and wind it on tight behind the flat gold tinsel. As you wind the hackle, keep the fibers flowing toward the back of the hook.

17. When you get to the tie-in area, take one or two turns of hackle, depending on how sparse or heavy you want it hackled at the front. Then tie it off.

18. With your thumb and index finger, pinch any fibers of hackle that stick up above the body of the fly, and pull them down and toward the back of the hook. Pull or pinch the fibers so they all flow toward the back of the hook. This clears the top of the hook of any hackle fibers where your wing will go.

19. To fold the hackle, take the red golden pheasant feather with the best side facing you, as shown in the photo. The middle finger and thumb on your left hand hold the butt end; your right thumb and index finger hold it by the tip. The index finger on your left hand will fold the fiber.

20. Using your left index finger and the tip of your left thumb, push the fibers on the left side of the feather back, and at the same time pinch the fiber with the left index finger and tip of your thumb. Start at the base of the feather and work toward the tip. Pinch the fiber and pull it toward the right side of the feather, in the process doubling or, as it is commonly called, folding the hackle.

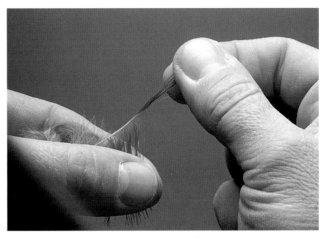

21. Depending on the size of the feather, you may need to fold the hackle several times to fold all the fibers from the left side of the feather behind.

22. When completed, your hackle should look like this—all fibers are flowing toward the right side of the feather.

23. Tie on the red golden pheasant throat hackle by the tip.

24. Wind on two turns of throat hackle, and then tie it off. As you did with the body hackle, take the fibers that make up the collar, and pull them down and toward the back of the hook. Strip off any fiber above the hook shank, leaving the top of the hook clear of fibers where the wing will be tied on.

25. The wing is a pair of bronze-mallard feathers, one right and one left feather. Try to select two of the same size and feather pattern.

26. Cut two sections of quill of matching length and width for the strips for the wings.

27. Each wing section will be tied on separately. Start with the far, or left, wing. Hold the wing section up to the fly to size the length of the wing—the wing should not extend past the rear of the hook. Set the wing on the shoulder of the fly and hold it in place with your index finger.

28. Holding the wing in place gently, take two or three turns of thread and tie it on the fly. The wing should be tied in by the gray section of the fiber; this area of the fiber is soft and ties in easily. Tying the bronze-mallard feathers this way keeps your wings from splitting, a common problem with this feather.

29. Take the closer, or right-hand, wing section, holding it on the shoulder of the fly with your thumb, and tie it on with two or three turns of thread. When done, your wings should appear as they do in the photo. Then cut off the butt ends of the fibers very neatly.

At this point you will finish off the fly and start making or forming the head. Before you start this, make sure your tying thread is flat and untwisted. You want a head that is small but still securely holds the materials. I wind my thread on the head area until I see that any materials tied in are covered with turns of thread, in the process making the shape of my head.

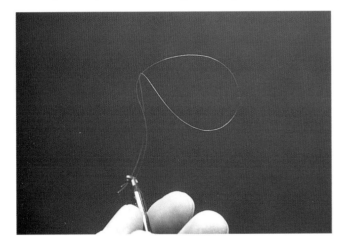

30. To finish off your fly, you must make a whip-finish. This secures your tying thread to the head of the fly. I use a loop of fine mono thread to do this.

31. Take the loop of fine mono, and lay it across your tying thread. Then form a loop as you did when you tied in the ribs of the fly.

32. Place the mono loop on the head of the fly with the loop end extending past the front of the fly, and make seven turns of thread.

33. Hold your thread with your fingertip so it doesn't unravel. Cut your tying thread and place the loose end through the mono loop.

34. Hold the loose end of your tying thread tight, and start to draw the loop of mono toward the back of the hook. The tying thread will be locked under the seven turns of thread that make up the whip-finish.

35. Cut off the tying thread. Your fly is completed, and the head is ready to be glued. I use Cellire on the heads of my flies, and depending on the size, it takes three to four coats of head cement to finish the head with a clear gloss, smooth finish.

AFTER EIGHT

Hook	Size 4 return-eye Partridge
Tag	Oval silver tinsel and orange silk
Body	Green seal fur
Rib	Oval silver tinsel
Hackle	Gray Spey hackle
Wing	Bronze mallard
Collar	Teal or guinea fowl dyed green
Head	Olive-green thread

The After Eight is a modern Spey pattern originated by Bob Warren. Bob says that this pattern is a good producer most of the season on normal water levels. Bob has fished the Miramichi River for the last twenty years and during this time developed several patterns for specific river conditions.

BLACK HERON

Hook	Size 1/0 blind-eye Partridge
Body	Black Berlin wool
Ribs	Flat gold tinsel with two threads of gold and silver beading between the bars of gold tinsel
Hackle	Black heron, substitute with black Spey feather
Wings	Bronze mallard

The Black Heron is described in A. E. Knox's 1872 book, *Autumns on the Spey*. I have also seen this pattern tied with wings consisting of strips of teal flank and a teal flank throat or collar.

BLACK KING

Hook	Size 1/0 blind-eye Partridge
Body	Three turns of orange Berlin wool, followed by black wool
Ribs	Far side, oval gold tinsel; near side, oval silver tinsel; both wound the reverse way, at equal distances apart
Hackle	Black Spey cock hackle, but wound from end of the body in the usual direction, from the root instead of from the point, crossing over the ribs at each turn
Throat	Teal, one turn only
Wings	Two strips of bronze mallard

This dressing for the Black King comes from George Kelson's 1895 book, *The Salmon Fly*. He mentions that it is one of the old standard flies for the Spey. The Black King is also included in A. E. Knox's book, *Autumns on the Spey*. Kelson's dressing differs from Knox's with the added section of orange wool and the oval tinsel wound the reverse way. Knox's dressing also includes a throat of guinea fowl. Knox states that the flies known as Kings are characterized by having alternate bars of flat gold and silver tinsel and no beading.

CARRON

Hook	Size 2/0 blind-eye Partridge
Body	Orange Berlin wool
Ribs	Flat silver tinsel, scarlet floss, and silver thread, reverse
Hackle	Black heron hackle, substitute with black Spey feather
Throat	Teal
Wings	Two strips of bronze mallard

This is the dressing for the Carron from Pryce-Tannatt's 1914 book, *How to Tie Salmon Flies*, although the fly first appeared in A. E. Knox's 1872 *Autumns on the Spey*. It is a very old pattern and strays slightly from the norm—old Spey patterns were generally somber in color. The original from Knox's book had no throat, and the body was ribbed with bars of silver tinsel. Pryce-Tannatt's Carron has flat silver tinsel ribs, scarlet floss, and silver thread, but the rest of the fly is the same as Knox's.

The fly is also included in George Kelson's 1895 book, *The Salmon Fly*. Kelson's pattern was the same as the one in A. E. Knox's book. This pattern may be the forerunner of the Red King.

CLARET-BROWN

Hook	Size 3/0 blind-eye long Dee
Tail	A few fibers of yellow macaw
Body	Three turns of orange pig's wool, followed by claret-brown pig's wool
Rib	Silver tinsel
Body hackle	Crown pigeon, from center, substitute blue-eared pheasant
Throat	Guinea fowl
Wings	Two strips of glentana gled, substitute cinnamon turkey, and a topping
Horns	Red macaw

The Claret-Brown is a pattern originated by George Kelson and appears in his 1895 book, *The Salmon Fly*.

COPPER CAROLINE

Hook	Size 1/0 return-eye Partridge CS10/1
Tail	Fibers from the red body feathers of the golden pheasant
Body	Olive-brown wool
Ribs	Flat and oval copper tinsel
Body hackle	Heron, substitute gray Spey hackle
Throat	Red golden pheasant body feather
Wing	Strips of bronze mallard

The Copper Caroline is basically the same basic pattern as the Lady Caroline but tied with ribs of copper tinsel. This pattern would also make a good steelhead or sea-run cut-throat fly.

COPPER REEACH

Hook	Size 2/0 blind-eye Partridge
Body	Black wool
Ribs	Flat and oval copper tinsel
Body hackle	Red Spey cock hackle
Throat	Teal
Wing	Strips of bronze mallard

The Copper Reeach is a pattern I designed based on the original Reeach patterns in A. E. Knox's book, *Autumns on the Spey*. I like the look of copper tinsel on a fly. A variation of this pattern is the Copper-Green Reeach, tied with a body of olive-brown wool.

COPPER SPEAL

Hook	Size 1/0 return-eye Partridge
Body	Black wool
Ribs	Flat and oval copper tinsel
Body hackle	Gray Spey hackle, substitute with blue-eared pheasant hackle, which also serves as throat
Wing	Strips of bronze mallard

The Copper Speal is a variation of the original Speal patterns as found in A. E. Knox's *Autumns on the Spey*.

CULDRAIN

Hook	Size 1/0 blind-eye Partridge
Body	Black Berlin wool
Ribs	Two bars of flat silver tinsel, set apart between two strands of silk, one orange and one yellow
Hackle	Black Spey cock hackle, also serves as throat
Wing	Bronze mallard or gray mallard

The Culdrain is another old Spey pattern from A. E. Knox's *Autumns on the Spey*. I have only seen it in Knox's book. Knox mentions that all the flies in his book were tied by the extremely skillful tier Shanks of Craigellachie. We will probably never know for sure if Shanks was the creator of the original Spey patterns, but there is a good chance he was. Shanks was probably a Spey-side gillie, adept at tying but not at keeping records of the flies he tied. He is credited with many of the original Spey patterns, such as Miss Grant.

This pattern is one of my favorites from *Autumns on the Spey*, with its multiple ribs of tinsel and silk.

DALLAS

Hook	Size 6/0 blind-eye antique
Body	Three turns of yellow Berlin wool, followed by black wool
Ribs	Oval silver tinsel, oval gold tinsel, red thread, and blue thread, all equal distances apart
Hackle	Black Spey cock's hackle from end of body, wound the reverse way and crossing over the ribs
Throat	Red hackle from golden pheasant
Wings	Two strips of plain cinnamon turkey
Head	Orange wool, picked out

The Dallas is included in George Kelson's *The Salmon Fly*, was christened by Mr. Little Gilmore, and was originated by John Dallas. Many of the old Spey patterns had several tinsel ribs and different colored threads, and this is a good example and a beautiful pattern. This is also one of the few true Spey patterns that used turkey for the wing. I think it's one of the classiest looking patterns, with ribs of tinsel and red and blue silk thread.

FITZGIBBON NUMBER TWO

Hook	Size 2 return-eye Bob Veverka Classic Salmon Hook
Body	Puce silk
Ribs	Gold and silver flat tinsel, and yellow-green silk thread
Body hackle	Brown pendant feather from a cock's tail, Spey cock
Wing	Brown spotted feathers from a turkey tail

The Fitzgibbon Number Two is an early Spey pattern Edward Fitzgibbon (Ephemera) lists in his 1850 book, *The Book of the Salmon*. He mentions that this was an old standard Spey spring fly even then. We don't know how old it actually is, but Spey flies were first tied sometime in the early 1800s. This is a very early Spey fly and by its dressing could be the fly that we know today as the Purple King. Fitzgibbon was the first to collect salmon flies and list them by the rivers they were tied for. Fitzgibbon says that these patterns were tied on hooks with long shanks and fine wire.

FITZGIBBON NUMBER THREE

Hook	Size 2 return-eye Bob Veverka Classic Salmon Hook
Body	Puce silk
Ribs	Flat gold and silver tinsel, and yellow-green silk thread
Body hackle	Brown pendant feather from a cock's tail
Wing	Brown-mallard (bronze-mallard) feather

The Fitzgibbon Number Three is an early Spey fly from Edward Fitzgibbon's *The Book of the Salmon*. This is the same pattern as Fitzgibbon Number Two but with a wing of bronze mallard. Spey flies were known for the bronze-mallard wing material, and it wasn't until later that the teal feather throat became characteristic of Speys. This could be the fly that evolved into the Purple King.

FITZGIBBON NUMBER FOUR

Hook	Size 2 return-eye Bob Veverka Classic Salmon Hook
Body	Cinnamon-brown silk
Ribs	Flat gold and silver tinsel, and yellow-green thread
Body hackle	Brown pendant feather from a cock's tail
Wing	Brown-mallard (bronze-mallard) feather

The Fitzgibbon Number Four is another early Spey pattern in Edward Fitzgibbon's *The Book of the Salmon*. He says that the above three flies were summer and autumn flies tied on hook sizes 5 and 6.

All three of the above patterns are very similar in their dressings with subtle color changes in the body. Many of the Speys were very similar except for minor changes in tinsel or body colors. The earliest Spey patterns had bodies that were black, olive, or purple with variations in tinsel color or different shades of body materials.

This pattern may have been one of the first flies that led to the development of the Green King.

GLEN GRANT

Hook	Size 2/0 blind-eye Ron Reinhold
Tail	Golden pheasant yellow rump feather, point
Body	Three turns of yellow wool, remainder black wool
Ribs	Silver lace and silver tinsel
Hackle	Black Spey cock hackle from end of body, but wound from the root the reverse way, crossing over the ribs
Throat	Teal
Wings	Two long jungle cock back to back, two reaching half way, two still shorter, and two strips of teal flank
Head	Yellow wool

The Glen Grant was one of a series of flies in George Kelson's *The Salmon Fly*. Kelson considered it an old standard on the Spey. This fly was originated by Major Grant, whose Castle Grant is on the Spey River at one of its finest stretches. Grant also originated Glen Grant's Fancy and Mrs. Grant. Kelson considered these modern Spey River patterns. Miss Grant is another pattern attributed to the Grant family, credited to Shanks.

GLEN GRANT'S FANCY

Hook	Size 4/0 blind-eye Partridge
Tag	Silver twist and red-claret silk
Tail	Topping (golden pheasant)
Butt	Black herl
Body	Light olive-green seal fur
Rib	Silver tinsel
Throat	Jay and teal
Wings	Tippet strands, guinea fowl, light mottled turkey, golden pheasant tail, mallard, and topping
Head	Black herl

George Kelson considered Glen Grant's Fancy a modern standard on the Spey and included it in *The Salmon Fly*. Another one of Major Grant's patterns, this one has a more complex wing. The Grants had a castle on the Spey and were considered authorities on fly fishing and fly patterns for the River Spey.

GOLDEN PHEASANT SPEY

Hook	Size 2 return-eye Bob Veverka Classic Salmon Hook
Tag	Oval copper tinsel
Tail	Golden pheasant crest over orange polar bear hair, tail as long as body of fly
Body	Half hot orange silk, ribbed with oval copper and veiled with yellow rump feathers from a golden pheasant, black ostrich herl butt at middle, and half oval copper tinsel
Hackle	Claret hackle followed by two red golden pheasant feathers

The Golden Pheasant Spey is a modern Spey fly originated by Bob Warren. Bob mentions that he finds this fly most effective in the fall in the sizes 2 and 4 (see After Eight Spey).

GOLD-GREEN FLY

Hook	Size 1/0 blind-eye Partridge
Body	Olive, composed of a mixture of red, green, and purple fine Berlin wool
Ribs	Three or four turns of flat gold tinsel, with a single strand of orange silk in between
Hackle	Red cock hackle
Throat	Teal
Wing	Bronze mallard

The Gold-Green Fly is one of the original patterns in A. E. Knox's *Autumns on the Spey*. Many of the patterns in Knox's book use a blend of Berlin wool for the body material. As the seasons progressed, more red was added to the mixture of wools.

GOLD-GREEN REEACH

Hook	Size 1/0 blind-eye Partridge
Body	Olive, composed of a mixture of red, green, and purple fine Berlin wool
Ribs	Three bars of flat gold tinsel, with three rows of very fine oval gold beading in between
Hackle	Red cock hackle
Throat	Teal or guinea fowl
Wing	Bronze mallard

The Gold-Green Reeach is one of the patterns in A. E. Knox's book, *Autumns on the Spey*, and the Gold Riach appears in George Kelson's *The Salmon Fly*. Many of the original Spey patterns were similar, but the blends of wool were slightly different. To a novice eye, they appeared the same, but the slight difference made all the difference in the way it fished during different seasons. No two fly tiers tied Spey flies the same way, and there was no constant dressing for any pattern.

GOLD HERON

Hook	Size 1/0 blind-eye Partridge
Body	Black Berlin wool
Ribs	Bars of flat gold tinsel, with one gold and one silver beading in between
Hackle	Very long gray heron, substitute with blue-eared pheasant
Wing	Bronze mallard

The Gold Heron was one of the early Spey patterns included in A. E. Knox's *Autumns on the Spey*. Syd Glasso originated a Steelhead Spey pattern of the same name (see chapter 8).

GOLD PURPLE FLY

Hook	Size 1/0 blind-eye Partridge
Body	Purple wool
Rib	Flat gold tinsel
Body hackle	Red Spey cock hackle, also serves as throat
Wing	Bronze mallard

The Gold Purple Fly is included in A. E. Knox's list of Spey patterns in *Autumns on the Spey*. Knox mentions that it was commonly called the Gold Purpy.

GOLD REEACH

Hook	Size 1/0 blind-eye Partridge
Tag	Orange silk
Body	Black wool or mohair
Ribs	Three bars of flat gold tinsel, with three rows of very fine oval gold beading in between
Body hackle	Red Spey cock hackle from the tail covets (soft and fine), along the body of the fly
Throat	Teal or guinea fowl
Wings	Brown mallard

The Gold Reeach is included in A. E. Knox's *Autumns on the Spey*, along with the Silver Reeach and the Gold-Green Reeach (see above). He notes that the flies for his book were tied by Shanks, who is also mentioned in George Kelson's book, but not in any book after Kelson. Not much is known about Shanks, but he is credited with many of the original Spey patterns.

This is a beautiful example of an old Spey fly. I also like to tie it with a throat of brown hooded merganser or northern shoveler flank feather because it blends nicely with the reddish body hackle. The modern substitute for the body hackle is schlappen.

GOLD RIACH

Hook	Size 1/0 return-eye Partridge
Body	Orange Berlin wool, three turns, followed by black wool
Ribs	Narrow gold tinsel, gold twist, and silver twist, wound in reverse way (toward head) and placed an equal distance apart, from different starting points
Hackle	Red Spey cock hackle, from the end of body, wound from the root of the feather and crossing entirely over the ribs
Throat	Teal, two turns
Wings	Two strips of bronze mallard with brown mottled points and gray mottled roots

The Gold Riach is included in George Kelson's book, *The Salmon Fly*. He credits the pattern to Mr. Riach and mentions that it kills best in spring and autumn. Some tiers confuse this with the Reeach patterns in A. E. Knox's book.

GOLD SPEAL

Hook	Size 1/0 blind-eye Partridge
Body	Black Berlin wool
Ribs	Three turns of flat gold tinsel, with a single strand of fine oval silver beading in between
Hackle	Red cock hackle, very soft, from the tail of the Spey cock
Wing	Bronze mallard

The Gold Speal is one of the original Spey patterns from A. E. Knox's *Autumns on the Spey*. His patterns are broken down into four groups: Speals, Reeachs, Kings, and Herons. Interestingly, Knox's book is the only one to include the Speals.

GREEN KING

Hook	Size 1/0 blind-eye Partridge
Body	Dull green, composed of a mixture of light and dark green, brown, and a little yellow Berlin wools
Ribs	Narrow gold tinsel, narrow silver tinsel, and light olive-green sewing thread, wound the reverse way at equal distance apart, from separate starting points. The sewing thread is left until the hackle is tied on. The two metal ribs run under the hackle, and the sewing thread is put over it, between the fibers.
Hackle	Red Spey cock hackle, wound from the end of the body from the root instead of the point, thus crossing over the metal ribs
Throat	Teal, two turns only
Wings	Bronze mallard

This dressing for the Green King is included in George Kelson's *The Salmon Fly*. Kelson mentions that patterns like the Green King were tied on long-shank hooks, and that it is dressed after the local insect of that name. The insect, an exceedingly large one at least twice the size of a hornet, appears in enormous numbers the end of April. Kelson says that salmon will rise to these.

Kelson also mentions that the fly he took the dressing from was tied by Charles Stuart from Aberlour, under the supervision of John Cruikshank.

Francis Francis's 1867 *A Book on Angling* lists the pattern with a body of a mixture of orange and olive-yellow mohair. In a letter to him from Mr. C. Grant of Aberlour, he states that the body of the Green King should vary from greenish in the spring to more reddish as the season progresses. Grant says the hackle should be a Spey hackle, brown with gray tips.

This pattern and the Purple King are the oldest Spey patterns mentioned in early salmon fly books.

GREEN KING

Hook	Size 1/0 blind-eye Partridge
Body	Olive, a mixture of red, green, and purple Berlin wool
Ribs	Alternate bars of flat gold and silver tinsel
Hackle	Red cock hackle
Shoulder	Teal
Wing	Bronze mallard

This is the original pattern dressing for the Green King from A. E. Knox's *Autumns on the Spey*. As you can tell by the above dressings, there was no set standard for dressing a Spey pattern. The Green Kings described by Francis, Kelson, and Knox all differ in the color or shade of the body materials and the ribs.

GREEN QUEEN

Hook	Size 6 treble Waddington shank
Tag	Narrow oval gold tinsel
Tail	Yellow rump feather from golden pheasant, point
Body	Dull green, composed of a mixture of light and dark green, brown, and a little yellow Berlin wool
Rib	Flat gold tinsel
Hackle	Crown pigeon or gray heron hackle, one side stripped, from second turn of tinsel, substitute with blue-eared pheasant hackle
Throat	Bittern white speckled feather dyed yellow
Wings	Dark cinnamon turkey with lightest points; or better still, gled

The Green Queen is a pattern that George Kelson originated and included in his book, *The Salmon Fly*. In bright weather, he preferred it as a general pattern to the Green King, but the Green King is the best fly on the Spey during the insect hatch. Kelson also mentions that the Green Queen is a capital fly on many other rivers.

This pattern has materials that were commonly used on both Spey and Dee patterns. I added a drooping jungle cock on the pattern that appears in the plates.

GRAY HERON

Hook	Size 1/0 return-eye Partridge
Body	One-third lemon Berlin wool, remainder black Berlin wool
Ribs	Flat silver tinsel, sparse, three turns; oval silver and oval gold tinsel
Hackle	Gray heron, or substitute
Throat	Speckled guinea fowl
Wings	Bronze mallard

The Grey Heron is included in Pryce-Tannatt's 1914 book, *How to Dress Salmon Flies*. It is also included in a much later book, *Classic Salmon Flies: History and Patterns*, by Mikael Frodin, published in 1991. Frodin's book contains many of the old classic salmon patterns with a lot of information and history about the patterns.

LADY CAROLINE

Hook	Size 1/0 return-eye Partridge
Tail	A few strands of golden pheasant red breast feather
Body	Two parts brown and one part olive-green Berlin wool mixed together
Ribs	Flat narrow gold tinsel, gold twist, and silver twist, wound the usual way, at equal distances apart, from separate starting points
Hackle	Gray heron, or substitute, wound from tail along flat gold tinsel
Throat	Golden pheasant red breast feather, two turns
Wings	Bronze mallard

The Lady Caroline first appeared in George Kelson's *The Salmon Fly*, although he calls it an old standard Spey pattern. It is one of only two original Spey patterns tied with a tail.

A much later book, *A Guide to Salmon Flies*, by John Buckland and Arthur Oglesby, published in 1990, says the fly was named after Lady Caroline Gordon-Lennox, daughter of the then Duke of Richmond and Gordon at Gordon Castle. The pattern's creator is not credited anywhere, but many speculate that it was Shanks, who is mentioned in Knox and in Kelson. Shanks originated Spey patterns and named them after women of the time, an example being the Miss Grant, which is the only other Spey pattern dressed with a tail.

When Roderick Haig-Brown first fished for steelhead, this was one of the Atlantic salmon patterns he used. It is still widely used today for both Atlantic salmon and steelhead and is probably the best known of the original Spey patterns.

MISS GRANT

Hook	Size 3/0 blind-eye Partridge
Tag	Silver twist
Tail	Teal, in strands
Body	Two turns of orange silk followed by olive-green Berlin wool
Rib	Silver tinsel
Hackle	Gray heron, from second turn, substitute gray Spey feather
Wings	Two strips of golden pheasant tail

The Miss Grant is included in George Kelson's *The Salmon Fly*. He calls it a modern Spey pattern, originated by Shanks, the accomplished artist who provided all the flies for A. E. Knox's *Autumns on the Spey*.

The Grant family had a castle located on the Spey, and Major Grant, who is credited with several Spey patterns, appears in *The Salmon Fly*. Miss Grant is a unique pattern that uses golden pheasant tail for the wing and has a tail of teal.

MRS. GRANT

Hook	Size 4/0 blind-eye Partridge
Tag	Silver twist and yellow silk
Tail	Topping and Indian crow
Butt	Black herl
Body	Copper tinseled chenille
Hackle	Red Spey cock hackle, from center
Throat	European jay
Wings	Tippet strands, bustard, golden pheasant tail, light mottled turkey, gray mallard, and a topping
Horns	Red macaw
Head	Black herl

Mrs. Grant is included in George Kelson's *The Salmon Fly* and is credited to Major Grant. Kelson calls it a modern Spey pattern.

MUDDY WATERS

Hook	Size 4/0 blind-eye Partridge
Body	Black seal fur
Ribs	Flat silver tinsel, yellow and red silk, equally divided
Body hackle	Black Spey cock hackle, also serves as throat
Wings	Two strips of bronze mallard

The Muddy Waters is a modern Spey fly pattern tied by Derl Stovall in the true Spey fly tradition. The ribs of yellow and red silk and the flat silver tinsel give it an old Spey fly look.

PITCROY FANCY

Hook	Size 2/0 blind-eye Partridge
Tag	Silver twist
Tail	Topping and strands of tippet
Butt	Scarlet wool
Body	Silver tinsel
Rib	Oval silver tinsel
Hackle	Gray heron, from center, or substitute
Throat	Guinea fowl
Wings	Tippet (large slips), light mottled turkey, pintail, mallard, and topping
Sides	Jungle cock
Head	Scarlet wool

The Pitcroy Fancy was included in George Kelson's *The Salmon Fly*. Kelson calls it a modern Spey pattern, originated by Mr. Turnbull, who also originated the Duchess and the Wilson.

PURPLE KING

Hook	Size 1/0 blind-eye Partridge
Body	Light purple mohair
Ribs	Gold and silver tinsel and silver twist over hackle
Hackle	Brownish black Spey cock hackle with light dun tips
Throat	Teal
Wings	Bronze mallard

The Purple King first appeared in Francis Francis's 1867 *A Book on Angling*. He mentions that Mr. C. Grant sent him examples of the Green and Purple Kings for his book. Grant says to mix purple, red, and scarlet wool to get the color for the body.

A. E. Knox in *Autumns on the Spey* lists the Purple King with a body of lake-colored wool, composed of scarlet and purple wool, and a hackle of gray or red cock, according to your fancy. Knox says that a variation called the Gold Purpy is ribbed with gold tinsel and has a body of purple wool.

The Purple King is also included in George Kelson's *The Salmon Fly*. Kelson calls it an old standard for the Spey and the best of the Kings for general use. In Kelson's dressing, the body is a mixture of one part blue wool and two parts red wool, and the body hackle is a red Spey cock.

Another version is listed in Pryce-Tannatt's *How to Dress Salmon Flies*. It has a body of purple Berlin wool with a ribbing of flat gold tinsel, purple floss, and gold thread. I have also seen it tied with red floss. Pryce-Tannatt also calls for a bronze-black Spey hackle. The tinsel is wound so the gold thread crosses over the hackle, and the flat gold and purple floss are wound the usual way.

The Purple King and the Green King are the oldest and most mentioned of the original Spey patterns. If I had to choose only one of the Purple Kings, it would be Pryce-Tannatt's, with its extra rib of purple floss. I change the hackle to a long black hackle.

RED KING

Hook	Size 1/0 blind-eye Partridge
Body	Brick-red Berlin wool
Ribs	Gold tinsel from far side, silver narrow tinsel from near side, wound the reverse way at equal distance apart
Hackle	Red Spey cock's hackle, from the end of body, wound in the usual direction crossing over the ribs
Throat	Teal, one turn only
Wings	Bronze mallard

The Red King is included in George Kelson's *The Salmon Fly*, published in 1895. Kelson mentions that it is an old standard Spey fly, and he describes the color of the body as brick red. The Green King was tied with more red in the body color as the season went on. The Red King is not included in the Spey dressings given by A. E. Knox in his 1872 *Autumns on the Spey*, which leads me to believe it is not one of the original Kings but was developed later.

ROUGH GROUSE

Hook	Size 3/0 blind-eye Partridge
Tail	A few fibers of yellow macaw's tail
Body	Short black Berlin wool
Rib	Silver tinsel
Hackle	Gray heron, from third turn, substitute with gray Spey hackle
Throat	Black-and-white speckled turkey as hackle (soft mottled brown body feather)
Wings	Black-and-white speckled turkey strips

In *The Salmon Fly*, George Kelson calls the Rough Grouse a splendid fly on the River Spey in dull, wet weather. Kelson also says that he sometimes does better with a fly tied using crown pigeon instead of gray heron. He mentions that this is Cruikshank's version.

SILVER-GREEN FLY

Hook	Size 1/0 blind-eye Partridge
Body	Olive, composed of a mixture of red, green, and purple fine wool
Ribs	Three bars of flat silver tinsel, with three rows of very fine silver beading in between
Hackle	Gray Spey cock hackle
Throat	Teal or guinea fowl hackle
Wing	Bronze mallard

The Silver-Green Fly is one of the original Spey flies that appeared in A. E. Knox's 1872 book, *Autumns on the Spey*.

SILVER-GREEN REEACH

Hook	Size 1/0 blind-eye Partridge
Body	Olive, a mixture of red, green, and purple fine Berlin wool
Ribs	Three bars of flat silver tinsel between three rows of fine silver beading
Hackle	Gray Spey cock hackle
Throat	Teal or guinea-fowl hackle
Wing	Bronze mallard

The Silver-Green Reeach is another fly included in A. E. Knox's *Autumns on the Spey*.

SILVER REEACH

Hook	Size 1/0 blind-eye Partridge
Body	Black Berlin wool
Ribs	Three bars of flat silver tinsel, with three rows of very fine silver beading in between
Hackle	Gray Spey cock hackle
Shoulder	Teal or guinea-fowl hackle
Wing	Bronze mallard

The Silver Reeach is a Spey pattern from A. E. Knox's book, *Autumns on the Spey*. All the Reeach patterns had a similar appearance with only very subtle changes in tinsel or body colors to fit certain circumstances throughout the season. By changing the color of the tinsel or body colors for a specific pattern, tiers found that certain shades of colors worked better at different times of the day or season.

SILVER SPEAL

Hook	Size 1/0 blind-eye Partridge
Body	Black Berlin wool
Ribs	Three turns of flat silver tinsel, and a single strand of fine gold beading in between
Hackle	Red Spey cock hackle
Wing	Bronze mallard

The Silver Speal is another of the original Spey patterns from A. E. Knox's *Autumns on the Spey*. I have not found the patterns for the Speal series of flies in any other book. They must be old patterns that went out of use when new patterns were introduced.

SPEY DOG

Hook	Size 4 blind-eye Ron Reinhold, Noble P
Body	Black pig's wool
Rib	Broad silver tinsel
Hackle	Large black feather with light dun tip, taken from the side of a Scotch cock's tail. The feather is dressed opposite of the tinsel, and gold tinsel is crisscrossed over the hackle.
Throat	Teal
Wings	Golden pheasant tail with bronze-mallard strips over

The Spey Dog is an early Spey pattern from Francis Francis's list of flies for the River Spey in *A Book on Angling*. He says it is usually dressed large for spring using long-shank Dee hooks. A variation uses brown hackle and turkey tail for the wing instead of golden pheasant tail. It is also dressed with orange silk between the tinsels.

The description of the hackle winding can be confusing. First you should tie in the flat tinsel the usual way, then crisscross the hackle over the flat tinsel in reverse, and then wind oval tinsel over the hackle stem the usual way. The tinsels are all wound the same way, but the hackle is not.

STODDART'S SPEY

Hook	Size 4/0 blind-eye Partridge
Tail	Tuft of yellow or orange wool or mohair
Body	Black and brown mohair or pig's wool
Ribs	Broad gold and silver lace
Hackle	Black feather of the male heron taken from the pendant
Wing	Brown mallard

Stoddart's Spey is included in Thomas Stoddart's 1847 book, *The Anglers Companion*. This is an early pattern that originally used a heron hackle and was dressed in the Spey style.

SWEEP

Hook	Size 6, 45mm treble Waddington shank
Tag	Silver tinsel
Tail	Golden pheasant crest
Butt	Black herl
Body	Black floss
Rib	Flat silver tinsel
Hackle	Black Spey hackle
Wing	Black crow or black goose quill
Topping	Golden pheasant crest
Cheeks	Jungle cock
Horns	Red macaw
Head	Black thread

The Sweep is a pattern John Henry Hale lists in *How to Tie Salmon Flies*, 1892 and 1919. Another dressing calls for cheeks of blue kingfisher, blue and gold macaw horns, and no crest. This is a very striking pattern, mostly black with the accent of the golden pheasant crests and the red macaw horns. It also appears in Joseph D. Bates, Jr., and Pamela Bates Richards's 1996 *Fishing Atlantic Salmon*.

CHAPTER 4

Dee Patterns

DEE FLIES WERE FIRST DESIGNED AND DRESSED ON the River Dee in northeastern Scotland. They are similar to Spey flies with long body hackles but are tied in much larger sizes with more brilliantly colored bodies. They are tied large but dressed slenderly. Special hooks were used, large hooks with longer shanks and a Limerick bend, called long Dee hooks. Dee flies were tied with tails, and many patterns contained tail veils. The earliest Dee patterns used the red body feathers from a golden pheasant for the tails. In time, golden pheasant crests were used for the tails, many times with tail veils of golden pheasant tippets or other accenting feathers.

The bodies were dressed with mohair, pig's wool, or more often seal fur, in very brilliant colors. The earliest Dee bodies were dressed with mohair or pig's wool, and later flies were dressed with seal fur, as the tiers began to feel that it was the best translucent material to use for fly bodies. Most Dee flies have multisegmented bodies of various colors of seal fur. Yellow, orange, red, claret, and blue are some of the most popular colors.

The body hackles were the longest gray and black heron hackles. Throat hackles were mainly teal, widgeon, and guinea-fowl flank feathers and red body feathers from the golden pheasant. Feathers with the longest fiber length were used for throats on Dee patterns.

Dee-strip wing flies got their name by the way the wings were tied—two strips of quill were tied on separately. When tied on properly, they had a scissorslike effect in the water. This style of wing created very enticing action for the fish. The wing and the long heron hackles made for a very mobile fly in the water.

Many of the Dee patterns were tied with jungle cock along the sides of the fly, set drooping along or below the body. Heads were tied as small as possible with black thread so that the water glided over the head and gave the wings the best possible action in the water.

Dee patterns are some of my favorite flies to tie. I love their look. Big hooks and long sweeping tails; bodies of translucent natural furs gleaming with broad turns of bright tinsel; and hackled with the longest of Spey hackles; throats of fine penciled duck flank; long, slender, shapely strips for wings; cheeked with jungle cock; and finished off with the smallest heads. The flies are perfection in motion, every part of the fly fulfilling maximum movement. They have a waspy look that is truly unique.

Many classic flies were tied for use on the River Dee, and some very important tiers were Dee tiers. Mr. Brown of Aberdeen ran a tackle shop and designed some of the original Dee flies. Charles Akroyd and Mr. Garden, mentioned in George Kelson's *The Salmon Fly*, originated a number of patterns that we consider classic Dee patterns today. Kelson himself also originated some of the Dee flies that appear in his book.

Contemporary fly tiers can use some of the larger low-water salmon hooks made by Partridge to dress their flies. Partridge has return-eye and blind-eye hooks that can be used to tie Dee patterns. Dee flies should be tied on hooks size 2/0 or larger—they just don't look the same when tied on smaller hooks.

Most materials—silks, tinsels, and fur dubbing for the bodies—are readily available. The best substitute for the original long heron body hackle is a large blue-eared pheasant hackle from the saddle or rump of the bird. No other legal feather has the long fiber length of blue-eared pheasant. The natural gray color of blue-eared pheasant hackles works for the patterns that use gray heron, but they can be dyed black for patterns that call for black heron. Wing materials can be procured from various types of turkey feathers in a range of cinnamon shades. One of my favorites is the eyed

Contemporary Dee and Eagle Flies

Doctor Forbes, Rossman	Speckle Dee, Stovall

Pink Ghost, Rossman

Sweep (Waddington shank), Veverka	Inchgarth (Waddington shank), Veverka

Tiger Blue, Rossman

Speckled Eagle, Veverka	Scarlet Eagle, Veverka

Contemporary fly tiers like the look of the long wispy Dee-style flies, and many tie them today with a little flair or personal touch that accents the look of this style of fly. Above are some old and new Dee patterns dressed on large, long-shank hooks called Dee irons. When tied on a Waddington shank, the flies take on an interesting and unique style. The original Eagle patterns were dressed the same as the Dee flies but used an eagle feather for the body hackle. Today we use various types of marabou hackles.

and barred feather from the argus pheasant. The fiber length is long enough to dress the largest flies and the texture is soft, so they take on a sweeping look when tied on as Dee-fly wings. Jungle-cock feathers for Dee flies should be taken from the sides of the neck so the natural curve of the feather adds to the look of the fly.

Joseph D. Bates, Jr., and Pamela Bates Richards's *Fishing Atlantic Salmon* includes both antique and contemporary Spey and Dee patterns. *A Guide to Salmon Flies*, by Arthur Oglesby and John Buckland, is another good reference for both Spey and Dee patterns, many tied by their originators.

WHITE-WINGED AKROYD DEE FLY

Hook	Size 6, 45mm Waddington shank treble hook
Tip	Oval silver tinsel
Tag	Yellow silk
Butt	Ostrich herl
Tail	Golden pheasant crest and tippet strands
Body	Rear half, light yellow–orange seal fur; front half, black silk
Ribbing	Oval silver or gold tinsel over yellow-orange seal fur, with yellow hackle; flat silver tinsel over black silk
Body hackle	Black heron feather, substitute black Spey feather
Throat	Guinea-fowl or teal flank
Wings	Strips of cinnamon turkey or white goose (many contemporary tiers use various types of feathers for the wings)
Cheeks	Jungle cock, drooping

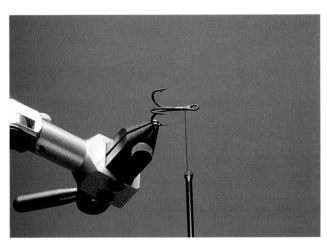

1. Place treble hook in vise, and start your tying thread just behind the eye of the hook.

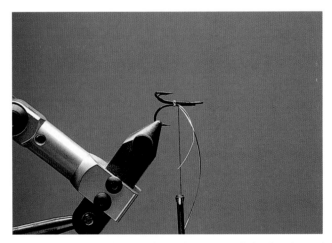

2. Wind your thread back to the point of the hook, and tie on the oval silver tinsel. Make three turns of tinsel, winding it toward the eye of the hook, and tie it off. Then bind down the ends of the oval tinsel with the thread, and finish with the thread just behind the eye of the hook.

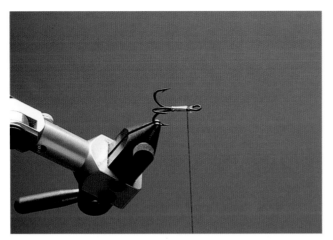

3. Tie on a strand of yellow silk, and wind it toward the bend of the hook. Then wind it back toward the eye of the hook and tie it off.

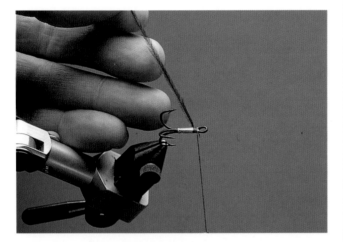

4. Tie on a piece of ostrich herl.

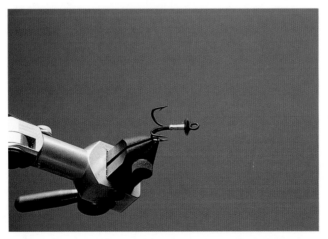

5. Take several turns of herl, until you feel the butt is the desired fullness, and tie it off.

Form the head with the tying thread, then whip-finish and add cement to complete the hook. Remove from vise.

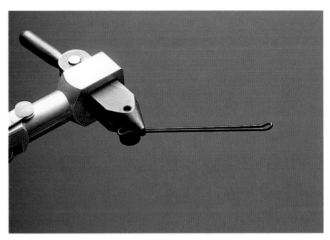

6. Place a 45mm Waddington shank in your vise. A rotary vise comes in handy when tying on Waddington shanks because various procedures require your vise to be angled or positioned differently.

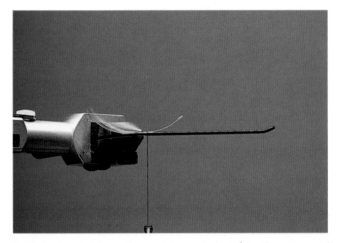

7. Select a golden pheasant crest that fits the size and shape of the shank, stripping off any excess fibers. Then, with two or three turns of tying thread, tie it on. Make sure it is tied on straight in the shape you desire.

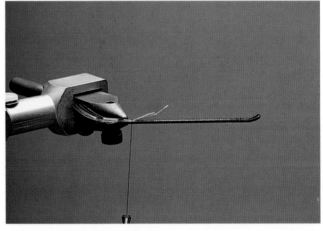

8. Select a golden pheasant tippet feather, and strip off about six to eight strands of fiber for the tail veil. To make the several strands as one, I either roll the fibers or fold them. Hold them up to the tail to size them—the tail veil should be half the length of the tail. Once they are the proper length, take two or three turns of thread and tie them on the top of the tail.

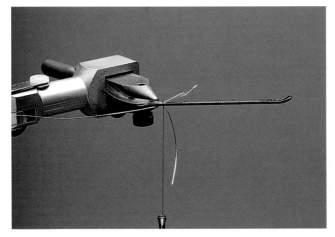

9. Loop the oval tinsel on your thread, and tie it on the back of the shank. This will make the rib for the back section of the fly.

10. Prepare the yellow hackle for the back section of the body by folding or doubling the hackle. Then tie it on the back of the shank by the tip of the feather with the fibers flowing toward the back of the fly.

11. The back section of the fly body is yellow-orange seal fur. Tie in a strand of yellow silk and dub the seal fur onto the silk. I use yellow silk as my dubbing thread because it makes dubbing much easier and gives this section of the fly a brilliant base color.

Then wind your tying thread to the middle of the shank, binding down all loose ends and forming a smooth underbody as you go.

12. Start winding the yellow-orange seal fur toward the center of the fly.

13. Tie it off.

14. Take the strand of oval tinsel, make five turns over the seal fur, and tie it off.

15. Tie in the yellow hackle by the butt end with the fibers flowing toward the back of the hook, and wind it along the back edge of the tinsel. Tie it off at the tie-in area at the center of the fly.

16. Loop on a strand of flat silver tinsel to make the rib for the front section of the body. Take a blue-eared pheasant hackle dyed black, fold the hackle, and tie it in by the tip of the feather with the fibers flowing toward the back. Then wind your tying thread toward the eye, binding down all loose ends as you go.

17. Tie in a strand of black silk at the eye.

18. Wind the silk to the center of the hook. Then reverse direction, wind the silk toward the eye, and tie it off. Try to keep the silk tight and smooth.

Take the flat silver tinsel, make four turns over the black silk, and tie it off.

19. Wind on the front body hackle along the back edge of the flat silver tinsel rib with the fibers flowing toward the back of the hook. At the tie-in area, take one or two additional turns of hackle, and tie it off. Cut off any excess tinsel and hackle stem.

Pinch the fibers and pull them down and toward the back of the hook to clear them from the top of the hook for the wing.

20. Prepare the guinea-fowl feather for the throat by folding or doubling the feather. Tie it on by the tip of the feather.

21. Take one to three turns of feather (depending on how sparse or heavy you want it), and tie it off.

With a pinch, pull the fibers down and back toward the back of the hook to clear them from the top of the shank for the wing.

22. Select two sections of wing quill that match in length and width. The wings on Dee flies are tied on one at a time. Start with the section for the left wing, the one on the far side of the fly. Size the wing against the fly; the wing should not extend past the back of the hook. Each wing section is tied onto the shoulder of the fly.

Hold the wing on the fly with your index finger, and tie it on with two or three turns of thread. Once it is tied on, make sure it is in the right position. If it is not, hold the main wing section and work or move the butt ends into the right position.

23. Size the right wing section, the one closest to you, against the left wing section, and tie on in the same manner.

24. Make sure the wings are in position—they should form a V when viewed from above. Cut off the butt ends of the fiber, and make enough turns of thread so the wings are securely tied on.

25. Select two jungle-cock feathers that are the same length and eye size for the cheeks. I usually take two feathers from the sides of a jungle-cock neck, one from

either side. The natural curve of those feathers accents the shape of the cheeks.

Put the two feathers back to back, and size them to the fly. Strip off any excess fiber, and make sure the feathers are the same length.

Tie on the feather for the far side of the fly. Catch a few fibers of the feather under the tying thread so you are not tying on only the stem. This prevents the feather from twisting along the side of the fly. Repeat the process on the feather for the side closest to you.

Make sure the jungle-cock cheeks are flat against the side of the fly and angling down below the body in the same position on both sides. Cut off any excess stem.

26. To make the head, take turns of thread to cover any material, while building your overall head shape. Keep the head as small as possible. Do a whip-finish, and cut off the tying thread. Apply head cement to finish the fly.

This Akroyd tied with a peacock wing quill shows how various types of wings change the overall look of a fly.

The wing on this Akroyd is speckled bustard tail feather.

The wing on this Akroyd is argus quill.

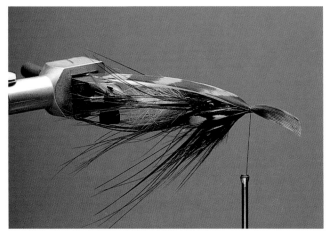

The wing on this Akroyd is florican bustard.

AKROYD

Hook	Size 2/0 blind-eye antique long Dee, Phillips
Tag	Silver tinsel
Tail	Topping and tippet strands
Body	Half light yellow–orange seal fur, half black floss, with a butt of black ostrich herl between the halves
Ribs	Oval silver tinsel over the yellow-orange seal fur, with a yellow-orange hackle; flat silver tinsel over the black floss
Hackle	Black heron hackle, substitute with dyed-black Spey feather
Throat	Black heron or teal, in some dressings guinea fowl
Wings	A pair of cinnamon turkey tail strips (white goose for White-Winged Akroyd)
Cheeks	Jungle cock, drooping

The Akroyd was originated in 1878 by Mr. Charles Akroyd from Duncraggie, Brora, in Sunderland. He called it "the poor man's Jock Scott." It is included in George Kelson's 1895 *The Salmon Fly*. Kelson mentions that this is a good Dee pattern for the early season. In snow water, the fly is dressed with double wings, as introduced by Mr. Garden of Aberdeen. This is perhaps the best known of the Dee patterns and is still widely used today on salmon rivers all over the world. It can also be dressed on tubes and Waddington shanks. A good book on this subject is *Tube and Waddington Fly Dressings* by Kenichiro Sawada, a very talented fly tier from Japan.

I tie two consecutive Akroyds on a very long shank hook size 8/0 to 12/0 to make a Double Akroyd.

BALMORAL

Hook	Size 3/0 blind-eye long Dee, Partridge, same as CS10/3 with longer shank
Tag	Silver twist
Tail	Topping and tippets in strands
Butt	Black ostrich herl
Body	Green and dark blue seal fur, divided equally
Ribs	Oval silver lace and flat silver tinsel
Hackle	Black heron from green seal fur, substitute with Spey feather dyed black
Throat	Widgeon
Wings	Two strips of plain cinnamon turkey
Cheeks	Jungle cock, drooping

The Balmoral is one of Mr. W. Garden's Dee patterns and is included in George Kelson's *The Salmon Fly*. Kelson says it is a favorite Dee pattern. Garden also originated the Gardener and the Glentana, his version of the Gled Wing.

I usually tie this pattern with strips of argus quill for the wing. Argus quill has a unique barred and spotted pattern, enough fiber length to tie any size Dee fly, and great mobility in the water. You can use a lighter shade of the seal fur to change the look of the fly.

This is one of my favorite Dee patterns. It is also included in *Fishing Atlantic Salmon* by Joseph D. Bates, Jr., and Pamela Bates Richards, *Tying the Classic Salmon Fly* by Michael D. Radencich, and the Winter 1998 issue of *Wild Steelhead* magazine.

CRANE

Hook	Size 3/0 blind-eye long Dee
Tag	Silver tinsel and orange silk
Tail	Yellow swan
Butt	Red wool
Body	Bright blue silk
Rib	Silver tinsel
Hackle	Gray heron feather, substitute with gray Spey feather
Throat	Guinea fowl
Wing	Two jungle-cock hackles topped with cuckoo dun hackles
Head	Red wool

The Crane was included in Francis Francis's 1867 *A Book on Angling* and John James Hardy's 1907 *Salmon Fishing*. The Crane was an Irish pattern that Francis Francis received from an angler he met on the River Suir. It is dressed on large hooks and used for rapid and high water.

DOCTOR FORBES

Hook	Size 3/0 blind-eye long Dee
Tag	Flat gold tinsel
Tail	Golden pheasant crest and tippet
Butt	Black ostrich herl
Body	Rear half, bright orange silk; front half, black silk
Ribs	Gold and silver tinsel
Hackle	Black heron over black silk, substitute with black Spey feather
Throat	Red body feather from a golden pheasant
Wing	Dark brown turkey

The Doctor Forbes is included in John James Hardy's 1907 book, *Salmon Fishing*.

DODGER

Hook	Size 3/0 blind-eye long Dee, Partridge
Tag	Silver thread
Tail	Red saddle feather from golden pheasant
Body	Orange, light blue, and scarlet mohair
Ribs	Medium flat silver tinsel followed by silver twist
Hackle	Gray heron, substitute with gray Spey feather
Shoulder	Teal, sparingly
Wing	Ginger speckled turkey strips, lightly toward tips

The Dodger appears in the article "Salmon Flies for Spring Fishing on the Dee, Aberdeenshire" by Mr. W. Murdoch for the March 14, 1885, issue of *The Fishing Gazette*. Mr. Murdoch is also credited with the Dunt Dee pattern, his most popular Dee pattern.

DUNT

Hook	Size 6, 45mm treble Waddington shank
Tag	Silver twist and light blue silk
Tail	Topping and teal feather
Body	Yellow, orange, and red-claret seal fur in equal sections
Ribs	Silver lace and flat silver tinsel
Hackle	Black heron from claret fur, substitute with dyed black Spey feather
Throat	Teal
Wings	Two strips of plain brown turkey with black bars and white tips
Sides	Jungle cock, short and drooping over throat hackle

Mr. William Murdoch, who is credited with the Dunt, states "there is not a better all-around fly of the plain sort than the Dunt put upon the Dee in spring or autumn" (George Kelson's *The Salmon Fly*, 1895). In Pryce-Tannatt's 1914 *How to Dress Salmon Flies*, the Dunt has a tail veil of jungle cock.

The Dunt differs from most Dees because it has a wing of white-tipped turkey. Most tiers use cinnamon turkey. Many early salmon patterns, such as the famous Toppy, used white-tipped turkey for the wings.

GARDENER

Hook	Size 4/0 blind-eye long Dee, Eugene Sunday
Tag	Gold twist and crimson silk
Tail	Topping and tippets in strands
Body	Yellow, green, and dark blue seal fur in equal parts
Rib	Flat silver tinsel
Hackle	Topping (golden pheasant crest) from yellow fur, as a hackle (some dressings call for an orange hackle)
Throat	Black heron or substitute
Wings	Two strips of plain cinnamon turkey
Sides	Jungle cock, short and drooping

The Gardener was originated by Mr. W. Garden, a dedicated Dee angler, and is included in George Kelson's *The Salmon Fly*. Kelson says this is one of Mr. Garden's best Dee patterns. Mr. Garden was a skillful fly tier who also originated the Glentana and the Balmoral Dee patterns.

This pattern has a small feature that sets it apart from all other Dee flies—the hackle for the body is a golden pheasant crest.

GHOST

Hook	Size 4/0 low-water blind-eye Partridge
Tag	Silver twist
Tail	Jay points, back to back
Butt	Black herl
Body	Half thin black silk butted with two turns of sliver tinsel and two golden pheasant toppings above and below, half black ostrich herl
Hackle	Natural black hackle from center
Wings	Two strips of shovel duck, substitute with bronze mallard
Horns	Blue macaw

The Ghost is included in George Kelson's 1895 book, *The Salmon Fly*. Kelson writes that this pattern is an old standard and has a reputation for killing fish on those occasions when pools have been overthrashed with ordinary patterns.

When I first saw this pattern, I thought it would make a nice conversion to a Dee. For the original, I tie the body hackle with a long Spey hackle and sometimes used a wing of bronze mallard because shovel duck is hard to find.

I also tie another pattern called the Purple Ghost, which appeared on the back cover of Judith Dunham's *The Atlantic Salmon Fly*. The Purple Ghost has a wing of long purple goose quill, purple body section and hackle, and a throat of guinea fowl dyed purple.

GLED WING

Hook	Size 3/0 blind-eye long Dee, Partridge
Tag	Silver tinsel
Tail	Red golden pheasant saddle feather
Body	One-third orange-yellow mohair and two-thirds claret-purple mohair
Rib	Broad silver tinsel
Hackle	Black heron from yellow mohair, or substitute
Shoulder	Teal
Wings	Strips of swallow-tailed gled or red dun turkey of the same color

The Gled Wing is an old Dee pattern (perhaps the first), credited to Mr. Brown in Francis Francis's 1867 *A Book on Angling*. Francis Francis says that the Gled Wing is considered the best of the local flies for the Dee, and that many of the Dee patterns were fashioned after this pattern.

This is the forerunner to the Glentana. The original pattern uses gled or kite, a type of hawk, for the wing, but when it was no longer found on Dee side, tiers changed the wing to strips of cinnamon turkey. Cinnamon turkey had a similar color but was not as effective as the original strips of gled. Cinnamon turkey is very close to the original color but lacks the darker markings that are on the tail of the gled. I think that the texture of the gled made a difference in the water, as all hawks or birds of prey have very soft feathers. The original material must have been very mobile in the water, and perhaps this is the attribute that the later material, the turkey tail, lacked.

GLENTANA

Hook	Size 1/0 blind-eye double Partridge Bartleet
Tag	Silver twist
Tail	Red breast feather of the golden pheasant
Body	One-third light orange seal fur followed by two-thirds light claret seal fur
Ribs	Silver lace and flat silver tinsel
Hackle	Black heron, from orange fur, or substitute black Spey feather
Throat	Widgeon
Wings	Two strips of plain cinnamon turkey, light points showing

The Glentana was originated by Mr. Garden of Aberdeen and is included in George Kelson's *The Salmon Fly*. Kelson calls it an old Dee fly (its forerunner is the Gled Wing). When the material for the wing, the gled, became extinct on Dee side, tiers substituted with cinnamon turkey.

The fly pictured in the plates is tied with wings of zebra turkey quill.

INCHGARTH

Hook	Size 6, 45mm treble Waddington shank
Tag	Silver thread
Tail	Saddle feather from a golden pheasant (gold)
Body	Three turns of golden orange mohair and four turns of fiery red mohair
Ribs	Silver tinsel and gold twist
Hackle	Golden yellow cock hackle from first turn of yellow mohair
Throat	Grouse hackle
Wings	Two strips of the black and tan feather from a peacock's wing

The Inchgarth is listed in the November 9, 1895, issue of *The Fishing Gazette*. The pattern fits the Dee style of fly, but I would change the body hackle or throat hackle to a longer-fibered hackle.

JOCK O' DEE

Hook	Size 3/0 blind-eye long Dee, Partridge
Tag	Silver tinsel
Tail	Topping and Indian crow
Body	Two-fifths, lemon floss; remainder, black floss
Ribs	Flat silver tinsel and twist
Hackle	Gray heron hackle from third turn of tinsel, or substitute
Throat	Widgeon
Wings	Two strips of cinnamon turkey tail

The Jock O' Dee is a pattern that first appears in Pryce-Tannatt's 1914 book *How to Dress Salmon Flies*. It must have been modeled after the Akroyd because it has the same colors on the body and the same material for the wing. It looks very similar to the colors in the Jock Scott as well, and the Akroyd was called the "poor man's Jock Scott."

KILLER

Hook	Size 3/0 blind-eye long Dee
Tag	Flat gold tinsel
Tail	Yellow rump feather from a golden pheasant
Body	Three turns of yellow, orange, dark blue, and scarlet seal fur
Hackle	Gray heron, substitute with gray Spey feather
Throat	Red body feather from a golden pheasant
Wing	Two strips of dun turkey

The Killer is included in John James Hardy's 1907 book, *Salmon Fishing*, and George Kelson's *The Salmon Fly*. Kelson mentions that the Tri-Color Dee pattern, when tied with a throat hackle of red body feather from a golden pheasant, is called the Killer.

MODEL GRAY HERON

Hook	Size 3/0 blind-eye, Partridge Bartleet traditional
Tag	Gold thread and topping (golden pheasant), colored silk
Tail	Fibers of golden pheasant tippet
Body	Orange pig's wool or mohair
Ribs	Broad flat gold tinsel and gold twist
Hackle	Gray heron, substitute with gray Spey feather
Shoulder	Teal
Wings	Cream-colored turkey strips

The Model Gray Heron is included in Mr. W. Murdoch's article "Spring Flies for the Dee" in the March 14, 1885, issue of *The Fishing Gazette*. Mr. Murdoch tied several flies in the Dee style—his most famous is the Dunt.

MOONLIGHT

Hook	Size 6/0 blind-eye, Eugene Sunday
Tag	Silver tinsel
Tail	Topping and a pair of jungle-cock feathers, back to back
Body	Front half, flat silver tinsel, veiled with blue chatterer above and below; rear half, black floss, on edge
Ribs	Fine oval silver tinsel over flat silver tinsel and broader oval gold tinsel over the black floss
Body hackle	Black heron hackle over black floss, or substitute
Throat	Speckled guinea fowl
Wing	Cinnamon turkey

The Moonlight is another Dee pattern in Pryce-Tannatt's book, *How to Dress Salmon Flies*, that is not mentioned elsewhere. The veils of chatterer on the rear half of the body make this pattern different from many others. I tie this fly with white wings, like in the White-Winged Akroyd, and sometimes with strips of argus quill (my favorite material for Dee wings). I also add the drooping jungle cock.

PEACOCK

Hook	Size 3/0 blind-eye Partridge Bartleet traditional
Tag	Silver tinsel
Tail	Two sprigs of tippet, 1/2 inch long
Body	Half orange and half light blue mohair
Ribs	Broad flat silver tinsel and silver twist
Hackle	Gray heron over blue mohair, substitute with gray Spey feather
Shoulder	Teal
Wings	Well-marked peacock strips for large flies, barred black-and-white turkey tail

The Peacock appeared in William Murdoch's article "Spring Flies for the Dee" in the March 14, 1895, issue of *The Fishing Gazette*. Francis Francis's 1867 *A Book on Angling* confirms that these are flies from Mr. W. Murdoch of *The Fishing Gazette*.

PINK GHOST

Hook	Size 3/0 blind-eye long Dee
Tag	Copper tinsel and light green floss
Tail	Golden pheasant crest and two Impeyan pheasant feathers, back to back
Butt	Bronze peacock herl
Body	Rear half, pink floss veiled with golden pheasant crests dyed pink; front half, pink seal fur
Hackle	Dyed pink Spey hackle and black Spey hackle
Throat	Guinea fowl
Wing	Pink turkey quill

The Pink Ghost, a variation of the original Ghost pattern, was originated by Paul Rossman.

RED WING or RED-WINGED HERON

Hook	Size 4/0 blind-eye Ron Reinhold Droughtwater Dee
Tag	Narrow silver tinsel
Tail	Fibers of golden pheasant tippet
Body	Light blue and rich claret mohair, equal parts
Ribs	Broad flat silver tinsel and silver twist
Hackle	Gray heron hackle, substitute with gray Spey feather
Shoulder	Teal, sparely tied
Wings	Dark brown turkey strips
Cheeks	Jungle cock

The Red Wing is included in William Murdoch's "Spring Flies for the Dee" in the March 14, 1895, issue of *The Fishing Gazette*.

SPECKLE DEE

Hook	Size 6/0 blind-eye long Dee
Tip	Fine oval silver tinsel
Tag	Orange silk
Tail	Golden pheasant crest
Butt	Peacock herl
Body	Orange silk, orange seal fur, magenta seal fur, and purple seal fur in equal sections
Ribs	Embossed silver and oval silver tinsel
Body hackle	Speckled bustard
Throat	Dyed magenta guinea fowl
Wings	Two strips of argus quill
Sides	Jungle cock

The Speckle Dee is a modern Dee pattern, originated by Derl Stovall of Madras, Oregon. Its unique feature is the speckled bustard body hackle.

TARTAN

Hook	Size 4/0 blind-eye Ron Reinhold Droughtwater Dee
Tag	Gold tinsel
Tail	Red rump feather from a golden pheasant
Body	Half orange pig's wool and half scarlet pig's wool, dressed thin
Rib	Broad gold tinsel
Hackle	Natural red cock hackle with gray heron hackle over, left full at the throat
Throat	Teal
Wings	Two long strips of silver-gray turkey, finely mottled

The Tartan is included in Francis Francis's *A Book on Angling*. He says that this fly was originated by Mr. Brown.

The early Dees were tied with pig's wool or mohair, but during George Kelson's time, tiers' favorite fly-body fur became seal fur. The Tartan is an early Dee pattern but probably not as old as the Gled Wing, since the Tartan wing is made with turkey tail and the earliest Dee patterns called for gled wing.

THUNDER AND LIGHTNING

Hook	Size 6, 45mm treble Waddington shank
Tag	Fine oval gold tinsel and yellow silk, dressed on treble hook
Butt	Black ostrich herl, also dressed on treble hook
Body	Black silk
Ribs	Flat gold tinsel and oval gold tinsel
Body hackle	Bright orange hackle
Wing	Black heron hackle wound as collar
Throat	Blue dyed guinea fowl
Head	Black thread

The Thunder and Lightning is included in Poul Jorgensen's 1978 book, *Salmon Flies*. The original pattern was created by James Wright, an expert Tweed tier. Dee patterns take on a different look when tied on Waddington shanks, but many of the Dee patterns can be converted to this style of fly. I have dressed many of the Dee patterns like this for fishing in Russia. The Akroyd tied in this style is my favorite. A great book about Waddington and tube-fly dressings is *Tube and Waddington Fly Dressings* by Kenichiro Sawada.

TIGER BLUE

Hook	Size 3/0 long blind-eye Dee
Tag	Oval copper tinsel and light blue silk
Tail	Golden pheasant crest and Indian crow
Body	Three equal sections of dark blue, medium blue, and rust-colored seal fur
Ribs	Double embossed copper tinsel
Hackle	Tiger heron, substitute hybrid pheasant hackle
Throat	Teal
Wing	Hybrid pheasant tail
Sides	Jungle cock, drooping

The Tiger Blue is a pattern by Paul Rossman. He designed it for John Kilmer using some of the hybrid feathers he is developing.

TRI-COLOR

Hook	Size 4/0 long blind-eye Dee, Eugene Sunday
Tag	Silver twist
Tail	Red breast feather of the golden pheasant
Body	Yellow, light blue, and scarlet seal fur
Ribs	Silver lace and flat silver tinsel
Hackle	Natural gray heron, from blue seal fur, or substitute
Throat	Widgeon or teal
Wings	Two strips of plain cinnamon turkey

The Tri-Color is included in George Kelson's *The Salmon Fly*. Kelson mentions that this pattern is a standard on the Dee, and when dressed with a red breast hackle from a golden pheasant for the throat and wings of white, the fly is known as the Killer.

He doesn't mention who originated it, but by its style and the colors and the use of red golden pheasant hackle for the tail and throat, it must be Mr. Brown or Mr. Garden of Aberdeen. The golden pheasant in the tail and body of multi-colored seal fur and turkey wing are the same style of these early Dee tiers.

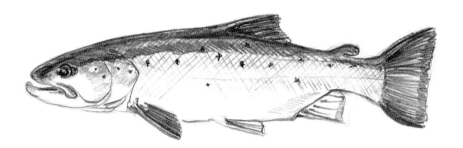

CHAPTER 5

River Don Patterns

RIVER DON FLIES ARE SIMILAR TO DEE PATTERNS but not as large, according to Francis Francis. The gled wings and tartans are standard flies on the River Don, varied by using brown or gray mallard wings. It is thought that they are a mix of Dee flies and the patterns used on the Spey with their wings of bronze mallard. Francis discusses six patterns by number, which were summer patterns, so they were tied smaller and sparser.

For hooks to tie River Don patterns, the modern hooks by Partridge, Alec Jackson, and Bob Veverka work well. Size should range from 2 to 2/0.

Number 1

Hook	Size 2/0 blind-eye Ron Reinhold
Tag	Silver tinsel
Tail	A few fibers of golden pheasant's rump and a small tuft of yellow crewel
Butt	Black ostrich herl
Body	Black pig's wool
Rib	Silver twist
Hackle	Black
Throat	Jay
Wings	Gled or dun turkey strips

Number 2

Hook	Size 2/0 blind-eye Ron Reinhold
Tag	Silver tinsel
Tail	A few fibers of gold pheasant's rump and a small tuft of yellow crewel
Butt	Black ostrich herl
Body	Two-fifths dark red pig's wool, three-fifths dark blue pig's wool
Rib	Silver twist
Hackle	Light blue at shoulder with grouse hackle over
Wings	Strips of red (cinnamon) dun turkey tail feather speckled with black

Number 3

Hook	Size 2/0 blind-eye Ron Reinhold
Tag	Gold tinsel
Tail	Tuft of orange crewel
Body	Two-thirds orange pig's wool, one-third black pig's wool
Rib	Narrow gold tinsel
Hackle	Halfway down, large cochy-bondu hackle with a well-marked center, also serves as throat
Wings	Strips of gray mallard with brownish points (bronze mallard)

Number 4

Hook	Size 2/0 blind-eye Ron Reinhold
Tail	A few fibers of golden pheasant's rump
Body	Half yellow pig's wool, half medium red pig's wool
Rib	Gold twist
Hackle	Halfway down, small black heron hackle fiber just long enough to cover point and bard, also serves as the throat
Wings	Bronze mallard

Number 5

Hook	Size 2/0 blind-eye Ron Reinhold
Tail	Small topping
Body	Purple-claret pig's wool
Rib	Silver twist
Hackle	Black heron dressed spare and only at the shoulder but longer in fiber than the bend of the hook, substitute with black Spey hackle
Wings	Two strips of gled or red turkey

Number 6

Hook	Size 2/0 blind-eye Ron Reinhold
Tag	Gold tinsel
Tail	Small bit of topping
Body	Brown-orange mohair
Rib	Gold tinsel
Hackle	Blue heron hackle, fibers should extend to the bend of the hook, substitute with gray Spey hackle
Wings	Two strips of bright speckled gray turkey

Francis Francis credits these patterns to Mr. Brown of Aberdeen. Brown ran a tackle shop there and is credited with several of the early Spey and Dee patterns. He is also credited with many of the summer patterns used on the Dee, including Jockie and Logie and Jeannie.

CHAPTER 6

Eagle Patterns

THE EAGLE PATTERNS ARE A SMALL GROUP OF flies set apart from other styles because of the eagle feather body hackles. The hackles were taken from the shin of the bird, had a marabou-like texture, and were used in their natural color or dyed yellow. Eagle patterns were used early or late in the season when the water was cold or slightly off-color.

The patterns were similar to Dee patterns; they were dressed on large hooks, the bodies were mohair or seal fur, and the wings were strips put on in the Dee fashion. Some later patterns had wings similar to full-dressed flies with married sections and tails and toppings of golden pheasant crests.

Many steelheaders from the Northwest tie similar patterns, simply called Marabous, for winter steelhead. They have long, mobile, marabou hackles dyed hot oranges and reds collared on the front of the fly. Many were developed and fished for early-run steelhead on the Skagit River. They are series of patterns tied for a specific river under certain river conditions, so perhaps a better name would be the Steelhead Eagles.

Contemporary fly tiers that want to tie eagle patterns can use hooks made by Partridge in size 2/0 or larger. For body hackles, use large marabou plumes, but look for hackles that have a fine stem. Hackles can be stripped on one side for a less bulky fly. A good modern substitute for the body hackle is mottled turkey marabou in its natural color. The colors and shades of the natural hackles range from off-white to gray, tan, and brown, and many have speckling or splashes that add to their appearance and are almost identical to the original material.

Wings can be tied with turkey quills or other large quills such as argus pheasant, peacock wing quills, and bustard quills. Heads on the original flies were tied with black thread.

The first eagles were tied by Mr. Brown of Aberdeen, as per Francis Francis in the 1867 *A Book on Angling*. Kelson includes a few more patterns in his book, and one of his favorites was the Quilled Eagle. To view some truly beautiful antique eagle patterns, see Joseph D. Bates, Jr., and Pamela Bates Richards's *Fishing Atlantic Salmon*.

AVON EAGLE

Hook	Size 6/0 return-eye double antique
Tag	Silver tinsel
Tail	Topping and tip of golden pheasant breast feather, best side under
Body	Lemon, bright orange, scarlet, and fiery brown seal fur in equal sections, dressed sparsely
Ribs	Broad silver tinsel and twist
Hackle	Eagle hackle (one side stripped) dyed yellow, substitute with yellow marabou hackle
Throat	Widgeon
Wings	A pair of golden pheasant sword feathers (back to back)
Sides	Jungle cock and two or three toppings

The Avon Eagle is a pattern from Pryce-Tannatt's 1914 book, *How to Dress Salmon Flies*. It does not appear in Kelson or earlier books. Joseph D. Bates, Jr., and Pamela Bates Richards's 1996 book, *Fishing Atlantic Salmon*, has beautiful examples of antique Avon Eagles. The originator of the pattern is a mystery. This is one of my favorite Eagle patterns.

BROWN EAGLE

Hook	Size 4/0 blind-eye custom Andrew J. Sobota
Tag	Silver twist and light blue floss
Tail	Green parrot, summer duck (wood duck), and fibers of tippet
Butt	Black herl
Body	Two turns of light brown floss, remainder orange seal fur
Rib	Oval gold tinsel
Hackle	Dark gray down of the golden eagle, from light brown silk, substitute gray marabou hackle
Shoulder	Teal flank
Wings	Strips of dark brown turkey feather with white tip
Horns	Red macaw

The Brown Eagle is a pattern I found in the November 6, 1895, issue of *The Fishing Gazette*.

FLOODTIDE

Hook	Size 4/0 blind eye
Tag	Fine oval silver tinsel and crimson silk
Tail	Topping and summer duck
Butt	Black herl
Body	Canary, yellow, dark orange, and crimson seal fur
Ribs	Flat and oval silver tinsel
Hackle	Dark orange yellow eagle, substitute with yellow marabou
Throat	Two turns guinea fowl dyed crimson
Wings	Two golden pheasant sword feathers (back to back), enveloping two extended jungle cock (back to back), bustard, Amherst pheasant tail, swan dyed yellow and crimson, and a topping
Cheeks	Jungle cock

The Floodtide was originated by George Kelson and is included in his book, *The Salmon Fly*. Kelson says that this is one of the best standards for use "on the top of a flood." For spring fishing he dresses the body with pig's wool, and for clear water he dresses it in a smaller size and uses a hen pheasant hackle dyed yellow instead of eagle.

I find similarities between this fly and the Black Dog—this pattern has an almost identical wing and is tied in the same style. Kelson broke with the norm and chose Amherst pheasant tail for the wing. Other patterns credited to Kelson that use Amherst are the Pearl, Prince's Mixture, and the Queen of Spring.

GOLDEN EAGLE

Hook	Size 3/0 long blind-eye Dee, Partridge
Tag	Gold twist and gold silk
Tail	Tippet in strands
Body	Gold and fiery brown pig's wool, divided equally
Rib	Gold tinsel
Hackle	Eagle hackle dyed gold, over one third of body, substitute with golden dyed marabou hackle
Throat	Teal flank
Wings	Two strips of silver mottled turkey

The Golden Eagle is included in George Kelson's book, *The Salmon Fly*. Kelson writes that it is a standard at Ringwood. This is a very handsome pattern with a golden hackle and silver mottled wings. This is an interesting pattern for a turkey quill wing—its light appearance with splashed markings make it a natural choice for Eagle and Dee patterns.

GRAY EAGLE

Hook	Size 6/0 return-eye double antique
Tag	Silver twist
Tail	Red breast feather of the golden pheasant
Body	Yellow, light blue, and scarlet seal fur
Ribs	Silver lace and flat silver tinsel
Hackle	Gray eagle from blue fur, substitute with gray mottled marabou hackle
Throat	Widgeon (teal for large patterns)
Wings	Two strips of brown mottled turkey feather with black bars and white points

Mr. Brown of Aberdeen is credited with originating the Gray and the Yellow Eagle. It is in Francis Francis's 1867 *A Book on Angling* and in George Kelson's *The Salmon Fly*. It is one of the earliest eagle patterns, if not the first.

NIGHTSHADE

Hook	Size 2/0 return-eye Partridge Bartleet Traditional Salmon Fly
Tag	Silver twist and pink silk
Tail	Orange toucan and red toucan
Butt	Black ostrich herl
Body	Light red–orange and dark red–orange pig's wool
Rib	Oval silver tinsel
Body hackle	Small eagle hackle or hen pheasant hackle dyed dark red–orange
Throat	Black partridge, gray speckled
Wings	Two strips of black-and-white mottled turkey

The Nightshade was originated by George Kelson and is included in his book, *The Salmon Fly*. He mentions that it is a good late-evening fly.

QUILLED EAGLE

Hook	Size 4/0 blind-eye Eugene Sunday
Tag	Silver twist and quill dyed yellow
Tail	Topping, two strands of peacock herl (sword feathers), bustard, and ibis
Butt	Black herl
Body	Quill dyed yellow, leaving space for four turns of orange seal fur at the throat
Rib	Oval silver tinsel
Hackle	Gray eagle hackle from center, substitute with gray mottled marabou hackle
Throat	Guinea fowl
Wings	Two tippets (back to back) veiled with extending jungle cock, a strip of ibis, bustard, and topping
Sides	Jungle cock (to center of former pair)

The Quilled Eagle was originated by George Kelson and is included in his book, *The Salmon Fly*. He mentions that this is one of his favorite patterns and he rarely uses any other eagle pattern. He also says that he sometimes ties it with an eagle hackle dyed yellow.

This is a brilliant-looking fly with a fluffy hackle, married wing, and unique body material of quill dyed yellow.

SCARLET EAGLE

Hook	Size 4 blind-eye Ron Reinhold Phillips
Tag	Flat silver tinsel
Tail	Golden pheasant crest veiled with Indian crow
Body	Three equal sections of yellow, red, and purple seal fur
Ribs	Flat and oval silver tinsel
Body hackle	Turkey marabou, mottled, dyed scarlet
Throat	Guinea fowl dyed red
Wing	Peacock wing quill dyed red
Horns	Red macaw

The Scarlet Eagle was designed by me. First it was dressed as a steelhead marabou pattern and tied in the style of the original Atlantic-salmon eagle patterns of long ago.

SPECKLED EAGLE

Hook	Size 2/0 antique long Dee
Tag	Flat silver tinsel
Tail	Golden pheasant crest and Indian crow veil
Body	Orange and claret seal fur
Ribs	Flat silver and oval gold tinsel
Hackle	Mottled turkey marabou
Throat	Speckled bustard hackle, from the neck
Wings	Speckled bustard quill with white tips

The Speckled Eagle is a pattern tied in the eagle tradition with a soft marabou body hackle of mottled turkey marabou and speckled bustard hackle for the throat.

YELLOW EAGLE

Hook	Size 6/0 return-eye double antique
Tag	Silver twist
Tail	Red breast feather from the golden pheasant
Body	Yellow, scarlet, and light blue seal fur
Ribs	Silver lace and flat silver tinsel
Hackle	Eagle hackle dyed yellow, from scarlet seal fur, substitute with yellow marabou hackle
Throat	Widgeon or teal flank
Wings	Two strips of gray mottled turkey tail with black bars and white points

The Yellow Eagle is a pattern credited to Mr. Brown of Aberdeen, as Francis Francis mentions in *A Book on Angling*, and George Kelson in *The Salmon Fly*. This is a very early eagle pattern and a standard on many rivers in the early spring or high-water conditions. The Gray and the Yellow Eagle were the first two eagle patterns originated.

YELLOW EAGLE (Halladale)

Hook	Size 8/0 blind-eye Eugene Sunday
Tag	Silver twist and yellow silk
Tail	Topping, widgeon, and green and red parrot
Butt	Black herl
Body	Three-fifths light yellow seal fur, two-fifths red-orange seal fur, well picked out
Ribs	Double oval silver tinsel
Hackle	Eagle hackle dyed yellow, from red-orange fur, substitute with yellow marabou
Throat	Guinea fowl
Wing	Two tippets extending to tag; red and yellow swan and golden pheasant tail; jungle cock on either side, full length of wing; gold-colored mohair on top; and topping over all
Cheeks	Jungle cock

The Halladale Yellow Eagle is a pattern that appears in the November 6, 1895, issue of *The Fishing Gazette*. It was also included in John James Hardy's 1907 book, *Salmon Fishing*.

CHAPTER 7

Spey-Type Patterns

NY NUMBER OF PATTERNS CAN BE CONVERTED TO Spey and Dee patterns by adding long body hackles. The following patterns are not listed as Spey or Dee patterns, but many display the long body hackles similar to Spey and Dee patterns. The patterns listed below contain all types of wings not commonly found on Spey patterns, from clumps of peacock herl to more complex married wings. Some of the patterns are very early salmon patterns and, I speculate, the fore-runners of some of the Spey and Dee patterns.

BEAULY SNOW FLY

Hook	Size 2 or 6, 45mm treble Waddington shank
Body	Very light blue pig's wool, rather sparsely dressed, substitute with seal fur
Ribs	Flat silver tinsel with gold twist
Hackle	Black heron hackle, long in fiber (should extend beyond hook bend), substitute with black Spey hackle
Wing	Large bunch of bronze peacock herl
Collar	Ruff of bright orange mohair

The Beauly Snow fly is named for the River Beauly and was originated by Mr. Snowie of Iverness, an expert on salmon flies. It was tied on very large, long-shank single hooks. Francis Francis mentions that, as long as the melting snow and ice lasts on the Beauly, there is no other fly that can compete with it. This is a striking pattern set off by its collar of bright orange mohair.

BLACK CREEPER

Hook	Size 4/0 low-water blind-eye Partridge
Tag	Silver twist and light blue silk
Tail	Ibis and powered blue macaw mixed in strands
Butt	Section 1. Hackle, black Spey hackle, cheeked with chatterer body, black chenille. Section 2. Black Spey hackle in center of body and cheeked as before. Section 3. Black Spey hackle, larger than before, and cheeked as before.

The Black Creeper is actually a grub pattern, but by adding longer body hackles it becomes a Spey-type fly. It is included in George Kelson's 1895 book, *The Salmon Fly*. It was also originated by him and is one of the many grub patterns that he listed and originated.

BLACK DOG (Original)

Hook	Size 3 blind-eye Ron Reinhold Noble P
Wings	Bluish feathers from a heron wing, intermixed with spotted reddish turkey tail feathers
Body	Lead-colored pig's wool
Rib	Small gold twist
Throat and hackle	Large black cock hackle
Head	Dark green mohair

The original Black Dog is in Alexander Mackintosh's 1808 book, *The Driffield Angler*. This early pattern was tied in the Dee fashion (with a long body or throat hackle) and used heron wing quill for a more complex wing. This pattern was either the forerunner of the Dee patterns or copied from Dee patterns in use at the time. It was changed into a more elaborate full-dressed pattern that was used on the Tay, as Francis Francis mentions in his 1867 *A Book on Angling*.

BLACK DOG (Tay Fly)

Hook	Size 3/0 to 5/0 blind-eye long Dee
Tag	Silver twist and canary silk
Tail	Topping and ibis
Butt	Black herl
Body	Black silk
Ribs	Yellow silk and oval silver twist running on each side
Hackle	Black heron or substitute from third turn of tinsel
Wings	Two red-orange hackles (back to back), enveloped by two long jungle cock, unbarred summer duck (wood duck), light bustard, Amherst tail, swan dyed scarlet and yellow, and two toppings

The original Black Dog is an old pattern that was at one time a simple strip wing, as Alexander Mackintosh mentions in his 1808 book, *The Driffield Angler*. This dressing of the Black Dog is included in George Kelson's 1895 book, *The Salmon Fly*. Kelson mentions that it is his father's old favorite, useful on high water on the Spey and Wye.

The fly pattern is also included in Francis Francis's 1867 *A Book on Angling*. Francis recommends it for the Tay, and he thought it was similar to many other Tay flies that have undergone changes. Francis Francis's pattern calls for red silk for the body and a long-fibered claret hackle. He says that it must be a dyed heron hackle. Francis Francis lists the Black Dog under flies used for the Tay River. The Spring flies used on the Tay are the largest size, he says, and they have undergone a thorough revolution. Francis mentions a Mr. Paton of Perth who is an authority on such matters. He remarks that even the Wasps and Black Dog, standard flies since the time of the oldest inhabitant, have changed. All the old plain wings, the long slips of dun turkey, have disappeared, and in their place are mixed wings with jungle cock, wood duck, and toppings.

We will never know for sure who converted the old standard Black Dog to a mixed-wing fly, but its wing is very similar to the Floodtide originated by Kelson. Most flies from this time period that used Amherst pheasant in the wing were originated by Kelson.

I also found a dressing for the Black Dog in *The Fishing Gazette*, dated December 7, 1895. It is the same pattern as described above with the following changes: It is ribbed with silver and gold oval tinsel with orange silk in between. The wing is bronze peacock herl, silver gray turkey, bustard, pintail, teal, wood duck, and mallard and swan feathers dyed red, yellow, and blue. It also uses jungle cock, golden pheasant crest, and horns of blue and gold macaw.

This was one of Syd Glasso's favorite patterns.

Spey Fly Conversions from George Kelson's *The Salmon Fly*, 1895, Veverka

Black Creeper	Ghost
Purple Ghost	Silver Spectre
Copper Caroline	

These patterns from *The Salmon Fly* have been converted to a Spey-style fly. Almost any pattern can be converted to a Spey fly by using longer-fibered hackles. Kelson himself changed the hackle type on certain patterns depending on the type of water he was fishing or the action he desired.

The Black Creeper is a grub pattern and was a natural choice for a Spey fly because it has a bold, dark silhouette and three body hackles. The Ghost and the Purple Ghost are basically the same pattern dressed in different colors. The original pattern, the Ghost, was already a slenderly tied fly, so by changing to a longer-fibered body hackle, it took on the look of a Spey fly. The Silver Spectre was a fly used in what Kelson described as flaked water, similar to the water that the Beauly Snow fly was developed for. Both have wings of peacock herl, but using a long throat hackle transforms the Silver Spectre into a Spey-style fly. The Copper Caroline is the same pattern as the original Lady Caroline but uses copper tinsel for the ribs

CAPTAIN WALTON

Hook	Size 4/0 blind-eye long shank, Pryce-Tannatt
Tag	Silver twist, cream and crimson silk
Tail	Ibis, powdered blue macaw, tippet, and peacock wing in strands
Butt	Black herl
Body	Claret silk, two turns, dark blue seal fur and black seal fur
Ribs	Flat and oval silver tinsel
Body hackle	Black heron from blue seal fur
Throat	Guinea fowl
Wings	Peacock wing dyed claret, blue macaw, red macaw, and teal in strands, golden pheasant tail, guinea fowl, and mallard
Sides	Jungle cock
Cheeks	Indian crow
Topping	Golden pheasant crest
Head	Black herl

The Captain Walton is a pattern tied with a Spey-type hackle for the body. George Kelson originated the fly and includes it in his book, *The Salmon Fly*. Kelson mentions that it was used on the Dee, Spey, and Beauly Rivers.

DUN WING

Hook	Size 2/0 blind-eye Eugene Sunday
Tail	Golden pheasant topping and sprigs of tippet
Body	Light orange, red-claret, and darkish blue and black pig's wool
Rib	Broad silver tinsel
Hackle	Black from red wool
Wings	Two strips of dun-brown turkey tail

The Dun Wing is an old Scottish pattern that was used on the River Tweed, according to Francis Francis's *A Book on Angling*. He mentions that it is a favorite on the Kirkcudbrightshire Dee, and when dressed on long large hooks, it is a good Tay fly. Francis directs the reader to *River Angling*, the capital work by John Younger, for information on the River Tweed. In the book, every water and cast on the Tweed is named and described.

Francis mentions that this fly was tied by James Wright of Sprouston, a first-rate artist. Wright would later start the move from drab flies to more gaudy flies. He originated the Black Ranger, Thunder and Lightning, Silver Gray, and some of the well-known classics of his time.

This pattern, along with the Toppy and other early fly patterns that were used on the Tweed, were the forerunners for flies copied from the Spey and Dee patterns. The style used to tie on the wings is the same.

ETHEL

Hook	Size 2/0 return-eye Partridge Traditional Salmon Fly
Tag	Gold twist and light yellow silk
Tail	Summer duck
Butt	Black herl
Body	Section 1. Light yellow silk, ribbed with fine silver tinsel, and butted with toucan, above and below, and black herl. Section 2. Red silk, ribbed with gold tinsel.
Throat	Black heron, substitute with black Spey feather
Wings	Two snipes (back to back) for underwing, veiled with peacock herl
Horns	Blue macaw
Head	Black herl

The Ethel is included in George Kelson's book, *The Salmon Fly*. It was originated by Mr. Turnbull, and Kelson mentions that it was a good fly on the Usk. Turnbull originated several patterns with long Spey hackles. It is in the class of Spey-type flies because of its black heron throat.

FITZGIBBON Number 2 (Carron)

Hook	Size 4 blind-eye Ron Reinhold Phillips
Tag	Silver tinsel, orange silk, and black ostrich
Tail	Two fibers of bustard
Body	Black floss silk
Rib	Silver twist
Body hackle	Black heron, or substitute
Wings	Bustard, peafowl, silver pheasant, and teal feathers
Horns	Blue and yellow macaw
Head	Black thread

The Fitzgibbon Number 2 is included in Edward Fitzgibbon's *The Book of the Salmon*. He mentions that it was used on the River Carron.

HIGHLAND GEM

Hook	Size 2/0, 3/0 blind-eye Ron Reinhold Brittannia
Tag	Silver twist and yellow silk
Tail	Ibis and summer duck topping
Butt	Black herl
Body	Section 1. Yellow silk, ribbed with narrow oval silver tinsel, and butted with golden bird of paradise or toucan above and below, and black herl. Section 2. Blue silk ribbed as before alongside broad, flat silver tinsel.
Hackle	Black heron over blue silk, or substitute
Throat	Guinea fowl
Wings	Amherst pheasant strips and three toppings
Horns	Black cockatoo, tail

The Highland Gem is a pattern that George Kelson originated, and it is included in his book, *The Salmon Fly*. He states that it is an excellent spring pattern on the Spey.

This is another pattern similar to Kelson's Black Dog and Floodtide, patterns tied in the Spey style with a long body hackle but with a more complex wing, which Kelson was known for. He used Amherst tail in the wings of his flies, which was unique as not many flies of that time used that material. He mentions in his book that his friend, Mr. George Horne of Hereford, raised golden and Amherst pheasants, so we know he had access to those materials. The horns in the original call for black cockatoo, but a good substitute is Amherst tail dyed red.

IKE DEAN

Hook	Size 3/0 long blind-eye Dee
Tag	Silver tinsel and pink silk
Tail	Golden pheasant crest
Butt	Blue chatterer wound as a hackle
Body	Section 1. Oval silver tinsel, veiled with golden bird of paradise. Section 2. Black silk ribbed with silver lace.
Hackle	Black heron over black silk, or substitute
Wing	Gray mallard, golden pheasant tail, blue and yellow swan, and two strips cinnamon turkey
Topping	Golden pheasant crest

The Ike Dean is included in George Kelson's book, *The Salmon Fly*. The original name for this fly was Ich Dien, and it was introduced on the Lochy by Kelson's father. It was one of the first fancy flies and became very popular a few years before the advent of the Butcher. The singular success attained on the upper pools of this river by the guide named Ike Dean led to the general use of the pattern on other rivers in Scotland, where the fly is known only by the name Ich Dien.

LORD JAMES MURRAY

Hook	Size 3/0 blind-eye Eugene Sunday
Tag	Silver twist and orange silk
Tail	Golden pheasant crest and kingfisher
Butt	Black ostrich herl
Body	Black silk
Rib	Silver tinsel and silver twist
Hackle	Black hackle
Shoulder	Black heron with orange hackle over, substitute with black Spey feather
Wings	Underwing, tippets; overwing wood duck, golden pheasant tail, pintail, mallard, bustard, and green and red swan
Head	Black thread

The Lord James Murray is included in Francis Francis's *A Book on Angling* and was used on the Tay. Many of the Tay flies were tied with heron hackles and had wings similar to the full-dressed patterns.

MCINTYRE

Hook	Size 3/0 blind-eye Partridge
Tag	Silver tinsel and golden yellow silk
Tail	Golden pheasant crest and Indian crow
Butt	Black ostrich herl
Body	Three turns of orange silk and four turns each of red, dark orange, red, and light blue seal fur
Rib	Silver tinsel
Hackle	Magenta hackle
Throat	Pale blue and black heron hackles
Wings	Two jungle cock enveloped by two tippets, golden pheasant tail, bustard, peacock wing, yellow, red, and blue swan, bronze mallard, and a topping
Cheeks	Chatterer
Horns	Red and blue macaw
Head	Black thread

The Mcintyre is included in John James Hardy's 1907 book, *Salmon Fishing*.

NIAGARA

Hook	Size 6/0 blind-eye Eugene Sunday
Tag	Gold twist and black silk
Tail	Two long strands of Amherst pheasant
Butt	Black herl
Body	Section 1. Yellow thread butted with yellow hackle. Section 2. Pea-green thread butted with pea-green hackle. Section 3. Red thread butted with red hackle. Section 4. Dark blue thread.
Ribs	First three sections, gold tinsel, fine oval; silver fine oval over dark blue
Throat	Dark orange hackle and black heron, or substitute
Wings	Two natural black saddle hackles back to back, veiled with teal, bustard, golden turkey, and mallard
Sides	Summer duck (wood duck)
Topping	Golden pheasant crest
Horns	Red macaw
Head	Red wool

The Niagara is included in George Kelson's book, *The Salmon Fly*. It was originated by Mr. Turnbull and is a Spey-like pattern with a throat of black heron hackle.

SILVER ARDEA

Hook	Size 4/0 blind-eye Ron Reinhold Jock Scott stout
Tag	Silver twist and yellow silk
Tail	Golden bird of paradise (three)
Body	Flat silver tinsel
Rib	Oval silver tinsel
Hackle	Bright red-claret thread
Throat	White heron, dyed light blue, or substitute
Wings	Mixed, peacock wing, bustard, golden pheasant tail, Amherst pheasant tail, black-and-white mottled turkey, red macaw, and dyed yellow and blue swan
Topping	Golden pheasant crest
Sides	Jungle cock
Head	Black herl

The Silver Ardea is included in George Kelson's book, *The Salmon Fly*. He mentions that this is the only standard pattern with extralong hackles over a silver tinsel body. The Black Ardea is a variation—the body is black silk instead of silver tinsel.

SILVER SPECTRE

Hook	Size 2/0 return-eye Partridge Traditional Salmon Fly
Tag	Oval silver tinsel
Tail	Red macaw (hackle strips) enveloped in two strips of summer duck (wood duck)
Body	Flat silver tinsel
Rib	Oval silver tinsel
Hackles	Section 1. Jay and black herl at butt. Section 2. Red macaw butted with black herl at center. Section 3. Black hackle at throat.
Wings	Copper peacock herl
Cheeks	Blue chatterer
Horns	Black cockatoo tail
Head	Black herl

The Silver Spectre is a pattern originated by George Kelson, which he includes in his book, *The Salmon Fly*. He states that it is his favorite for flaked water. I like to tie this fly with a long black Spey hackle for the throat, making it into a Spey-type fly. It is similar to the Snow fly with its peacock herl wing but with a more complex and colorful body and various colored hackles. This is a beautiful fly tied in small sizes.

SIR RICHARD

Hook	Size 6 treble Waddington shank
Tag	Silver thread and orange silk
Tail	Topping and Indian crow
Butt	Black herl
Body	Black silk
Ribs	Flat silver tinsel and fine oval silver tinsel
Hackle	Black heron, substitute with black Spey hackle
Throat	Speckled guinea fowl
Wings	Scarlet, orange, and blue swan, bustard, florican, mottled gray turkey, and golden pheasant tail; short strip of speckled guinea fowl on sides of wing
Cheeks	Blue chatterer
Topping	Golden pheasant crest
Horns	Blue and yellow macaw

The Sir Richard is included in Pryce-Tannatt's 1914 book, *How to Dress Salmon Flies*. He mentions that small flies are tied with a black body hackle and larger sizes are tied with black heron for the body hackle.

This pattern is also included in George Kelson's *The Salmon Fly*. Kelson adds jay in addition to the throat, and the wing is different: dark mottled turkey, golden pheasant tail, peacock wing, parrot, ibis, and bronze mallard. The rest of the fly is the same. Kelson mentions that it is a useful standard on any river.

SPRING FLY (Bainbridge)

Hook	Size 4 blind-eye Ron Reinhold Noble P
Body	Orange silk
Rib	Broad gold twist
Body hackle	Smokey dun
Wing	Dark mottled-brown feather from a bittern

The Spring fly is described in George Bainbridge's 1816 book, *The Fly Fishers Guide*. Bainbridge's book is the first to show plates of salmon flies. He includes the Spring, Summer, Quaker, Wasp, and Gaudy flies, very early patterns that long remained standards. Their style is similar to that of the early Spey and Dee patterns.

STEELHEAD DOG

Hook	Size 2/0 blind-eye antique long Dee, Phillips
Tag	Silver tinsel and red silk
Tail	Golden pheasant crest and Indian crow
Butt	Black ostrich herl
Body	Section 1. Oval silver tinsel, veiled with Indian crow top and bottom, and black ostrich herl. Section 2. Purple silk ribbed with oval gold tinsel.
Body hackle	Black Spey hackle
Throat	Orange hackle
Wings	Underwing, jungle cock, golden pheasant tail, and orange goose
Sides	Jungle cock
Topping	Golden pheasant crest
Head	Black thread

The Steelhead Dog is a fly that was originated by me in the tradition of the Black Dog Atlantic-salmon pattern. It is my version of a full-dressed steelhead fly.

SUMMER FLY (Bainbridge)

Hook	Size 5 blind-eye Ron Reinhold Phillips
Tail	Mottled feather from the drake and a little floss
Body	Dark sable thread
Rib	Gold wire
Body hackle	Dusky red hackle, thickly wound
Wing	Cormorant, or the mottled feather from a mallard, very dark (bronze mallard)

The Summer fly is described in George Bainbridge's book, *The Fly Fishers Guide*, the first book to have illustrated plates of salmon flies.

TOPPY

Hook	Size 4 blind-eye Ron Reinhold Phillips
Tag	Crimson silk or mohair
Tail	Yellow mohair
Butt	Two turns of red hackle
Body	Black pig's wool or bullock's hair
Rib	Gold or silver tinsel
Hackle	Black hackle on body and throat, substitute with black Spey hackle
Wings	Two strips of black turkey with white tips
Head	Crimson mohair

The Toppy is an early Tweed fly. A fly similar to the Toppy is in John Kirkbridge's 1837 book, *The Northern Angler*, and John Younger's 1840 book, *River Angling for Trout and Salmon*. Younger listed this fly by number, but surely it was the Toppy or his version of the pattern. William Scrope names the pattern in his 1843 book, *Days and Nights of Salmon Fishing on the Tweed*, and makes the fly famous. It is also included in Edward Fitzgibbon's 1850 book, *The Book of the Salmon*, and is pictured in the plates.

Francis Francis also includes it in his *A Book on Angling*. He mentions that it is an old noted Tweed fly. George Kelson includes it in *The Salmon Fly* with a tail of toucan and ibis, a butt of claret herl, body, three turns of red-claret silk, butted with a red-claret hackle, and followed by black seal fur.

I feel this pattern is similar to the style of Spey and Dee flies. The wing style is the same, put on one at a time, with strips of turkey, and splayed over the body like a pair of scissor blades.

WASP FLY

Hook	Size 1/0 blind-eye Partridge
Tag	Silver twist and orange yellow silk
Tail	Guinea fowl and black partridge tippet
Butt	Black herl
Body	Yellow and dark blue pig's wool
Rib	Embossed gold tinsel over rear half and silver tinsel over blue pig's wool
Hackle	Golden hackle over yellow, black hackle over blue
Shoulder	Jay
Wings	Two strips of brown speckled turkey tail

The Wasp fly is an old pattern, as George Bainbridge mentions in his 1816 book, *The Fly Fishers Guide*, the first book to contain color prints of salmon flies.

In 1867, the fly appears again in Francis Francis's *A Book on Angling*. Francis also mentions the Claret, Black, and Blue Wasp patterns under flies for the Tay.

This pattern is very similar in color and construction to a later Dee fly, the Akroyd.

WHITE WING

Hook	Size 6 treble Waddington shank
Tag	Silver twist
Tail	Golden pheasant topping and tippet strands
Body	Yellow, orange, claret, and black seal fur
Ribs	Silver lace and flat silver tinsel
Hackle	Natural black from second turn of tinsel, substitute with Spey hackle
Throat	Blue hackle
Wings	Two strips of white swan

The White Wing is included in Francis Francis's *A Book on Angling*. He mentions that it is a good Tweed fly for nighttime fishing. It is also included in George Kelson's book, *The Salmon Fly*. Kelson mentions that this is an old Tweed fly—it was originated by James Wright (1829–1902), who was considered a great fly tier in his day. Other patterns that James Wright originated include the Doctors, Black Ranger, Thunder and Lightning, and the Silver Gray.

WILSON

Hook	Size 2/0 blind-eye Ron Reinhold Phillips
Tag	Silver twist and cream silk
Tail	Two strips of summer duck (wood duck)
Butt	Black herl
Body	Silver tinsel
Rib	Oval gold tinsel
Throat	Vulturine guinea fowl and black heron, or substitute
Wings	Egyptian goose, bustard, silver speckled turkey, gray mallard, and topping
Cheeks	Indian crow and chatterer

The Wilson is included in George Kelson's 1895 book, *The Salmon Fly*. It was originated by Mr. Turnbull and named after Mr. Wilson of Moffat. Kelson mentions that it is a superb killer on most rivers.

CHAPTER 8

Steelhead Spey Patterns

STEELHEAD SPEYS WERE ORIGINATED IN THE PACIFIC Northwest by Syd Glasso of Forks, Washington. Glasso created his series of Spey patterns for the steelhead rivers of the Olympic Peninsula. His flies were inspired and fashioned after the original Atlantic-salmon Spey patterns. He converted the original flies to steelhead patterns by tying them in bright fluorescent colors that attract steelhead. The original Spey patterns were very somber colors; Glasso's steelhead Speys are the punk rockers of Spey-fly patterns. Glasso's flies flowed and had an elegant look to them and were finished off with the smallest, neatest heads.

Glasso only tied on the finest salmon hooks. He looked for hooks with fine return eyes and slightly longer shanks. Low-water salmon hooks fit the bill. The bodies were tied very sparsely with hot orange floss and seal fur. He relied heavily on the original heron body hackle, but on many patterns he dyed the hackles more brilliant colors. He also used many different types of hackles for the throats. (A modern substitute for heron hackle is a blue-eared pheasant hackle.) The wings usually consisted of four hackle tips. For his strip-wing flies he used bronze mallard, widgeon, dyed goose, and heron quill.

His classic ten patterns appeared in Trey Combs's book, *Steelhead Fly Fishing and Flies*. All steelhead Spey flies evolved from these patterns. All were Spey patterns except for two, the Sol Duc and the Sol Duc Dark, which would be considered reduced steelhead classics, fashioned after classic Atlantic-salmon patterns. They were tied with tails and toppings like the classics.

His tying has influenced and inspired many fly tiers, since he started tying Spey patterns in the late 1950s. Other Spey fly tiers influenced by Glasso included Dick Wentworth, Walt Johnson, Pat Crane,

Andy Anderson, and Mark Canfield. They all fished with Glasso and took a liking to the flies he tied and fished. All of the Steelhead Spey patterns originated after this time were influenced by his flies.

After Glasso died, there was a resurgence in the art of tying classic Atlantic-salmon flies and Spey flies for steelhead. The new flies, though, had a different style, sparsely dressed with sleek, low-set wings, that gave the flies a racy look. This too can be attributed to the work done by Glasso.

During the mid- to late-1980s the East and West Coasts were in a classic Atlantic-salmon craze, and many tiers were attempting to tie a flawless salmon fly. In the process, some beautiful patterns were developed. This enthusiasm flowed over into the flies that were tied for steelhead, and many brightly colored, finely tied steelhead patterns emerged as well.

Many anglers tie and fish Spey flies today—they can be found in use on many of the steelhead rivers of the West Coast. And they are catching on for the steelhead of the Great Lakes as well. They have a very fishy look to them, and many anglers are drawn to them for that reason. Orange and black are basic steelhead colors, but many new patterns contain purple, now a highly regarded color among steelhead fly tiers. Purple is as dark as black but has a hint of color.

Many different styles of Speys are used for steelhead: the simple but effective collared patterns such as the Spider series and the Spade patterns tied by Alec Jackson; the marabou series of flies tied by Bob Aid, John Farrar, and George Cook; Randall Kaufmann's series of flies that use marabou hackle for the body hackle, simply called marabou Speys. All of these patterns could be classified as a type of Spey pattern, similar to the original salmon Speys because they have a soft hackle that moves in the water. Other contempo-

Joe Howell Steelhead Speys

Green Butt Spey	Black Vulture
Winter Spey	Golden Eagle
Fontanalis Spey	Snow Queen
Harvest Moon	
	Autumn Spey
North Fork Spey	Silver Streak Spey

Joe Howell lives and fishes along the North Umpqua River in southern Oregon. Howell likes to fish Spey flies in some of the deeper, slower pools with a six-inch strip that pulsates the hackles of a Spey pattern and proves enticing to a wild steelhead. Joe is a true historian on matters concerning steelhead, the fishermen, and the fly tiers who developed the patterns for the North Umpqua River.

rary Spey tiers include Dave McNeese, Steve and Karen Gobin, Joe Howell, Deke Meyer, Bill Chinn, Mark Waslick, and Brad Burden, with new tiers emerging every year.

Steelhead Spey flies should be dressed sparsely; heavily dressed flies are bulky and sink slowly. A Spey fly should sink quickly, get to where the fish are holding, and be ready to fish. The hook should act as a keel for the fly. If dressed too heavily, most won't track properly in the water.

Hooks are the hardest item to find. Some of the old low-water hooks are perfect, but they are rare. Some new hooks that can be used for steelhead Speys are the salmon hooks made by Partridge, Alec Jackson's Spey Fly Hook, and Bob Veverka's Classic Salmon Hook. They are best in sizes 2, 1, and 1/0, although many tiers choose to tie them larger. What I look for in a hook is a fine return eye with a low pitch (a sleeker profile), a straight shank with a slightly longer length, and a straight hook point, preferably with a nice, graceful bend.

Most materials used to tie Speys are readily available—silks, tinsels, furs, and quills—but the hackle for the body is somewhat hard to find. All types of hackles have been used—ring-necked pheasant rump hackles, marabou, duck hackles, and different types of eared pheasant hackles, which prove to be the best in color and fiber length and come close to the original heron material. Herons are water birds, so their feathers' water resistant properties made them a natural choice

for flies. The only difference between heron hackles and the modern substitute is the texture of the feather. Look for blue-eared pheasant hackles with nice thin stems and enough length to wind three or four turns on the fly.

For more examples of steelhead Spey styles, take a look at *Steelhead Fishing and Flies* and *Steelhead* by Trey Combs.

ORANGE HERON

Hook	Size 1, 1/0, 2/0
Tag	Flat silver tinsel
Rib	Flat and oval silver tinsel
Body	Half hot orange flat waxed nylon, half hot orange seal fur or substitute
Body hackle	Gray Spey hackle
Throat	Teal flank
Wings	Four hot orange hackle tips
Head	Red thread

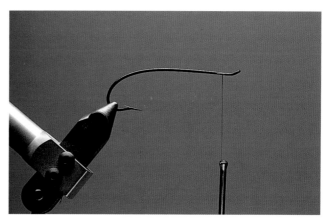

1. Start with a size 1 or 1/0 return-eye salmon hook, and place it in the vise with the shank on a straight horizontal plane. Start the tying thread at the return wire about one-eighth inch back from the eye.

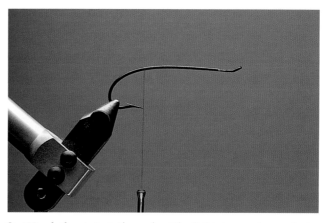

2. Wind the tying thread with tight turns toward the back of the hook, stopping above the hook point.

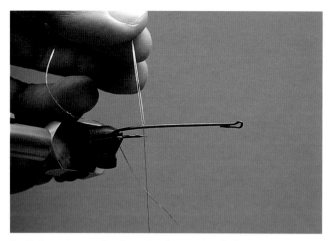

3. Take a strand of oval silver tinsel, loop it on your tying thread, and tie it on the rear of the hook shank.

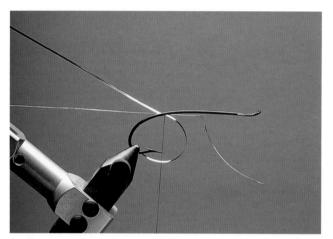

4. Do the same with a strand of flat silver tinsel. Then wind your thread tightly, covering the loose ends of the tinsel toward the center of the fly. Try to keep these wraps as smooth as possible.

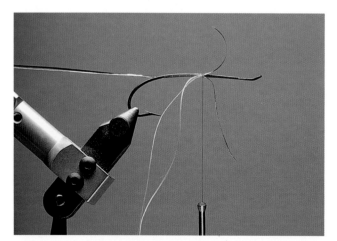

5. With your tying thread at the center of the fly, loop on two fine strands of hot orange silk.

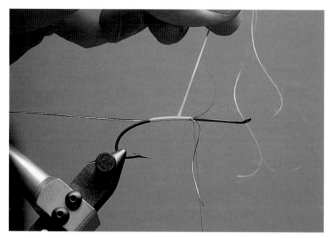

6. Wind the strands of silk toward the back of the hook; then reverse the silk, and wind it forward to the center of the fly. Again, keep this as smooth as possible. Tie off and leave the running ends of the silk on; these will be used for the front section of the body.

7. The body hackle is a blue-eared pheasant hackle in its natural slate-gray color. Prepare the hackle by folding it and tying it on by the tip end of the stem at the center of the fly body. The fibers should flow toward the back of the hook. Wind your tying thread toward the front of the fly, keeping it tight and smooth, and stop where you started just behind the return eye.

8. Twist the hot orange dubbing onto the loose ends of hot orange silk.

9. Wind the silk dubbing toward the eye of the hook and tie it off.

10. Take two turns of the flat silver tinsel on the hook shank behind the hook point and the end of the fly body (this forms the tip of the fly body). Then proceed with the flat tinsel rib toward the eye of the fly, making five evenly spaced turns of tinsel. The third turn of tin-

sel should land just in front of the body hackle stem. Tie off the flat silver tinsel.

Wind the oval tinsel rib tightly behind the flat silver rib and tie it off.

11. Wind the body hackle behind the turns of tinsel, keeping the hackle fibers flowing toward the back of the hook. At the tie-in spot, take one or two more turns of hackle and tie it off. Cut off any remaining stem and fiber.

12. With your thumb and index finger, pinch the hackle fibers and pull them down and toward the back of the hook. This clears the top of the fly of any fibers that would interfere with the wing.

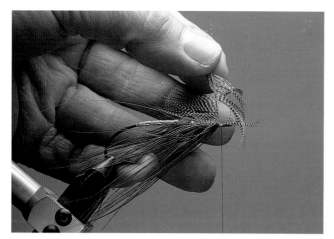

13. Prepare the teal flank feather by folding or doubling the feather. Tie in the folded feather by the tip of the stem with the fibers flowing toward the back.

14. Take one or two turns of hackle for the throat, and tie it off. Cut off the waste ends. As you did with the body hackle, pinch the fibers and pull them down and back toward the rear of the hook. Make sure the top of the fly is cleared of any fibers.

15. I usually take my hackle tips for the wing from Chinese necks, as they have small narrow hackles that fit a fly this size and style. Select two sets of matching hackles from each side of the neck (each set is made up of two hackles). Make sure you select hackles that are the same length and width. Place them back to back, put them up to the fly to size them, and strip off any excess fiber.

16. Tie each set of wings on separately starting with the left wing, the one on the far side of the fly. Put the wing up to the fly and size it to the hook—the wing should not extend past the back or bend of the hook.

The first section of the wing should be tied on the shoulder of the fly, riding low (tenting) the body of the fly.

Hold it in place with your fingertip, take a few turns of thread, and tie it on. Before tying in the next side of the wing, make sure it is in the right position.

17. Take your right wing section, the side closest to you, and repeat step 16.

18. This is the top view of the wing positions. When both wing sections are tied on, they should be low along the body of the fly and tenting it.

If the wings are not sitting correctly, take them off and try again until you get them aligned properly. If they look correct, take some turns of thread to make them secure. Then cut off the waste ends of the stems very neatly.

Side view of wing positions.

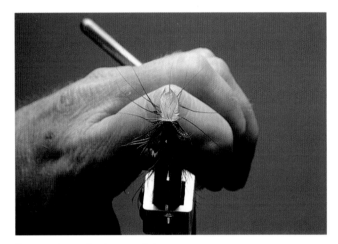

Front view of wing positions.

Form the head of the fly, taking enough turns of thread to cover any of the hackle stems while forming the overall head shape. Then do a whip-finish, and trim the thread. Try to keep the overall size of the head as small as possible, as this is the signature of this style of fly. Add head cement to finish the fly.

Brad Burden Steelhead Speys

Fireant Spey

Golden Demon Spey   Black Gordon Spey

Hot Peacock Spey

Fireplum Spey   Surveyor

Red Wing Spey

Sorcerer   Nighthawk Spey

Raven

Brad Burden is a very talented fly tier from Oregon who has spent years perfecting his fly tying and learning the rivers of Oregon where he fishes for steelhead with Spey rods and flies. Brad likes to include bold contrasting colors and incorporate a strong silhouette into his flies. They are fine examples of today's style of steelhead flies—finely tied, low precisely set wings, and that classic steelhead Spey swept-back look.

AUTUMN SPEY

Hook	Size 3 Alec Jackson Spey Fly Hook
Tag	Flat gold tinsel
Tail	Golden pheasant crest
Butt	White ostrich herl
Body	Fluorescent orange floss
Rib	Fine oval gold tinsel
Body hackle	Blue-eared pheasant hackle
Collar	Natural guinea-fowl hackle
Wings	Two matching slips of white goose quill
Head	Florescent orange Danville 6/0 thread

The Autumn Spey was originated by Joe Howell, who owns and runs the Blue Heron Fly Shop along the banks of the North Umpqua River in southern Oregon. Joe has lived and fished and tied flies all his life along the North Umpqua.

Fishing the river all his life, he has learned many things about it and the fish that run it. Joe knows all the best water and how to fish it. He has developed many fly patterns over the years for the steelhead of the Umpqua, some of which are Spey patterns.

He usually fishes Speys in slower-moving water, with an occasional slow six-inch pull-pause action to impart a little pulse to the long, flowing hackle fibers. He prefers to fish Speys on sinking-tip lines.

BLACK GORDON SPEY

Hook	Size 1 Alec Jackson Spey Fly Hook
Tag	Fine oval silver tinsel
Tail	Dyed red golden pheasant crest
Body	Rear half, red floss; front half, black angora goat
Rib	Fine oval silver tinsel
Body hackle	Long black Spey hackle
Throat	Teal flank
Wing	Two pairs of matched black hackle tips
Head	Black thread

The Black Gordon Spey is one of Brad Burden's variations of the North Umpqua's classic steelhead fly, the Black Gordon. Brad finds that it is very effective with lots of movement and good strong steelhead colors.

It belongs to a series of classic patterns that were converted to Spey flies. The original Black Gordon steelhead pattern was created by Clarence Gordon in the late 1930s for use on the North Umpqua River. He was a well-known, fine fly tier and fly fisherman.

BLACK HERON

Hook	Size 2, 1, or 1/0 low-water salmon
Body	Rear two-thirds, black floss; front third, black seal fur
Ribs	Flat silver tinsel and oval silver tinsel
Hackle	Gray heron or substitute
Throat	Teal flank
Wing	Four matching black hackle tips or two strips of dyed black goose quill
Head	Black thread

This version of the Black Heron was originated by Syd Glasso. Glasso tied two styles of the Black Heron: one with four black hackle tips for the wings, the other with two sections of black wing quill. This is a pattern that appeared in *Flyfishing* magazine (October 1982) in an article written by Walt Johnson.

BLACK AND RED SPEY

Hook	Size 3/0 blind-eye Eugene Sunday
Body	Half red silk, half black seal fur
Ribs	Flat silver tinsel with a gold oval rib
Hackle	Black Spey feather
Throat	Silver pheasant hackle dyed red
Wing	Bronze mallard
Head	Black thread

The Black and Red Spey was originated by Mark Sagester from Eugene, Oregon. Mark fishes Spey rods and Spey flies throughout the West Coast steelhead rivers. One of his favorites is the North Umpqua in southern Oregon.

Many steelhead fly tiers use gut eyes (Dacron loops) because they feel the flies swim differently than those tied with standard return-eye hooks. Steve Gobin was the first to use this method.

BLACK VULTURE

Hook	Size 3 Alec Jackson Spey Fly Hook
Tag	Flat silver tinsel
Tail	Golden pheasant crest
Butt	Dyed red ostrich herl
Body	Black floss
Rib	Fine oval silver tinsel
Body hackle	Dyed black blue-eared pheasant hackle
Collar	Large dot guinea-fowl hackle dyed blue
Wing	Matching slips of guinea-fowl wing quill
Sides	Jungle cock
Head	Red 6/0 Danville thread

The Black Vulture was originated by Joe Howell for the steelhead of the North Umpqua River in southern Oregon (see Autumn Spey).

BROWN HERON

Hook	Size 2, 1, or 1/0 low-water salmon
Body	Rear two-thirds, orange floss; remainder, orange seal fur
Ribs	Medium flat silver tinsel with a fine oval silver rib
Hackle	Gray heron, one side stripped, or substitute
Throat	Teal flank
Wings	Bronze-mallard or widgeon flank
Head	Red thread

The Brown Heron is a steelhead Spey originated by Syd Glasso. It is included in the plates of Trey Combs's book, *Steelhead Fly Fishing and Flies*. This fly is very similar to the original Spey patterns, with a heron body hackle, throat of teal flank, and bronze-mallard wings. The bright orange body transformed it into a steelhead Spey.

CLARET SHOVELER

Hook	Size 1 or 1/0 low-water salmon
Body	Half flat silver tinsel, half claret-purple seal fur
Rib	Three turns of medium oval gold tinsel
Body hackle	Reddish brown Spey hackle
Throat	Shoveler duck flank
Wings	Two strips of argus pheasant quill
Head	Claret 6/0 Danville thread

I originated the Claret Shoveler. The name comes from the body color and the hackle used for the throat of the pattern. Shoveler Duck has a beautiful rich color that runs from cinnamon to a rich rusty brown, with markings of dark chocolate brown. It is very soft in texture and has a thin, pliable stem. I like the way it accents the color of the claret-purple seal fur.

The wings of argus quill have a beautiful barring effect. The fiber is very soft and easy to tie in, and it makes a nicely flowing shape for a Spey-fly wing. It is also very mobile in the water.

COAL CAR SPEY

Hook	Size 1/0 and 3/0 Partridge CS10/1
Tag	Flat silver tinsel
Rib	Oval silver tinsel
Body	Rear half, fluorescent fire orange and red floss; front half, black crystal chenille
Body hackle	Black marabou palmered through black crystal chenille
Wing	Four black hackle tips
Head	Black thread

The Coal Car was originated by Randall Kaufmann, in a series simply called marabou Speys. The original Coal Car pattern is tied with a black hackle for the throat. This steelhead pattern was developed for the Deschutes River in central Oregon.

COPPER HERON

Hook	Size 1 or larger low-water salmon
Body	Rear half, flat copper tinsel; front half, hot orange seal fur
Rib	Oval copper tinsel
Body hackle	Gray Spey hackle, blue-eared pheasant
Throat	Teal or widgeon flank
Wing	Strips of bronze mallard or widgeon flank
Head	Red thread

I originated the Copper Heron, which is similar to the Gold Heron but tied with copper tinsel for the body. I like the look of copper tinsel on a fly; it adds a different effect to a fly pattern.

COURTESAN

Hook	Size 2 Bob Veverka Classic Salmon Hook
Body	Two-fifths, orange floss, remainder, orange seal fur
Rib	Flat silver tinsel
Hackle	Long, soft, brown hackle (also serves as throat)
Wings	Four matching orange hackle tips
Head	Red thread

The Courtesan is a Syd Glasso Spey fly that appears in Trey Combs's book *Steelhead Fly Fishing and Flies*. It is similar to the Orange Heron, but it has a brown body hackle and no teal for the throat.

Glasso tied Spey patterns for steelhead in the 1950s, a time when it was rare just to see another fly fisherman on the steelhead rivers of the West Coast. His knowledge about fly patterns came from books written about Atlantic salmon (Atlantic salmon have habits similar to steelhead). He read and studied the fly patterns of Tavener, Pryce-Tannatt, and Kelson. According to these sources, Speys should be fished in high, cold, and off-color conditions, much like steelhead water. The conversion from Atlantic salmon to steelhead patterns was natural, but Glasso took it to a new level. He strived for highly refined patterns tied to perfection.

DEEP PURPLE SPEY

Hook	Size 2 Partridge, Wilson
Body	Deep purple mohair
Rib	Flat silver tinsel
Body hackle	Dark brown Chinese pheasant rump hackle
Throat	Deep purple hen hackle
Wings	Red golden pheasant body feathers

The Deep Purple Spey was originated by Walt Johnson and was a derivative of Ken Mcleod's Purple Peril. Walt says that the best hackles for the body hackle come from wild ring-necked pheasants. Walt Johnson is one of the last true pioneers in steelhead fly fishing. While fishing with Syd Glasso, he made a note of the Spey flies that Syd fished, and from that he created Spey patterns of his own design.

FIREANT SPEY

Hook	Size 1 1/2 Alec Jackson Spey Fly Hook
Tag	Fine oval silver tinsel
Tail	Dyed red golden pheasant crest
Body	Rear half, red floss; front half, black seal fur
Rib	Medium oval silver tinsel
Body hackle	Black Spey hackle
Throat	Dyed red teal flank
Wings	Four matching red golden pheasant body feathers
Topping	Dyed red golden pheasant crest
Cheeks	Jungle cock
Head	Black thread

The Fireant Spey was originated by Brad Burden. Brad developed this pattern before his Fireplum and has always thought the pair of contrasting flies nicely complement each other. Both patterns fish well throughout the season.

FIREPLUM SPEY

Hook	Size 1 1/2 Alec Jackson Spey Fly Hook
Tag	Fine oval silver tinsel
Tail	Dyed purple golden pheasant crest
Body	Rear half, red floss; front half, purple seal or angora goat
Rib	Medium oval silver tinsel
Body hackle	Black Spey hackle
Throat	Dyed red teal flank
Wing	Four matching dyed purple golden pheasant body feathers
Topping	Dyed purple golden pheasant crest
Cheeks	Jungle cock
Head	Black thread

The Fireplum Spey was originated by Brad Burden of Oregon. This is one of his favorite flies, combining the very effective steelhead colors of purple and red. Brad fishes this fly with confidence in all types of water year-round.

FONTANALIS SPEY

Hook	Size 1 1/2 Alec Jackson Spey Hook
Tag	Flat gold tinsel
Tail	Golden pheasant crest
Body	Fluorescent orange floss
Rib	Medium oval gold tinsel
Body hackle	Blue-eared pheasant dyed orange
Collar	Hot orange dyed guinea hackle
Wing	Married slips of orange, black, and white goose shoulder
Sides	Long jungle cock, slightly drooping
Thread	Fluorescent orange 6/0 Danville prewaxed thread

The Fontanalis Spey was originated by Joe Howell after Canadian tier B. A. Gulline created the Brook Trout pattern, better known as the Trout Fin pattern. The original pattern was thought to match the color of the fins of a northern brook trout.

FREIGHT TRAIN SPEY

Hook	Size 1/0 and 3/0 Partridge CS10/1
Tag	Flat silver tinsel
Rib	Oval silver tinsel
Body	Rear half, fluorescent fire orange and red floss; front half, black crystal chenille
Body hackle	Purple marabou hackle palmered through black crystal chenille
Wing	Four white hackle tips
Head	Black thread

The Freight Train Spey was originated by Randall Kaufmann and is part of his series of marabou Spey patterns.

GOLDEN ARGUS SPEY

Hook	Size 1/0 low-water salmon
Body	Flat copper tinsel
Body veil	Vibrant golden pheasant crests (small feathers located at the base of the crests where they meet the tippets, also used as a toucan substitute)
Hackle	Light orange hen hackle, sparse, and a longer claret hen hackle, followed by a reddish brown Spey hackle
Throat	Teal flank
Wings	Argus pheasant quill
Head	Black 6/0 Danville thread

I originated the Golden Argus Spey. I tied this fly at a time when I was borrowing some feathers and ideas from Atlantic-salmon flies. The wing of argus pheasant quill is unique. The body veils were taken from Preston Jenning's flies, the translucency coming from the golden pheasant crests. A copper tinsel body displays a brilliant hot spot in the fly, similar to the back section of the body on the classic Jock Scott.

GOLDEN DEMON SPEY

Hook	Size 1 ½ Alec Jackson Spey Fly Hook
Tag	Medium flat gold tinsel
Tail	Golden pheasant crest
Body	Medium flat gold tinsel
Rib	Fine oval gold tinsel
Body hackle	Dyed orange long Spey hackle
Throat	Dyed orange guinea fowl
Cheek	Jungle cock
Wing	Dyed ginger badger hackle tips for underwing, bronze-mallard strips over
Topping	One or two golden pheasant crests
Head	Black thread

The Golden Demon is a Spey fly developed by Brad Burden and based on the classic steelhead pattern of the same name. Brad finds it a good summer run fly on sunlit runs.

The original Golden Demon pattern originated in New Zealand and was brought to the States by Zane Grey. Other patterns were added by the famous C. Jim Pray, a fly tier from California who developed patterns for steelhead in the 1930s. One of his best was the Silver Demon, which was heavily fished on the steelhead rivers of northern California and southern Oregon.

GOLDEN EAGLE

Hook	Size 1 ½ Alec Jackson Spey Fly Hook
Tag	Flat silver tinsel
Tail	Golden pheasant tail, three to four strands of pink Krystal Flash
Rib	Medium oval silver tinsel
Body	Fluorescent fire orange angora goat blended with blue pearl Flashabou
Hackle	Double-dyed marabou, fluorescent hot orange with tips dyed red
Collar	Guinea fowl
Wings	Narrow strips of argus pheasant quill
Thread	Fluorescent orange

The Golden Eagle is an eagle substitute pattern tied by Joe Howell for the North Umpqua River in Oregon. There are several eagle patterns used for steelhead. Many marabous were originated for the wild steelhead that run the Skagit River in Washington state. They are close to eagle patterns, and could be called steelhead eagles, with a marabou plume as the substitute for the eagle wound on as a collar or a body hackle. Most patterns combine several colors or shades of colors blended into a multishaded pattern of red, orange, and purple.

GOLDEN ORANGE CROW

Hook	Size 2 Dave McNeese Salmon Iron
Body	Flat silver tinsel
Body veil	Veiled top and bottom with Indian crow
Hackle	Yellow-brown Spey feather
Throat	Orange hen hackle
Wings	Five or six golden pheasant toppings

I originated the Golden Orange Crow in the mid-1980s, at a time when I was using some classic materials to tie Spey patterns. I also tie this pattern with horns of Amherst pheasant tail dyed red. It was fashioned after the series of Atlantic-salmon patterns called the Sun flies, flies tied with wings made of several golden pheasant crests.

The Dave McNeese Salmon Iron is a hook designed by Dave McNeese and made by the Partridge Hook Company in England. Dave owned a shop in Salem, Oregon, when he designed the hook. The shop was a mecca for all things steelhead and salmon during the 1980s. He dyed feathers the most brilliant colors for steelhead flies and stocked all types of tying materials. His hooks only lasted for one run, but at the time he gave his patrons a new style of hook to tie on. Dave tied beautiful steelhead flies and was very interested in flies and fly-tying history.

GOLDEN SPEY

Hook	Size 2 Partridge, Wilson
Body	Fluorescent yellow floss, deep yellow seal fur
Rib	Flat embossed gold tinsel
Body hackle	White-black Spey hackle, dyed golden olive
Throat	Dyed toucan orange hen hackle
Wing	Two light brown hackles
Topping	Golden pheasant crest

The Golden Spey is a steelhead Spey pattern originated by Walt Johnson. Through many years of steelhead fishing, Walt has developed a series of Spey patterns inspired by Syd Glasso.

GOLD HERON

Hook	Size 1 low-water salmon or size 2 Bob Veverka Classic Salmon Hook
Body	Flat gold tinsel and hot orange seal fur
Rib	Oval gold tinsel
Hackle	Gray heron or heron dyed brown, substitute schlappen dyed brown
Throat	Widgeon flank
Wings	Widgeon flank
Head	Red thread

The Gold Heron was originated by Syd Glasso. There is also an Atlantic-salmon pattern by the same name, the only difference being the material used for the wing and the body color; the original used bronze mallard for the wing and had a black wool body.

Glasso chose unique feathers to tie flies—all were of the finest quality, but some were never before used in fly tying. He used various duck flank feathers, which were very rarely used by any other tiers. I don't know if he did this on purpose or by accident. He might have just used what was available to him and tried to match some of the original materials in color and markings. I like to think he tied with purpose.

GREEN-BUTT SKUNK SPEY

Hook	Size 1 ½ Alec Jackson Spey Fly Hook
Tag	Flat silver tinsel
Tail	Dyed red golden pheasant crest
Butt	Dyed chartreuse ostrich herl
Body	Black floss
Rib	Medium oval silver tinsel
Body hackle	Dyed black blue-eared pheasant
Collar	Natural speckled guinea-fowl hackle
Wings	White goose quill
Sides	Jungle cock, drooping
Head	Black thread

This Green-Butt Spey was tied by Joe Howell. There are many different variations of this standard steelhead pattern converted to a Spey fly. This is one of the best steelhead flies, with its bold silhouette and bright green accent. The original pattern was credited to Dan Callaghan, who fishes the North Umpqua River and is known for the photographs he takes there.

GREEN-BUTT SPIDER

Hook	Size 2 low-water salmon
Tip	Flat silver tinsel
Tag	Fluorescent green floss
Body	Black silk
Collar	Natural black hackle, teal flank
Head	Black thread

This Green-Butt Spider was tied by Merlin Stidham, a fellow tier and friend of Syd Glasso. This fly was given to me by Alec Jackson. Merlin Stidham is not mentioned in any books, but by the look of his flies you can see he was a fine fly tier. This would be considered a Spey-type fly. It comes from a series of Spider flies, sparsely tied flies collared with a soft hackle, usually some type of duck flank feather. Mallard flank is standard.

Al Knudson is credited with the first Spider pattern. Many other flies were tied from this pattern, with different colors and materials but the same basic design—the body and the collar hackle.

HARVEST MOON

Hook	Size 1 ½ Alec Jackson Spey Fly Hook
Tag	Flat gold tinsel with a fine oval gold rib
Tail	Golden pheasant crest
Butt	Black ostrich herl
Body	Fluorescent orange floss
Rib	Medium oval gold tinsel
Body hackle	Dyed black blue-eared pheasant hackle
Collar	Large dot guinea fowl dyed orange
Wings	Matching pairs of Whiting Farms hen hackle, dyed hot orange (white hackle with natural black edge)
Sides	Jungle cock, tied long and drooping
Head	Florescent fire orange 6/0 Danville thread

The Harvest Moon was originated by Joe Howell for the steelhead of the North Umpqua River (see Autumn Spey).

HOT PEACOCK SPEY

Hook	Size 1 ½ to 5 Alec Jackson Spey Fly Hook
Tag	Fine oval silver tinsel and fluorescent red floss
Tail	Golden pheasant crest, short (optional)
Body	Peacock herl
Rib	Medium oval silver tinsel
Body hackle	Gray Spey hackle from second turn of tinsel
Throat	Teal flank, sparse
Wing	Two strips of bronze mallard
Cheeks	Jungle cock
Head	Black thread

The Hot Peacock Spey is a steelhead Spey originated by Brad Burden, who fishes the fly on the steelhead rivers of Oregon. Brad mentions that he never saw a Spey fly tied with a peacock herl body, but he likes the buggy look of the peacock herl and the movements of the material in this fly. With the red floss in the body, the fly offers contrasting colors, flash, and movement.

LADY CAROLINE

Hook	Size 2, 1, or 1/0 low-water salmon
Tag	Medium flat gold tinsel
Tail	Red golden pheasant body feather fibers
Body	Blended angora goat, half brown and half olive (seal fur, wool, or other mixed blends of furs can be substituted)
Ribs	Fine oval gold tinsel, counterwrapped with fine oval silver tinsel
Body hackle	Gray Spey hackle
Throat	Red golden pheasant body feather
Wings	Bronze mallard

This is the classic Atlantic-salmon Spey pattern used for steelhead fishing and probably the first classic Spey pattern used for steelhead fishing. Haig-Brown mentions that he used classic Atlantic-salmon patterns when he first fished for steelhead, and one of the patterns was the Lady Caroline.

This fly is still widely used and is one of the most popular original Spey patterns. Its somber color looks natural when fished. It is also a good fly for sea-run cutthroat.

LOW AND CLEAR SPIDER

Hook	Size 3 gold Alec Jackson Spey Fly Hook
Tag	Copper tinsel
Tail	Golden pheasant tippets
Body	Tan fur
Rib	Fine copper tinsel
Collar	Lemon wood duck
Wing	Pine squirrel tail
Cheeks	Jungle cock
Head	Red thread

This Low and Clear Spider was originated by Mark Canfield, a talented fly tier who was inspired by the flies of Syd Glasso.

MIDNIGHT SPEY

Hook	Size 2 or 1 low-water salmon
Tag	Flat silver tinsel
Body	Rear half, purple floss; front half, purple seal fur
Rib	Flat silver tinsel
Hackle	Blue schlappen
Underwing	Purple goose quill
Wing	Green, blue, and purple goose quill, from bottom

The Midnight Spey was originated by Scott Noble. He's a very fine fly tier and fly fisherman from the state of Washington, whose flies are designed with Syd Glasso's and Walt Johnsons work in mind.

MR. GLASSO

Hook	Size 1 low-water salmon
Tip	Flat silver tinsel
Body	Hot orange floss and hot orange seal fur
Rib	Medium flat silver tinsel
Hackle	Black heron or substitute
Throat	Guinea fowl dyed hot orange
Wing	Four hot orange hackle tips
Topping	Dyed hot orange golden pheasant crest
Head	Wine-colored 6/0 thread

The Mr. Glasso is a steelhead Spey fly that Dick Wentworth originated in honor of Syd Glasso, his mentor and teacher in some of life's small pleasures, including fly tying and fishing for the steelhead of the Olympic Peninsula. On March 14, 1981, Dick caught a 21-pound, 8-ounce steelhead on the Sol Duc River on a Mr. Glasso Spey fly. Dick also originated the Quillayute Spey pattern.

This is a brilliant fly with hot dyed orange silk and seal fur. A modern substitute for the black heron hackle is a dyed black blue-eared pheasant hackle.

NIGHTHAWK SPEY

Hook	Size 1 1/2 Alec Jackson Spey Fly Hook
Tag	Fine oval silver tinsel and yellow floss
Tail	Golden pheasant crest and kingfisher
Butt	Red wool
Body	Medium flat silver tinsel
Rib	Fine oval silver tinsel
Body hackle	Long black Spey hackle
Throat	Same as body hackle
Wing	Black goose quill
Side	Jungle cock
Cheek	Kingfisher
Topping	Golden pheasant crest
Horns	Scarlet macaw
Head	Red thread

This Nighthawk Spey was developed and used by Brad Burden. It is a variation of the classic Atlantic-salmon pattern. He finds that it lends itself well to a steelhead Spey pattern. The original pattern used black crow for the wing material and is often tied as a low-water pattern.

NORTH FORK SPEY

Hook	Size 1 1/2 Alec Jackson Spey Fly Hook
Tag	Flat silver tinsel
Tail	Black-and-white barred wood duck flank section
Butt	Dyed red ostrich herl
Rib	Medium oval silver tinsel
Body	Black floss
Body hackle	Dyed black blue-eared pheasant hackle
Collar	Natural guinea-fowl hackle
Wing	Two matching pairs of silver badger neck hackles
Sides	Jungle cock
Head	Black thread

The North Fork Spey is one of Joe Howell's Spey patterns named after the North Umpqua River.

ORANGE HERON

Hook	Size 1 low water
Body	Hot orange floss and hot orange seal fur
Ribs	Flat and oval silver tinsel
Hackle	Gray heron, substitute with gray Spey feather
Throat	Teal flank
Wing	Four hot orange hackle tips
Head	Red thread

Syd Glasso is best remembered for the Orange Heron steelhead Spey-fly pattern. Its forerunner is the Silver-Orange Heron, the same pattern but with wings of gray hackle tips. This fly pattern is still very popular today on steelhead rivers.

Many fly tiers are judged by their attempts at this pattern—it's not one of the easiest patterns to tie correctly, but when tied well it's one of the most beautiful and deadly patterns for steelhead.

The original shown on page 55 was tied by Syd Glasso and given to me by Joe Bates in a trade for some rare Atlantic-salmon patterns. It is one of my most cherished fly patterns. The plates also contain an Orange Heron tied by Pat Crane, a fellow friend and fly tier who fished and tied with Syd Glasso. Crane tied his patterns with orange goose quill for the wing.

POLAR SHRIMP

Hook	Size 1 low-water salmon
Tag	Silver tinsel
Tail	Red golden pheasant body fibers
Body	Orange (or red) floss and orange (or red) seal fur
Rib	Oval silver tinsel
Hackle	Long red or orange hackle
Throat	Red golden pheasant body hackle
Wings	White hackle tips, white goose quill, white arctic fox tail
Head	Red thread

The Polar Shrimp is an old steelhead standard transformed into a Spey fly. It was amazing to see how Syd Glasso could take a standard pattern, work his magic, and turn it into an entirely different style of fly. By changing some of the materials and the length, almost any pattern can be changed into a Spey fly.

This pattern was included in Trey Combs's book *Steelhead Fly Fishing and Flies*.

The original Polar Shrimp pattern was a standard used in the 1930s and popularized on the rivers of northern California. The original pattern is credited to Clarence Shoff of Kent, Washington. He sold flies to Zane Grey and fly-tying materials to Jim Pray in the late 1930s.

PURPLE CROW

Hook	Size 1/0 Dave McNeese Salmon Iron
Body	Two equal sections of copper tinsel, butt of red wool at center
Body veil	Two sets of Indian crow, one long and one short, eight feathers in all, substitute with double-dyed red feathers
Throat hackles	Brown Spey hackle and purple hen hackle
Wings	Two strips of purple goose quill

I originated the Purple Crow, a bright pattern with body veils of Indian crow. This pattern is from a series of flies I tied while fully immersed in the art of tying the classic Atlantic-salmon patterns. I used some of the rarer feathers found in classic Atlantic-salmon flies for my steelhead Spey patterns.

PURPLE HEART SPEY

Hook	Size 1/0 low-water salmon
Body	Rear half, red silk; front half, purple seal fur
Rib	Wide oval silver tinsel
Body hackle	Purple Spey hackle
Throat	Red body feather from golden pheasant
Wings	Two strips of purple goose quill
Head	Red thread

The Purple Heart Spey was originated by me in honor of all the Americans who fought in the Vietnam War, those who came home and especially those who didn't.

PURPLE HERON

Hook	Size 2 low-water salmon
Body	Rear half, red silk; front half, purple seal fur
Rib	Medium oval silver tinsel
Body hackle	Gray Spey hackle
Throat	Teal flank
Wing	Four purple hackle tips
Head	Red thread

The Purple Heron is a pattern by Derl Stovall, who lives and fishes on the Deschutes River in Oregon.

PURPLE SOL DUC SPEY

Hook	Size 1 Allcock low-water salmon
Body	Rear half, fluorescent red silk; front half, purple seal fur
Ribs	Flat silver and narrow oval silver tinsel
Body hackle	Purple Spey hackle
Throat	Black Spey hackle
Wing	Two red hackle tips flanked by two purple hackle tips

The Purple Sol Duc Spey was originated by me and tied in the Syd Glasso tradition. Purple is a great color for steelhead flies. This is a modern addition to the series of flies originated by Syd Glasso for the Sol Duc River.

QUILLAYUTE

Hook	Size 1 low-water salmon
Tag	Flat silver tinsel
Body	Orange floss and orange seal fur
Rib	Medium flat silver tinsel
Hackle	Teal flank from second turn of tinsel
Throat	Black heron, sparse, substitute with blue-eared pheasant dyed black
Wing	Four matching golden pheasant body feathers
Topping	On later flies, a topping of golden pheasant crest dyed hot orange

The Quillayute was originated by Dick Wentworth of Forks, Washington. Dick fished and tied with Syd Glasso, who was his schoolteacher at one time. He tied this fly in the Glasso style and tradition, and they fished it for summer run steelhead. Dick is a fine tier and creator of some beautiful steelhead Spey patterns.

RAVEN

Hook	Size 1 1/2 Alec Jackson Spey Fly Hook
Tag	Medium flat silver tinsel
Tail	Dyed red golden pheasant crest
Body	Black angora goat
Rib	Fine oval silver tinsel
Body hackle	Black hen hackle
Throat	Black hen hackle
Wing	Dyed black goose quill
Head	Black thread

The Raven was originated by Brad Burden for the steelhead rivers of Oregon. This pattern was developed with a dark silhouette and has lots of movement. Brad finds that this is a good pattern as a follow-up fly to a Muddler or a light-colored fly to contrast the Raven's bold, dark silhouette.

RED SHRIMP

Hook	Size 1 low water
Body	Fluorescent orange floss and seal fur
Rib	Silver tinsel
Hackle	Brown rump feather from a ring-necked pheasant
Throat	Red hackle
Wing	Narrow strips of turkey quill dyed red

The Red Shrimp was originated by Walt Johnson and introduced in 1963. Johnson feels that steelhead are creatures of habit that respond to food they recently took in the sea, so he ties flies that represent sea creatures like shrimp. Steelhead are anadromous, and, just out of the sea, their response to the Red Shrimp may be triggered by their competitive search for ocean food.

Walt Johnson is one of the true pioneers of fly fishing for steelhead. He fished through the heyday of steelhead fishing, enjoyed its golden years, and is still at it today. His knowledge of the fish, fisherman, and fly patterns comes from over fifty years of pursuit of wild steelhead.

RED WING SPEY

Hook	Size 1 1/2 Alec Jackson Spey Fly Hook
Tag	Fine oval silver tinsel
Tail	Dyed red golden pheasant crest
Body	Rear two-thirds, black floss; front third, black ostrich herl
Rib	Fine oval silver tinsel
Body hackle	Long black Spey hackle
Throat	Long black Spey hackle
Wing	Dyed red goose shoulder
Head	Black thread

The Red Wing Spey was originated by Brad Burden as a Spey variation of the Hairwing. Brad fishes this pattern on the steelhead rivers of Oregon.

ROYAL BLUE AND BRONZE SPEY

Hook	Size 2, 1, or 1/0 low-water salmon
Tag	Flat silver tinsel
Body	Half royal blue silk, half purple seal fur
Rib	Three turns of medium oval silver tinsel from center of body
Hackle	Dark purple Spey hackle, more black than purple
Throat	Guinea fowl dyed purple
Wings	Two strips of bronze mallard
Head	Red 6/0 Danville thread

I originated the Royal Blue and Bronze Spey, a very dark pattern in the water, yet it still has a hue of color. It's a striking pattern.

ROYAL SPEY

Hook	Size 1 low-water salmon
Tag	Silver tinsel overlaid with cerise floss
Body	Peacock herl divided by a narrow band of pink fire fiber
Body hackle	White-black heron hackle dyed pink
Wing	Two light blue hackles, set low over the body
Cheeks	Lady Amherst tippets dyed blue
Head	White thread

The Royal Spey is another of the Speys originated by Walt Johnson. Others include the Deep Purple and the Golden Spey.

SIGNAL LIGHT SPEY

Hook	Size 1/0 and 3/0 Partridge CS10/1
Tag	Flat silver tinsel
Rib	Oval silver tinsel
Body	Rear, fluorescent fire orange and fluorescent green floss; front, black crystal chenille
Body hackle	Purple marabou hackle palmered through black chenille
Wing	Four black hackle tips
Head	Black thread

The Signal Light Spey was originated by Randall Kaufmann and belongs to his marabou series. Randall ties and fishes the rivers of the Northwest for steelhead and chases bonefish in the off-season. He has authored a number of books on fly fishing.

SILVER HERON

Hook	Size 1 low-water salmon, or Size 2 Bob Veverka Classic Salmon Hook
Body	Flat silver tinsel and black seal fur
Rib	Oval silver tinsel
Hackle	Gray heron, one side striped, substitute with gray Spey hackle
Throat	Guinea fowl
Wing	Strips of gray heron wing quill, substitute with dyed gray goose or turkey quill
Head	Black thread

The Silver Heron was originated by Syd Glasso. This pattern appears in the plates of Trey Combs's book *Steelhead Fly Fishing and Flies*. Trey's book on steelhead is a classic, a must-have on the history of steelhead fly fishing. It includes information on all the early steelhead fly fishermen and fly tiers and their fly patterns. Most important are the fly patterns and their history. All of the original steelhead flies tied by their originators are pictured in the fly plates. This is the first book that describes the flies by Syd Glasso, some very special flies by one of the finest fly tiers that ever lived.

Trey also went on to do an updated version, *Steelhead: Fly Fishing*, that was published in 1989. This includes all the history up to the present day, with lots of information on the steelhead rivers of the West Coast.

SILVER STREAK

Hook	Size 1 1/2 Alec Jackson Spey Fly Hook
Tag	Flat silver tinsel
Body	Flat silver tinsel
Rib	Medium oval silver tinsel
Body hackle	Natural gray blue-eared pheasant hackle, long
Cross-rib	Fine oval silver tinsel to secure the hackle on the slick texture of the flat silver tinsel body
Collar	Barred teal flank
Wing	Bronze-mallard slips
Sides	Jungle cock, drooping

The Silver Streak is one of Joe Howells's Spey patterns for the North Umpqua River in Oregon.

SNOW QUEEN (Winter Blue Spey)

Hook	Size 1 1/2 Alec Jackson Spey Fly Hook
Tag	Flat silver tinsel
Tail	Dyed red golden pheasant crest
Butt	White ostrich herl
Rib	Medium oval silver tinsel
Body hackle	Bleached white blue-eared pheasant hackle
Body	Danville fluorescent blue rayon floss
Collar	Dyed blue guinea-fowl hackle
Wing	White goose shoulder
Sides	Jungle cock
Head	White thread

The Snow Queen is another of Joe Howell's Speys that he fishes for winter-run steelhead on the North Umpqua River in Oregon.

SOL DUC

Hook	Size 4 Wilson dry fly
Tip	Flat silver tinsel
Tail	Golden pheasant crest
Body	Half fluorescent orange floss, half fluorescent orange seal fur
Rib	Flat silver tinsel
Hackle	Yellow hackle from second turn of tinsel
Throat	Teal flank, one turn
Wing	Four matching fluorescent orange hackle tips
Topping	Golden pheasant crest
Head	Red thread

The Sol Duc was originated by Syd Glasso and belongs to a series of flies that he tied for the Sol Duc River. There are three flies in the series: Sol Duc, Sol Duc Dark, and Sol Duc Spey. The Sol Duc was included in Trey Combs's book *Steelhead Fly Fishing and Flies*.

On Febuary 22, 1959, Syd Glasso caught an 18-pound, 12-ounce steelhead on the Sol Duc River that was the largest fly-caught steelhead in the United States for that year. The fly he used was the Sol Duc.

SOL DUC DARK

Hook	Size 1 low-water Partridge
Tip	Narrow oval silver tinsel
Tail	Amherst pheasant crest
Body	Fluorescent orange floss and fluorescent orange seal fur
Ribs	Flat silver tinsel and fine oval silver tinsel
Hackle	Yellow hackle from second turn
Throat	Teal flank, one turn
Wing	Four matching red golden pheasant body feathers
Topping	Lady Amherst pheasant crest
Head	Red thread

The Sol Duc Dark was originated by Syd Glasso in a series of patterns that he developed for steelhead fishing on the Sol Duc River. These patterns represent years of work and an evolutionary trend toward more effective and refined patterns.

SOL DUC SPEY

Hook	Size 1/0 Partridge
Tip	Narrow oval silver tinsel
Body	Fluorescent orange floss and fluorescent orange seal fur
Rib	Flat silver tinsel
Hackle	Very long webby yellow hackle (similar in features to the old Spey cock hackles)
Throat	Black heron, substitute with black Spey feather
Wings	Four matching hot orange hackle tips
Head	Red thread

The Sol Duc Spey is a pattern from a series of flies originated by Syd Glasso for the Sol Duc River. This is my favorite fly from the series. The long yellow body hackle and black throat contrast one another and give this pattern a special look. A hot orange body hackle could also be used for variation.

SORCERER

Hook	Size 1 ½ Alec Jackson Spey Fly Hook
Tag	Fine oval gold tinsel
Tail	Golden pheasant crest
Butt	Four or five dyed black goose quill fibers, twisted and wound on
Body	Rear two-thirds, flat embossed copper tinsel; front third, black angora goat
Rib	Fine oval gold tinsel
Body hackle	Long black Spey hackle
Throat	Guinea fowl
Cheek	Jungle cock
Wing	Dyed black goose quill
Head	Black thread

The Sorcerer was originated by Brad Burden from Bill McMillan's suggestion that Brad should consider designing a fly with copper in it. McMillan said, "There's something about copper and steelhead." After some thought and experimentation, the Sorcerer was the result.

SPADE

Hook	Size 3, 5, 7, or 1 ½ Alec Jackson Spey Fly Hook
Tail	Dik-Dik deer
Body	Peacock herl spun on oval tinsel and wound on
Collar	Grizzly hackle
Head	Red thread

The Spade is one of the beautiful little steelhead patterns that Alec Jackson ties for the steelhead of the rivers of the Pacific Northwest. Alec has a unique way of doing the bodies on his steelhead patterns. He spins several strands of ostrich or peacock herl onto oval tinsel and wraps it on for the body of the fly, which produces a beautiful, tightly wound body material.

SPECTRAL SPIDER

Hook	Size 3 gold Alec Jackson Spey Fly Hook
Tail	Fluorescent yellow Antron fibers
Body	Pearlescent Mylar
Rib	Flat silver tinsel
Wings	Cerise, orange, green, and blue Antron fibers, sparse, layered from bottom, flanked by two cream badger hackles
Hackle	Several wraps of stiff grizzly hackle, overwrapping Spider fashion with barred mallard flank
Cheek	Kingfisher

The Spectral Spider was originated by Walt Johnson. The original Spider pattern was by Al Knudson.

The idea for the Spectral Spider came from the patterns that Preston Jennings mentions in *A Book of Trout Flies*. He expressed great interest in the role light refraction plays in trout's vision. Water and sunlight can create a prismatic effect, which he duplicated in the rainbow-hued series of flies he developed, called the Iris series. The flies are the Lord, Lady, and Muddy Iris.

STEELHEAD SUNRISE

Hook	Size 1/0 low-water salmon
Body	Flat silver tinsel
Body veil	Small golden pheasant crest veiling the body top and bottom
Hackle	Yellow and orange Spey hackle
Throat	Red body hackle from a golden pheasant
Wings	Orange goose quill

I originated the Steelhead Sunrise, a bright pattern to go with the Steelhead Sunset. The two patterns use the contrasting colors of orange and purple, two of the most important colors in steelhead fly patterns.

The Sunset and Sunrise patterns belong to a series of flies I developed with strong steelhead colors, sometimes blended with hackles layered so the next color is one shade darker than the previous.

STEELHEAD SUNSET

Hook	Size 2, 1, or 1/0 low-water salmon
Body	Flat silver tinsel
Body veil	Small golden pheasant crests top and bottom, encasing the body
Hackle	Hot orange hen hackle, slightly longer fibered red hen hackle, and dyed purple Spey hackle
Wings	Two strips of purple goose quill
Head	Red 6/0 Danville thread

The Steelhead Sunset was originated by me. I like purple on a steelhead fly and an inner color that runs from orange to red and then purple. At the middle a translucent inner glow of the golden pheasant crests veils the body, picking up light.

For the Spey hackle I use a dyed purple feather, a white- or brown-eared pheasant rump hackle, for example. It should be long enough so that it extends slightly past the hook bend. I usually tie flies in the size 2 to 1/0 range.

This pattern was included in Trey Combs's book *Steelhead: Fly Fishing* and in *Flies for Steelhead* by Dick Stewart and Farrow Allen.

SUMMER SPIDER

Hook	Size 4 low-water salmon
Tip	Silver tinsel
Tag	Orange silk
Tail	Red hackle fibers
Butt	Peacock herl
Body	Orange silk
Rib	Fine oval silver tinsel
Throat	Hungarian partridge hackle
Wing	Four red golden pheasant body feathers
Head	Red thread

This Summer Spider was tied by Merlin Stidham, a friend of Syd Glasso. This fly is used for summer-run steelhead when the water is low and clear.

SURVEYOR

Hook	Size 1 1/2 Alec Jackson Spey Fly Hook
Tag	Medium flat silver tinsel
Tail	Dyed purple golden pheasant crest
Body	Purple angora goat
Rib	Fine oval silver tinsel
Body hackle	Dyed purple long hen hackle
Throat	Dyed claret hen hackle
Wing	Red squirrel tail underwing with bronze mallard over
Cheek	Jungle cock
Head	Black thread

The Surveyor is a pattern developed by Brad Burden, inspired by the Purple Peril. It displays a bold silhouette and incorporates the excellent steelhead colors of purple and claret.

THUNDER AND LIGHTNING

Hook	Size 2/0 Partridge
Body	Flat silver tinsel
Hackle	Soft marabou-like webby hen hackle, orange and very sparse black Spey hackle
Throat	Guinea hackle dyed kingfisher blue
Wings	Two strips of bronze mallard
Head	Black or claret thread

The Thunder and Lightning Spey is a fly that comes from the Atlantic-salmon pattern of the same name. The original Atlantic-salmon pattern was created by James Wright back in the mid-1800s. Thunder and Lightnings are still used today for Atlantic salmon. On some of my steelhead T&Ls I use bronze-mallard quill dyed a hot orange.

WINTER SPEY

Hook	Size 1 1/2 Alec Jackson Spey Fly Hook
Tag	Flat gold tinsel
Body	Fluorescent orange floss
Rib	Medium oval gold tinsel
Body hackle	Dyed orange blue-eared pheasant
Collar	Guinea-fowl hackle
Wing	Two pairs fluorescent orange hackle tips
Thread	Fluorescent fire orange 6/0 Danville thread

The Winter Spey was originated by Joe Howell for winter steelhead on the North Umpqua River in Oregon, where he lives and owns the Blue Heron Fly Shop. Joe has lived and fished there all his life, and he knows the river and its steelhead. More important, he knows the history of the river and the fly patterns used and developed there.

MATERIAL SOURCES

American Angling
23 Main Street
Salem, New Hampshire 03079
American Angling carries a full line of materials to tie Atlantic-salmon flies and runs classes to learn how to tie salmon flies. It also has a catalog.

Blue Heron Fly Shop
Joe Howell
North Umpqua River
109 Hargis Lane
Idleyld Park, Oregon 97447
(541) 496-0448
Joe owns and runs the Blue Heron Fly Shop along the banks of the North Umpqua River, a beautiful river with a good run of Wild Steelhead. Steelhead country is in his front yard. He ties fine steelhead flies and carries a large selection of steelhead fly-tying materials. He has a vast knowledge of the history of the Umpqua River system, the people who fish it, and the flies developed to catch its Steelhead.

Castle Arms (fisherman's fur and feathers)
P.O. Box 30070
Springfield, Massachusetts 01103
(413) 567-8268
Phil Castleman has a series of salmon and streamer fly hooks, return-eye hooks, and various styles of blind-eye hooks. Phil buys and sells a wide variety of salmon-fly materials, from the most common to the rarest plumage. He sends out a newsletter a few times a year that lists items for sale. If there's something you need, Phil probably has it somewhere.

Classic Outfitters
861 Williston Road
South Burlington, Vermont 05403
The outfitters carry a full line of quality hooks and materials to tie salmon flies, from hairwings to full dress.

Creekside
345 High Street SE
Salem, Oregon 97301
(888) 588-1768
Rich Younger runs Creekside shop and carries an extensive line of materials to tie steelhead and salmon flies. This was formerly Dave McNeese's shop, and Rich has carried on where Dave left off, supplying some of the finest materials available to tie steelhead flies.

Dazzle Dub
4463 - 196A Street
Langley, British Columbia
V3A 6A3 Canada
Dazzle Dub has a wide range of synthetic dubbing materials that can be used on Spey and Dee patterns.

Hunters Angling Supplies
Box 300
New Boston New Hampshire 03070
(603) 487-3388
Hunters Angling Supplies was started by Bill Hunter in the late 1970s and is now run by Nick Wilder. The shop is known for its fly-tying materials and fly-tying classes. It is always a good source for all types of fishing and flies and most importantly, salmon-fly materials. It has an extensive catalog.

Alec Jackson
Box 386
Kenmore, Washington 98028
Alec sells a number of hook styles to tie salmon and steelhead flies. He also carries a line of silk in various colors for steelhead and salmon flies.

Lagartun
16741 S. Old Sonoita Highway
Vail, Arizona 85641

Lagartun makes twelve-strand silk used for the tags and bodies of salmon flies. This is one of the finest quality silks I have used. It's dyed in all the major salmon colors. Lagartun also supplies all types of tinsel: gold, silver, and copper finishes in flat, oval, and round.

Ron Reinhold Gold Label Blind Eye Hooks
4446 Westridge Drive
Williamsburg, Michigan 49690
(616) 938-9211

Ron makes a series of blind-eye hooks that rival the original antiques. He can duplicate any of the old antique hooks or any of your favorite hook styles. He has a catalog.

Salmon Fly Tying Scissors
Jeff Becker
(631) 696-9767

A great pair of scissors with sharp fine points, they work great and cleanly cut any of the materials used in tying salmon flies.

Gary Selig
(610) 682-6255

Gary supplies many Atlantic-salmon fisherman with his custom-tied Spey-rod leaders.

BIBLIOGRAPHY

BOOKS

Bainbridge, George C. *The Fly Fishers Guide*. Liverpool, 1816.

Bates, Joseph, Jr., and Bates, Pamela Richards. *Fishing Atlantic Salmon*. Mechanicsburg, Pa.: Stackpole Books, 1996.

Combs, Trey. *Steelhead Fly Fishing and Flies*. Portland, Oreg.: Salmon Trout Steelheader, 1976.

———. *Steelhead: Fly Fishing*. New York: Lyons & Burford, 1991.

Dunham, Judith. *The Atlantic Salmon Fly*. San Francisco: Chronicle Books, 1991.

Ephemera (Edward Fitzgibbon). *The Book of the Salmon*. London: Longman, Brown, Green, and Longmans, 1850.

Francis, Francis. *A Book on Angling*. London: Longmans, Green & Co., 1867.

———. *A Book on Angling*. John Culler & Sons, 1995.

Frodin, Mikael. *Classic Salmon Flies*. New York: Bonanza Books, 1991.

Jorgensen, Poul. *Salmon Flies*. Harrisburg, Pa.: Stackpole Books, 1978.

Kaufmann, Randall. *Fly Patterns of Umpqua Feather Merchants*. Glide, Oreg.: Umpqua Feather Merchants, 1998.

Kelson, George M. *The Salmon Fly*. London, 1895.

Knox, A. E. *Autumns on the Spey*. London, 1872.

Meyer, Deke. *Advanced Fly Fishing for Steelhead*. Portland, Oreg.: Frank Amato Publications, 1992.

Oglesby, Arthur, and John Buckland. *A Guide to Salmon Flies*. Ramsbury, Marlborough, and Wiltshire, England: The Crowood Press, 1990.

Pryce-Tannatt, Dr. Thomas Edwin. *How to Dress Salmon Flies*. London: A. & C. Black, 1914.

Radencich, Michael D. *Tying the Classic Salmon Fly*. Mechanicsburg, Pa.: Stackpole Books, 1997.

Sawada, Kenichiro. *Tube and Waddington Fly Dressing*. Japan: Tulchan Books.

Scrope, William. *Days and Nights of Salmon Fishing on the Tweed*. London, 1843.

Stoddart, Thomas T. *The Anglers Companion*. Edinburgh and London, 1847.

Taverner, Eric. *Fly Tying for Salmon*. London: Seeley Service & Co., 1942.

———. *Salmon Fishing*. London: Seeley Service & Co., 1931.

Younger, John. *River Angling*. Edinburgh, 1840.

PERIODICALS

"The Creel." *The Bulletin of the Flyfishers Club of Oregon* 8, no. 1 (December 1970).

Flyfishing and Tying Journal, Frank Amato Publications.

INDEX

Page numbers in italics indicates sidebars and illustrations.

Leaping Salmon *by Chet Reneson*